FM 21–100

WAR DEPARTMENT

BASIC FIELD MANUAL

SOLDIER'S HANDBOOK

July 23, 1941

Including C1, May 4, 1942

NOTE.—*No initial distribution will be made of this manual as it contains only minor changes to the December 11, 1940, edition. Replacement of copies now in the hands of individuals is not authorized.*

WAR DEPARTMENT,
WASHINGTON, July 23, 1941.

FM 21-100, Soldier's Handbook, is published for the information and guidance of all concerned. Its purpose is to give
the newly enrolled member of the United States Army a convenient and compact source of basic military information and
thus to aid him to perform his duties more efficiently.

[A. G. 062.11 (7-23-41).]

BY ORDER OF THE SECRETARY OF WAR:

G. C. MARSHALL,
Chief of Staff.

OFFICIAL:

E. S. ADAMS,
Major General,
The Adjutant General.

DISTRIBUTION:

C and H (5); X.

(For explanation of symbols see FM 21-6.)

FOREWORD

You are now a member of the Army of the United States. That Army is made up of free citizens chosen from among a free people. The American people of their own will, and through the men they have elected to represent them in Congress, have determined that the free institutions of this country will continue to exist. They have declared that, if necessary, we will defend our right to live in our own American way and continue to enjoy the benefits and privileges which are granted to the citizens of no other nation. It is upon you, and the many thousands of your comrades now in the military service, that our country has placed its confident faith that this defense will succeed should it ever be challenged.

In the transition from civil life to the life of a soldier you may, at first, feel somewhat confused. It is the purpose of this handbook to help you over these rough spots as rapidly as possible and to lay the foundations for your successful career as a soldier.

Making good as a soldier is no different from making good in civil life. The rule is the same and that is—know your own job and be ready to step into the job of the man ahead of you. Promotion is going to be very rapid in this Army. Be ready for it. You will have little time to learn the duties of a noncommissioned officer after you become one. You will be expected to know those duties and show that you know them. At a moment's notice you may have to take charge of your squad as a corporal—and in a critical hour. In the same way when you are a sergeant you cannot tell under what conditions and at what hour you may have to take the place of your lieutenant. You want to know what is expected of you and be ready to do it.

The things that a trained soldier must know, and the way in which they are done, will be taught you as rapidly as you can absorb them. The basic military information is described and explained in this handbook so that it may be available constantly to you during the first weeks of your service. By mastering the contents your future progress will be much more rapid.

In making yourself an efficient soldier you are helping to build a defense for our country that nothing can destroy. You are repaying your obligation to the United States for all the benefits of the past and are declaring your faith in our future. If you will make a part of yourself the following characteristics of the good soldier, you will be doing your part in upholding the glorious reputation of the Army of the United States:

Be obedient.—Obedience means to obey promptly and cheerfully all orders of your commissioned and noncommissioned officers. At first you cannot be expected to know the reason for everything you are ordered to do. As you remain longer in the service and you understand more of the reasons for military training you will find that everything has been figured out as the result of experience in the past. Ways and methods which have been successful in the past are continued until some new way proves to be better, and then the change will be made. Cheerful obedience leads to a better performance of your duties. It makes it easier for all of your comrades to do their part. It means better teamwork.

Be loyal.—Loyalty means that you must stand by your organization through thick and thin. Boost your organization at every opportunity. Be loyal and true to your officers, your noncommissioned officers, and your comrades. In this way you will be loyal to your country.

Be determined.—Determination means the bulldog stick-to-it-iveness to win at all costs. During your training keep everlastingly at the most difficult tasks and never give up until you have mastered them. Determination to win means success in battle.

Be alert.—Alertness means being always on your guard. A good soldier may be pardoned for failure, but never for being surprised. Should the unexpected happen, use your head and do something, even if it is wrong, rather than "lie down."

Be a member of the team.—Teamwork means that each man in the squad, platoon, company, troop, or battery gives everything in his power to make for the success of the whole unit. Success in battle depends on teamwork just as much as success in a football game depends on the pull-together spirit of the football team. Unless you play your own special part the team may not win.

RECORD OF THE SOLDIER

Name _____   _____
Army serial No. _____
Grade _____ Organization _____
Height _____ _____ Weight _____
Born _____   _____
            (Place)   (Date)
In case of emergency notify _____
                                         (Name)

_____ _____ _____
     (Address)   (Town)   (State)
Beneficiary (6 months' pay) _____
                                        (Name)

_____ _____ _____
(Relation)   (Street and number   (Town and state)
            or rural route)
Government insurance _____ _____
                    (Amount)   (Policy number)
Other insurance _____ _____
                (Amount)   (Policy number)
Bank account _____ _____
        (Name of bank)   (City and State)

_____ _____
    (Church)   (Town and State)
Rifle number _____
Pistol number _____
Company number _____
Watch _____

_____
Regimental commander's name _____
Battalion commander's name _____
Company commander's name _____
Chaplain's name _____
Platoon commander's name _____
Squad leader's name _____

TABLE OF CONTENTS

	Paragraphs	Page

TABLE OF CONTENTS

FM 21-100

BASIC FIELD MANUAL

✤

SOLDIER'S HANDBOOK

———

Prepared under direction of the
Chief of Staff

UNITED STATES
GOVERNMENT PRINTING OFFICE
WASHINGTON : 1941

rights and property of others. A soldier who has learned to respect the rights of his comrades has made a big step forward in his training as a soldier and as a citizen.

SECTION II

RELATIONSHIP WITH NONCOMMISSIONED OFFICERS AND OFFICERS

■ **4.** For every business, every game, every group activity, and in every walk of life there is a leader, a "boss," an executive, or some directing agency. In the Army these group leaders are the officers and the noncommissioned officers.

■ **5.** The President of the United States is the Commander in Chief of the Army. He appoints officers, with the consent of the Senate, to assist him in the details of running the Army. He gives them certain authority and makes them responsible for certain groups or organizations in accordance with their grade and length of service.

■ **6.** You have a commander in charge of your company, battery, or troop, who is responsible for everything your company does or fails to do. He must see that you are properly trained, and that you are fed, clothed, and sheltered. He must look after your health, your comfort, and your amusements. He could not possibly attend to all these details alone. Suppose that your company commander had to go to every individual soldier, give him special instructions, explain what to do and what not to do, draw rations, issue equipment, keep all your records, and do all of the many things which you require. You can see that many things would be neglected and that you would suffer for lack of proper training, food, equipment, and amusements. To assist him in all the details of running the company he asks the regimental commander to appoint noncommissioned officers who are given certain authority and are made responsible for certain things. You are thus a part of a great organization or business in which the officers and the noncommissioned officers are the executives, the "bosses," and the foremen.

■ **7.** The first thing to appreciate is that you are subject to the orders of officers and noncommissioned officers placed over you. The officers and noncommissioned officers are *entitled*

to be, and they *must be* obeyed and respected by all soldiers
under them.   Make it a rule that you will obey them promptly,
cheerfully, and carefully.   A military order is usually sharp,
positive, and brief.   If you do not understand what is wanted,
it is your duty to ask questions, but do not quibble over small
details as to your "rights."   The man who is always thinking
of his "rights," rather than his duty, makes a poor soldier.

■ 8. If you believe that you have been given an unlawful order
you should obey first and make a report to your commanding
officer afterward.   Disobedience or failure to obey a lawful
order, which you may believe to be unlawful, may lead to
severe consequences.

■ 9. The Articles of War, the soldier's law, authorize your
commanding officer to impose certain punishments for minor
offenses.   That is, he can withhold certain privileges, restrict
you to the area of barracks or camp for a week, or require you
to perform extra duty or hard labor for as much as a week.
However, he does not delegate this authority to his noncommissioned officers.   A noncommissioned officer is not authorized to administer any form of punishment to a member of his
command.   A noncommissioned officer may require you to
sweep the barracks floor, wash the squad-room windows, and
the like, but he does this by regular detail from all the
members of your company, not as a punishment.

■ 10. It is the duty of a noncommissioned officer at all
times and under all circumstances, whether on duty or off
duty, to check promptly all disputes, quarrels, or disorderly
conduct which might bring discredit upon the service.   He
is required to enforce the orders and regulations governing
the conduct of soldiers.   In the absence of an officer, a noncommissioned officer may place a soldier under arrest until
he can be seen by his company commander.

■ 11. It can be seen that officers and noncommissioned officers must be specially selected.   They hold positions of
responsibility and honor, but they belong to the same military organization that you do.   The relationship between
all military men is one of comradeship, friendliness, and
helpfulness.   In no walk of life does "comradeship" mean
so much as in the military service and nowhere are obedience and respect for authority so important as in the Army.

As a soldier you must accept constituted authority, which is nothing more than team play. In your relationship with officers and noncommissioned officers you are expected to be loyal and truthful. Always be frank but courteous. By being courteous and respectful to constituted authority you are exhibiting qualities of a good soldier.

SECTION III

RELATIONS WITH CIVILIANS

■ 12. In his off-duty activities, whether in peace or war, the good soldier is always careful to be courteous and considerate toward civilians. You must realize that your organization and the Army will be judged by the conduct and appearance of its members in public. Any misconduct on your part in a public place will bring discredit not only upon yourself but also on the military service. You must take pains on every occasion to win the respect and confidence of all with whom you come in contact.

■ 13. When on duty your relations with civilians are governed primarily by the orders and instructions of your commanding officer. Here also, whether in peace or war, you should treat civilians with all courtesy and consideration consistent with a strict observance of your orders and the accomplishment of your military mission.

■ 14. The American Red Cross acts as the medium of communication between the Army and the civil community. This organization has chapters or representatives in all parts of the United States and its foreign possessions. If you should be concerned about the welfare of your family or conditions in your home, explain the situation to your company commander. He will help you in obtaining the assistance of the Red Cross through the Red Cross field director at your station or serving your unit.

SECTION IV

MILITARY OBLIGATIONS

■ 15. *a.* Every man who enters the Army of the United States, whether through voluntary enlistment or operation of the Selective Service Law, accepts certain solemn obligations. These obligations require that he bear true faith and allegiance to the United States of America; that he serve them faithfully against all their enemies; and that he will obey the orders of the President of the United States and the officers appointed over him (the soldier) according to the rules and Articles of War.

b. Your legal status has changed from that of a civilian to that of a soldier. You have become subject to military law and cannot again become a civilian until you receive your discharge by proper authority. As a civilian you could quit your job and seek other employment at will. As a soldier you have given up that privilege during the period of your service. During your off-duty hours as a civilian you could go when and where you pleased without asking permission from anyone. As a soldier you must first get permission before leaving your proper station.

c. The reasons for these differences in your status as a civilian and as a soldier are important but easy to understand. The military organization to which you now belong is a team that must be constantly trained and ready for duty in any emergency. If its members could go and come whenever they cared to there would be no assurance that this military team would be on hand when needed.

■ 16. As a soldier, then, you must keep in mind and faithfully fulfill your obligations. If you do so you will find the service pleasant and profitable, and will leave it as a veteran with a clean record which will entitle you to the benefits accorded by law to an honorably discharged ex-serviceman. Soldiers who constantly fail to fulfill these obligations are likely, sooner or later, to get into trouble, to lose the respect and regard of their comrades, to suffer punishments, and perhaps, finally to return to civil life dishonored and disqualified for any of the benefits with which the Government rewards honorable and faithful service.

SECTION V

THE ARTICLES OF WAR

■ 17. The Articles of War are part of the military laws enacted by Congress to control the conduct of those in military service of the United States. They govern the administration of military justice. They define the offenses for which soldiers may be tried by court martial, prescribe the composition and procedure of courts martial, and fix the limits of punishment that may be imposed by these courts.

■ 18. The Articles of War are read to every soldier shortly after he enters the service and at regular intervals thereafter, so that no one will be able to excuse himself for a violation of any of them upon the ground of ignorance of their provisions.

■ 19. However, as a good soldier, resolved to observe fully and in good faith the obligations of the oath of enlistment above discussed, you do not need to spend much time studying the detailed provisions of the Articles of War. As a general rule, they prohibit and penalize only such conduct as the person of ordinary intelligence will readily recognize to be wrong. The man who is resolved to do the right thing and carries out that resolution at all times, is very unlikely to violate any of the Articles of War. Should doubt ever arise in your mind as to whether anything you plan to do is improper or a violation of the Articles of War, don't hesitate to take the question to some more experienced comrade, to your first sergeant, or to your immediate commanding officer. They will be glad to advise you.

SECTION VI

POST AND STATION ACTIVITIES

■ 20. Although you have exchanged your civilian community for a military community, you will find many of the same activities on your post or station that you have known in civil life. For example, your own organization will probably have a barber and a tailor. All soldiers are required to have a short haircut known as a "military" haircut. This is done for sanitary reasons and to secure uniformity. Your organization barber is approved by your organization commander, and is required to maintain a sanitary establishment, which is inspected regularly by the post surgeon. Your organization tailor is prepared to clean and press your uniform and make necessary alterations and repairs. Both of these activities are maintained for the service and convenience of the members of your organization. The prices are fixed by the post commander so that they will be well within your means. You will be given credit by these activities and can pay for whatever service you have received at the end of each month.

■ 21. The *post exchange* is the community store, owned jointly by you and all other men on your post. It is operated under the supervision of the commanding officer and the post exchange officer entirely in your interests. All profits made in this store come back to you and your comrades in the form of recreational activities, the furnishing of your organization day room, and other similar benefits. No individual shares in these profits, and under Army Regulations, profits may be expended only for the welfare of the soldiers as a whole. The post exchange will probably operate a general store, a shoe repair shop, a barber shop, and a tailor shop. Your organization orderly room will issue you, on credit, a certain amount of post exchange coupons each month, which will be accepted by all post exchange activities. The cost of these coupons will be collected at the pay table at the end of the month.

■ 22. There will also be a *motion picture theater* on your post operated by the United States Army Motion Picture Service, at which will be shown one or two shows each night, or as announced from time to time. There will also be occasional free shows. The price of attendance for the regular shows is small, and payment may be made in cash, post exchange coupons, or in theater coupons. Theater coupon books may be obtained on credit and paid for at the end of the month in the same manner as post exchange coupon books.

■ 23. A *photograph shop* will also probably be operated by your post exchange. The photographer will make a specialty of taking photographs of soldiers at a very small cost, for which he will accept either cash or post exchange coupons. At your early convenience, have your photograph taken in your uniform, and send it home to a member of your family. They will be glad to have it and so will you, after you have returned to civil life.

■ 24. You will find that suitable provision has been made for a center of divine worship, devotions on Sunday, religious holidays, and other allied services. In newly established or temporary camps, you may find that the chapel is improvised in the recreation building or tent, in other available shelter, or outdoors. In any event, religious practices and allegiance have their place in the Army as well as in civil life. The *chaplain* of your organization, either through his own or the efforts of his associates, will assist you in maintaining your normal and regular religious practices. Meet your chaplain early in your Army experience and make him your confidant and advisor.

■ 25. There are also a number of other recreational activities on your post in which you are encouraged to participate during your off-duty hours. These will probably include bowling alleys, shooting galleries, baseball fields, and basketball and volley ball courts. They are provided for your enjoyment, and you should take advantage of them at every opportunity. Your first sergeant will be glad to explain how you can use them and where to obtain the necessary equipment.

■ 26. Your organization has a bulletin board just outside of the orderly room or organization headquarters tent. Make it a practice to read the contents of the bulletin board several times each day. On it will be posted various company and guard details as well as announcements as to the uniform and equipment to be worn on different occasions, the time and place where you will receive your pay, motion picture programs, and other items of interest to you.

CHAPTER 2

MILITARY DISCIPLINE AND COURTESY

SECTION I

MILITARY DISCIPLINE

■ 27. The average civilian or recruit coming into the Army, often misunderstands the meaning of the words *military discipline*. He thinks of them as being connected with punishments or reprimands which may result from the violation of some military law or regulation. Actually, discipline should not be something new to you for you have been disciplined all of your life. You were being disciplined at home and in school when you were taught obedience to your parents and teachers, and respect for the rights of others. On your baseball or other athletic team you were disciplining yourself when you turned down the chance to be a star performer in order that the team might win; you were acquiring discipline in the shop, or other business, when your loyalty to your employer and your fellow employees was greater than your desire to secure your own advancement. All of this was merely the spirit of team play; that is, you were putting the interests of the "team" above your own in order that the "team" might win.

■ 28. The word "company," "troop," or "battery" is merely the military name for a *team,* and military discipline is nothing more than this same spirit of team play. It is the most important thing in the Army. In civil life lack of discipline in a young man may result in his getting into trouble which will cause his parents and teachers regret or sorrow; it may cause a member of an athletic team to be "sent to the bench," or cause an employee to lose his job. In the Army it is far more serious. Here lack of discipline in a soldier may not only cost him his life and the life of his comrades, but cause a military undertaking to fail and his team to be defeated. On the other hand a team of a few well-disciplined soldiers is worth many times a much larger number of undisciplined individuals who are nothing more than an armed mob. History repeatedly shows that without discipline no body of troops can hold its own against a well-directed and well-disciplined enemy.

■ 29. In your work in the Army you may wonder why the officers and noncommissioned officers insist on perfection in what appears to be minor details. Why do rifles have to be carried at just the same angle; why do you have to keep accurately in line; why must your bed be made in a certain way; why must your uniform and equipment be in a prescribed order at all times; why must all officers be saluted with snap and precision? These things are part of your disciplinary training. Their purpose is to teach you obedience, loyalty, team play, personal pride, pride in your organization, respect for the rights of others, love of the flag, and the will to win.

■ 30. So you see that being disciplined does not mean you are being punished. It means that you are learning to place the task of your unit—your team—above your personal welfare; that you are learning to obey promptly and cheerfully the orders of your officers and noncommissioned officers so that even when they are not present you will carry out their orders to the very best of your ability. When you have learned these things and prompt and cheerful obedience has become second nature to you, then you have acquired *military discipline*—the kind of discipline which will save lives and win battles.

Section II

MILITARY COURTESY

■ 31. In your home and school you were taught to be polite and considerate in your speech and attitude to your parents, your teachers, and your comrades. That was courtesy. Military courtesy is the same thing except that the military man is so proud of his profession and has such high respect for the men who belong to it that in the Army courtesy is more carefully observed than in civil life. Military courtesy is a part of military discipline. The disciplined soldier is always courteous whether on duty or off, whether to members of the military service or to civilians. To help you in quickly becoming a well disciplined and efficient member of your team, the following are some of the more common occasions on which you may have an opportunity to demonstrate your military courtesy. The rules are few and simple, but they have an important bearing on your career as a soldier.

a. The *military salute* is the courteous recognition between members of the armed forces of our country. The salute is a privilege enjoyed only by members of the military service in good standing; prisoners do not have the right to salute.

b. The salute is given when you meet a person entitled to it. Those entitled to it are all officers of our Army, Navy, Marine Corps, and Coast Guard. It is also customary to salute officers of friendly foreign countries when they are in uniform.

c. The salute should be given when you can easily recognize that the person is an officer and entitled to it. Usually this is at a distance of not more than 30 and not less than 6 paces, in order that the officer may have time to recognize and return it.

d. When you execute the salute turn your head so that you observe the officer and look him straight in the eye. The smartness with which you give it indicates the pride you have in your profession. A careless or half-hearted salute is discourteous. (See fig. 31.)

e. In posts, camps, or stations, the salute is always given whenever you recognize an officer, even though one or both of you are in civilian clothes. It is likewise given whether or not you are wearing a head covering. For rule when outside post, camp, or station see paragraph 32*j*.

f. If the officer remains in your immediate vicinity without talking to you, no further salute is necessary when he departs. If a conversation takes place however, you should again salute when either you or he leaves.

g. (1) If you are one of a group of soldiers, not in formation, call the group to attention as soon as you recognize an officer approaching, unless some other member of the group has already done so. If the group is out of doors, all members of the group salute; if indoors or in a tent, all remove their head covering and stand at attention unless otherwise directed.

(2) If the group is in formation out of doors, it is called to attention by the one in charge and he alone gives the salute.

(3) If you meet an officer on a staircase or in a hallway, halt and stand at attention.

h. The salute is given only at a halt, or a walk. Either mounted or dismounted, always bring your gait down to a walk before saluting. Except in the field under campaign conditions, always dismount before speaking to or replying to a dismounted officer.

i. If you report to an officer in his office, first remove your headdress, unless you are carrying your rifle or sidearms, and enter when told to do so. March up to within two paces of the officer's desk, halt, salute, and state, "Sir, Private ———— reports to ————." (For example, "Sir, Private Jones reports to the Company Commander.") After reporting, carry on the conversation in the first and second person. When the conversation is ended, salute, make an about face, and withdraw. Unless you are carrying your rifle or sidearms, always remove your headdress when entering a room where an officer is present.

j. If you are driving a motor vehicle, salute only when the vehicle is halted. If it is an animal-drawn vehicle, salute only when both hands are not required to control your team. Any other soldier in the vehicle salutes whether the vehicle is at a halt or in motion, unless there are a number of soldiers in the vehicle in charge of an officer or noncommissioned officer. In this case only the officer or noncommissioned officer gives the salute.

k. When you are dismounted and not in formation and the National Anthem is played, or "To the Colors," sounded, at the first note face the music, stand at attention and give the salute. At "Escort of the Color" or "Retreat," face toward the color or flag. If you are in civilian clothes and wearing a headdress, stand at attention, remove your headdress and hold it over your left breast. If you are in civilian clothes and not wearing a headdress, stand at attention and execute the hand salute. Hold the salute until the last note of the music. If you are mounted and not in formation, halt and give the salute while mounted. Vehicles in motion will be brought to a halt. If you are riding in a passenger vehicle or on a motorcycle, dismount and salute. In other types of military vehicles, as for example troop carriers, trucks, and escort wagons, all individuals except the person in charge of the vehicle remain seated or standing (depending on whether they are riding seated or standing) in the vehicle at attention. The person in charge of the vehicle, unless he is a tank commander or the driver of a horse-drawn vehicle, dismounts and renders the salute. Tank commanders salute from their vehicles. Drivers of horse-drawn vehicles remain in their vehicles and salute only if both hands are not required to control their teams. Individuals leading animals or standing to horse stand at attention but do not salute. The same respect is shown the national anthem of any other country when it is played on special occasions.

l. If you are passing, or being passed, by an uncased national color, render the same honors as when the National Anthem is played.

m. Whenever you are present but not in formation while personal honors are being rendered, salute and remain in that position until the completion of the ruffles, flourishes, and march.

n. (1) In garrison, if posted as a sentinel with a rifle, you will salute by presenting arms. During the hours when challenging is prescribed, the first salute is given as soon as the officer has been recognized and advanced.

(2) While posted as a sentinel, if you are talking to an officer, do not interrupt your conversation to salute another officer. However, if the officer to whom you are talking salutes his senior, you will also salute. A mounted or dismounted sentinel armed with a pistol salutes by executing the hand salute, *except* that when challenging you execute "Raise pistol" and retain that position until the challenged party has passed.

o. If you are attending a military funeral not as a member of a formation, and whether in uniform or civilian clothes, stand at attention, remove your headdress, and hold it over your left breast at any time the casket is being moved by the casket bearers and during the services at the grave, including the firing of volleys and the sounding of taps. During the prayers, bow your head. If the weather is cold or inclement, keep your headdress on and give the hand salute whenever the casket is being moved by the casket bearers, and during the firing of volleys and sounding of taps.

■ 32. The following situations will assist you in remembering when you do not or need not salute:

a. If you are in ranks and not at attention and an officer speaks to you, come to attention, but do not salute. The officer or noncommissioned officer in command of your unit will give the salute for the entire organization to the person entitled to it.

b. If an officer enters the mess room or mess tent, you remain seated, "at ease," and continue eating unless the officer directs otherwise. If the officer speaks directly to you, remain seated "at attention" until the conversation is ended, unless he directs otherwise.

c. Members of details at work do not salute. The officer or noncommissioned officer in charge will salute for the entire detail.

d. When actually taking part in games you do not salute.

e. When standing to horse or leading a horse do not salute.

f. In churches, theaters, or other places of public assemblage, or in a public conveyance, do not salute. Indoors, salutes are not given except when reporting to an officer.

g. Do not salute when carrying articles with both hands or when you are otherwise so occupied as to make saluting impracticable.

h. If you are posted as a mounted or dismounted sentinel and are armed with a pistol, do not salute after challenging. Stand at "Raise pistol" until the officer you have challenged has passed.

i. When on a march in campaign, or under simulated campaign conditions, do not salute.

j. Off duty, and when you are not in a post, camp, or station, the salute is optional unless you are addressed by an officer.

■ 33. While officers and noncommissioned officers will usually address you by your last name, always use their title in addressing them. The following titles are used in the military service:

a. All general officers are addressed as "General"; lieutenant colonels are addressed as "Colonel" and both first and second lieutenants as "Lieutenant."

b. All chaplains, regardless of grade, are officially addressed as "Chaplain."

c. Warrant officers are addressed as "Mister."

d. Members of the Army Nurse Corps are addressed as "Nurse."

e. Noncommissioned officers are addressed as "Sergeant" or "Corporal." Master sergeants, technical sergeants, and staff sergeants are all addressed as "Sergeant."

■ 34. As the result of the observance of military courtesy in our Army for many years, certain customs have come into existence which are recognized as our unwritten law of conduct. Every civilian community, school, or business has its own customs, and a newcomer should learn them as quickly as possible so that he will not be embarrassed. In the same way, you will discover that your own organization probably has its own local customs, many of which date from some event in the organization's history, and of which it is very proud. You should become familiar with these customs as early as possible. The following are a few of the general customs which are observed throughout our Army, and which you should know:

a. If you wish to speak to your company, battery, or troop commander, first obtain permission from your first sergeant. The company commander will always see you, but he may be busy at the time or the first sergeant may be able to answer your question.

b. If you wish to deposit some of your money on pay day, notify your first sergeant before reporting to receive your pay.

c. When you report to your company commander for pay, halt directly in front of him and salute. After receiving your pay count it quickly, execute a right or left face and depart.

d. Do not salute with one hand in your pocket, while smoking, or with your coat unbuttoned or partly unbuttoned.

e. If you should be accompanying a dismounted officer walk on his left; if both you and the officer are mounted ride on his left.

15

CHAPTER 3

INSIGNIA

Section I

ARMS AND SERVICES

■ 35. Insignia.—Each of the various arms and services in our Army has a particular "mark" of its own, which is worn by all of its members. It serves to distinguish those members from all other soldiers of the Army and is a part of the uniform. These various marks are called insignia and usually consist of two types: the metal insignia which you will wear on the lapel of your coat, and the colored hat cord which you will wear on your service hat.

■ 36. To assist you in becoming quickly familiar with the various types of insignia and so that you can tell at a glance to which arm or service a soldier may belong, they are shown in figure 1.

■ 37. Hat Cord.—At a distance it will be easier to recognize the arm or service to which a soldier belongs by the color of his hat cord. You should be familiar with the following colors and the arm or service which they identify. Where two colors are given, the cord is of the first color and the acorns and keeper are the color of the piping.

    a. Air Corps—Ultramarine blue piped with golden orange.

    b. Cavalry—Yellow.

    c. Chemical Warfare Service—Cobalt blue piped with golden orange.

    d. Coast Artillery Corps—Scarlet.

    e. Corps of Engineers—Scarlet piped with white.

    f. Field Artillery—Scarlet.

    g. Finance Department—Silver-grey piped with golden yellow.

    h. Infantry and tanks—Blue.

    i. Medical Department—Maroon piped with white.

REGULAR ARMY & ORGANIZED RESERVE
(Not assigned to regiment)
(With regimental number)

NATIONAL GUARD
(Not assigned to regiment)
(With regimental number)

Arm or Service

Distinctive Insignia

AIR CORPS

CAVALRY

CHEM. WARFARE SERVICE

COAST ART. CORPS

CORPS OF ENGINEERS

FIELD ARTILLERY

FINANCE DEPARTMENT

INFANTRY

MEDICAL DEPARTMENT

NAT. GUARD BUREAU

ORDNANCE DEPARTMENT

QUARTERMASTER CORPS

SIGNAL CORPS

DETACHED ENLISTED MEN

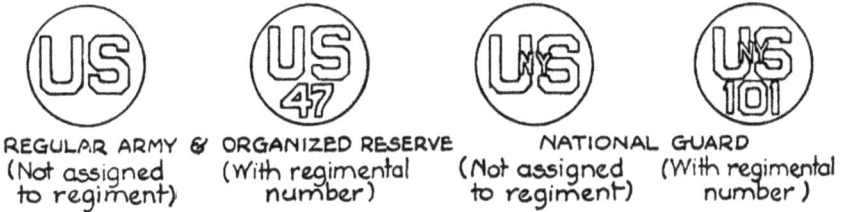

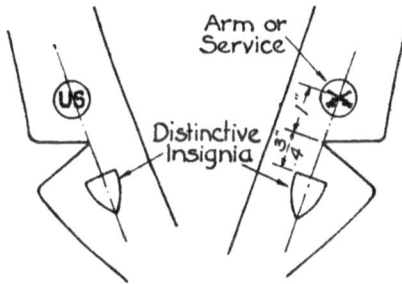

FIGURE 1.—Collar insignia for enlisted men.

j. Military Police—Yellow piped with green.

k. Ordnance Department—Crimson piped with yellow.

l. Quartermaster Corps—Buff.

m. Signal Corps—Orange piped with white.

■ 38. ARM BAND.—In addition to the identification marks described above, sometimes you will see certain soldiers wearing arm bands to show the particular type of work they are doing. These arm bands are called "brassards" and are worn on the left sleeve above the elbow. You will want to know the following brassards and what they mean:

a. Blue, with the letters, "MP" in white—Military Police.

b. Red, with the word "Fire" in white—Members of fire departments.

c. White, with red cross in center—Geneva Convention Red Cross.

d. White with green cross in center—Veterinary Green Cross.

■ 39. SERVICE STRIPE.—Each enlisted man who has served honorably in the military service for 3 years wears the service stripe. This stripe is worn 4 inches from the end of the left sleeve of the service coat. For each additional period of 3 years, another service stripe is worn.

■ 40. Wound and war service chevrons are worn only by those entitled to them. They are worn only on the woolen service coat, with the wound chevrons on the right sleeve and the service chevrons on the left sleeve. They are worn point down. When service stripes are worn the war service chevron is above the uppermost service stripe. (See fig. 2.)

■ 41. BADGE.—Soldiers are classified according to the qualifications attained in the use of weapons. The different classifications are: expert, sharpshooter or 1st class gunner, and marksman or 2d class gunner. Should you attain one of these classifications you will be entitled to wear a badge (fig. 3) which is issued by the War Department. A bar, attached to the bottom of the badge, shows the weapon with which you have qualified. Should you qualify with more than one weapon, you will be entitled to wear an additional bar for each weapon.

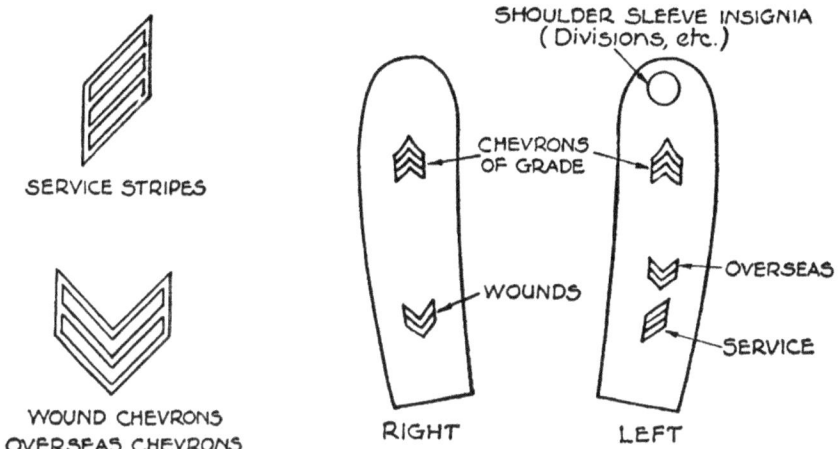

FIGURE 2.—Wearing of sleeve insignia.

FIGURE 3.—Badges for qualification in use of weapons.

Other bars to be attached to basic badges are as follows:

MACHINE RIFLE	SMALL BORE M. G.
AUTO. RIFLE	SUBMACHINE GUN
SMALL BORE RIFLE	GRENADE
BAYONET	COAST ARTY.
PISTOL-D	FIELD ARTY.
PISTOL-M	C. W. S. WEAPONS
SMALL BORE PISTOL	MINES
MECHANIZED VEHICLE	AERIAL GUNNER
WEAPONS	AERIAL BOMBER
INF. HOWITZER	ANTIAIRCRAFT WEAPONS
MACHINE GUN	

19

Section II

OFFICERS AND NONCOMMISSIONED OFFICERS

■ 42. Commissioned officers and noncommissioned officers also wear the insignia of the arm or service to which they belong and in addition certain other distinguishing marks which show their grade or authority in the Army. The insignia of grade worn by all officers on each shoulder loop of the coat, overcoat, or olive-drab shirt when worn without the coat, are shown in figure 4.

COLONEL (Silver) LT. COL. (Silver) MAJOR (Gold) CAPTAIN (Silver) 1ST LIEUT. (Silver) 2ND LIEUT. (Gold)

FIGURE 4.—Insignia of rank for officers (worn on shoulder loops).

■ 43. A general officer wears two bands of black braid just above the lower edge of each sleeve of the overcoat.

■ 44. Officers of the General Staff Corps wear a band of black braid 3 inches from the end of each sleeve of the service coat. All other officers wear a similar band of brown braid. All warrant officers and enlisted men who served honorably as officers in the World War wear a similar band of forest green braid.

■ 45. Noncommissioned officers wear chevrons of olive-drab material on a dark blue background. They are worn on the sleeve between the elbow and the shoulder of the olive-drab shirt, the coat, the overcoat, and the fatigue uniform. The chevrons for the different grades are shown in figure 5.

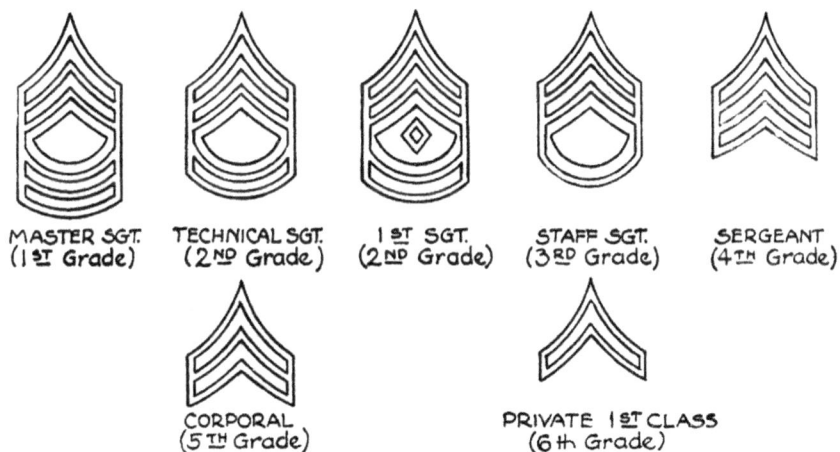

FIGURE 5.—Chevrons (insignia of grade) for noncommissioned officers and privates, first class (worn on sleeves).

CHAPTER 4

ORGANIZATION

■ 46. You are going to hear the word "organization" used constantly in your military service and it will help you to have an early understanding of just what the word means in the Army. If you think about it for a moment you will realize that, actually, organization is nothing new, for you have probably been familiar with its meaning for a long time in civil life. In your factory, shop, or office you remember how men were grouped according to the machine they operated or the type of work they did. The same thing was true in school where students were grouped by classes according to their progress and the number that each teacher could instruct. You are familiar with the way in which your local police and fire departments are divided into precincts or districts located in different parts of the city with one particular man in charge of each station.

■ 47. All of this grouping and arranging is for just one purpose—to get things done in the best way possible and without waste of time or effort. If every shop or office worker did only the things he wanted to do, and in his own way, his business would soon fail for he could not turn out his orders on time. If every student studied only the things he was interested in and only when he felt like it, we would soon be a nation of poorly educated people. If each time a fire occurred, the fire chief had to telephone the different firemen and tell them what to do, there would be little chance of saving many buildings. So, in order to direct the business workers, students, and firemen in their efforts, and to produce efficiency instead of confusion, they are divided into groups of a size which experience has shown one man can control. In charge of these groups are the foremen, chief clerks, teachers, or other group leaders you remember in civil life.

■ 48. The same arrangement exists in the Army and for the same purpose. You have been assigned to a company, troop, or battery of a certain regiment. In charge of your company, troop, or battery is an officer who is responsible for feeding, clothing, and training you and your comrades, and, finally, leading you to victory on the battlefield. He is your team captain. Your company, troop, or battery has in it from 100 to 200 men. If it were always going to be on the drill field, or in the barracks, the company commander could probably control it with his voice. But your team may not always remain in an area where the company commander can directly control it. It is training for the time when, if called upon, it will meet and defeat the enemy on the battlefield. There the distances and noise will make it impossible for the company commander to control directly more than a few men. So, to make sure that all the members of the team are exerting their efforts toward the same end, your company, troop, or battery is divided into a number of smaller groups called squads, sections, and platoons.

■ 49. *a.* In the Infantry and Cavalry the *squad* is the largest unit that can be effectively controlled by the voice and signals of its leader—the corporal or sergeant. In size it will vary from 4 to 16 members, depending upon the kind of squad it is. It takes its name from the principal weapon within the squad. For example, in a "rifle squad" the members are armed with the rifle; in a "machine-gun squad" the principal weapon is the machine gun which members of the squad serve, and in a "mortar squad" the principal weapon is the mortar. The squad is small enough so that the leader can directly control all of its members.

b. In the Field Artillery and Coast Artillery Corps the *section* is the smallest fighting unit. In these arms, squads are sometimes used for purposes of drill or administration. For combat, however, the members of the section are usually close enough to the gun they serve so that their leader, the sergeant, can control them.

■ 50. Next above the squad or section is the *platoon*, which is commanded by a lieutenant. A platoon includes several squads, or two sections, and has a strength of 40 or 50 soldiers. By the time we have reached a unit of this size you can see how difficult it would be for the lieutenant to control directly the actions of all members of the platoon while they are scattered over a large area in combat. He can easily control them, however, through his orders to his section or squad leaders.

■ **51.** *a.* Finally we come to your *company, troop,* or *battery.* It usually consists of 3 or 4 platoons and is commanded by a captain. Because of the way your company is "organized" it is possible for the company commander to control and direct efficiently the company as a whole through his orders to the platoon, section, and squad leaders and still have time to plan for the future care and welfare of the company. It would not be possible for him to do this if he did not have such an "organization," but had to spend his time constantly running back and forth, issuing orders to 200 individuals.

b. The organization of your company which has been discussed above deals with it as a fighting team. But to be able to fight effectively, it must be fed, clothed, and supplied with the necessary equipment. To assist the company commander in doing this, he has a company headquarters, whose principal noncommissioned officers are the first sergeant, the mess sergeant, and the supply sergeant. The first sergeant corresponds to the executive, or chief clerk, in a civilian office. He handles all of the administrative details of the company and publishes the orders of the company commander. The mess sergeant with his cooks secures and prepares the food you eat, and the supply sergeant issues you your clothing and equipment and exchanges it when it has become worn out or damaged. Your company is a carefully organized business with the various jobs so distributed that the largest possible number of men can be made available for its principal job of fighting.

■ **52.** The same considerations followed in the organization of your company, troop, or battery are carried on upward to your regiment. In the Infantry, Field Artillery, and Coast Artillery Corps, usually 4 companies or batteries are grouped to form a battalion, but there may be only 2 or 3. Similarly, in the Cavalry, troops are grouped as squadrons. These larger units, battalions or squadrons, are commanded by a major or lieutenant colonel. The regiment is composed of 2 or more—generally 3—battalions or squadrons and is commanded by a colonel. So you see how each unit from the 4-man squad up to the 500- or 1,000-man battalion fits into a definite place in the big regimental team. Each unit is so organized that one man will be able to control and direct it so that the full power of the team will be directed toward a common purpose.

■ 53. In certain arms of the Army you may find that one or more of the various units described above are not included in the organization for combat of that arm. In the Air Corps you will not find the squad, section, or platoon as fighting teams but only organized temporarily for drill and administrative purposes. The unit to which you will be assigned is a squadron, commanded by a major. The squadron, however, will be divided into sections which are named for the duties the members of that section perform. For example, the administrative section handles the squadron headquarters, mess, and transportation; the technical section does the engineering, supply, communication, photography, and repairs; and the flight section operates and maintains the aircraft of the squadron.

■ 54. In the same way, in certain armored units the smallest organization will be the crew of a scout car, tank, or personnel carrier, which will consist of 4 or more men, one of whom will be an officer or noncommissioned officer. Also certain other units such as chemical, antitank, and military police organizations will vary in size and numbers. But you will not be confused, in whatever organization you may be, if you will remember the purpose for which the Army is organized in every arm or service. It is necessary to secure the efficient control of all members of the team for success in battle.

CHAPTER 5

CLOTHING

SECTION I

ALLOWANCES

■ 55. When you enlisted or were inducted into the Army, you made a contract with your Government. Your part of the contract was to serve faithfully the United States of America against all their enemies. It was an obligation you were glad to assume in return for the many privileges you and your family have received as citizens of a free nation. As its part of the contract the Government agreed to pay, feed, clothe, and give you medical care during the time you were in the military service.

■ 56. You will be issued, without charge, all the articles of clothing necessary for the duties you will be required to perform. Whenever any item of this clothing is no longer serviceable, you may turn it in to your supply sergeant, who will replace it without charge. You must remember, however, that these articles of clothing are the property of the United States and are issued for your use while you are in the military service. If they are lost, damaged by your neglect, or unlawfully disposed of, the Government will require you to pay for them.

SECTION II

CARE OF CLOTHING

■ 57. Always remember that your uniform is more than a mere suit of clothes that is worn to cover and protect your body. It is the symbol of the honor, the tradition, and the achievements of our Army. The civilian or soldier who is careless in his dress and appearance is probably careless in everything else. You owe it to your comrades, your organization, and your Army to be neat and careful in your appearance, for officers and men of other organizations will judge your company by the impression you make.

■ 58. By being careful of your uniform, you have many advantages over a careless soldier. Your clothing will last longer, you will be neater and better dressed, and you will make a better impression on your comrades and officers.

■ 59. The following information will assist you in the care of your clothing:

a. Whenever you wear the uniform, either on or off duty, be sure that it is complete and that it conforms to the instructions of your post, camp, or station. Have your shirt, coat, and overcoat buttoned throughout. Keep your uniform clean, neat, and in good repair.

b. Dandruff, dust, or cigarette ashes on a uniform give a bad impression. If possible, keep a whisk broom in barracks for brushing your uniform. Promptly replace missing buttons and insignia.

c. Keep your woolen uniforms pressed. This not only improves the appearance of clothing, but actually increases its life.

d. Clothing not in use should be hung in wall lockers whenever available. If there are no wall lockers, fold your clothing carefully and put it away where it will not accumulate dust. Uniforms that have become wet or damp should not be folded until they are dry. It is also a good idea to inspect clothing before putting it away. Missing buttons and rips should be attended to as soon as you take off your clothing instead of waiting until it is again needed.

e. Grease spots on uniforms are unsightly and unmilitary. The sooner a grease spot is removed, the easier. Usually it helps to place a folded clean towel under the soiled part of the cloth during the cleaning. The cleaning should be done by dampening a clean white cloth with a good commercial cleaning fluid and rubbing gently back and forth in a straight line over a larger area than the spot until dry. This usually prevents leaving a ring on the fabric. Turpentine will remove

paint spots from clothing if used promptly, before the paint
gets dry.

f. Insignia and buttons having a gold finish should be
cleaned with ammonia and water. Don't use an abrasive, as
it will remove the gold plating. Rubber bands, manila paper,
or any material containing sulfur, if near medals, insignia, or
buttons, will tarnish them.

g. Have your woolen uniform dry-cleaned for summer
storage. Place adequate moth preventive between folds and
store during summer in locker trunk or storage space as nearly
airtight as possible.

h. (1) In cleaning your boots or shoes, first remove all dirt
or mud by scraping with a dull instrument such as a sliver of
wood. Do not use a piece of glass or a knife. Next, wash
them with a sponge saturated with a heavy lather of castile
soap. Never use hot water or allow the leather to soak in
water. Wipe off the lather with the wet sponge and rub the
leather thoroughly and vigorously with a clean cloth until
nearly dry. Drying by exposure to the sun, fire, or strong
heat will cause the leather to stiffen and crack and is forbidden. Stuffing the toes with crumpled paper helps in the
drying and tends to hold them in shape. After boots or
garrison or dress shoes have dried, a good polish should be
applied, provided that it has been authorized by the garrison
or unit commander. In the case of work shoes an application
of dubbing should be well rubbed in.

(2) For other articles of leather equipment, clean as described above. In the case of unfinished leather, while it is
still moist give it a very light coat of neat's-foot oil by rubbing
with a soft cloth moistened with the oil. Any oil not absorbed
by the leather should be wiped off. If more than a light coat
of oil is given, the leather will be greatly darkened and will
soil your clothing. If the leather is to be polished it should be
cleaned as described above and then polished with a good
grade of polish in the proper color.

Section III

WEARING THE UNIFORM

■ **60.** The manner in which your uniform should be worn is shown in figure 6.

① Field service.
② Garrison service, mounted.
③ Garrison service, dismounted.
④ Overcoat.

FIGURE 6.—Uniforms for enlisted men.

CHAPTER 6

ARMS AND EQUIPMENT

SECTION I

RESPONSIBILITY FOR CARE

■ 61. The arms and equipment which are issued to you are the property of the United States. They are entrusted to your care for military use during your period of service in the Army. You are responsible for them and it is your duty to see that they are properly cared for in the manner in which your officers and noncommissioned officers will instruct you. At various times you will attend inspections where your company commander, or other officers, will carefully check over your arms and equipment to see that you are taking the proper care of them and that they are clean and in condition for immediate active service. You will find that a little attention each day to the care and cleaning of your arms and equipment will save you time and effort in preparing for these inspections.

■ 62. Your safety and comfort in the field will depend upon the manner in which you keep your arms and equipment. You must take particular care not to lose them, as you may not be able to replace them by the time you will need them most. Before dark, place everything where you can quickly find it in the dark. Remember that carelessness in the protection and condition of your arms and equipment may cost you your life or health, or that of a comrade.

■ 63. Since these articles are the property of the United States, the Government will require you to pay for them should they be lost, damaged, or destroyed through your carelessness.

SECTION II

NOMENCLATURE AND CARE AND CLEANING OF U. S. RIFLE, CALIBER .30, M1

■ 64. The United States rifle, caliber .30, M1, is gas-operated, clip-fed, and air-cooled. It weighs about 9 pounds and the bayonet an additional pound. The clip holds 8 rounds. The rifle fires each time you squeeze the trigger. The rifle is provided with a safety lock. (See fig. 7.)

a. Disassembling.—The method of disassembling your rifle given below is sufficient for cleaning purposes. You should learn more detailed disassembling at your first opportunity. If you do not receive instructions as to disassembling, go to your squad leader, who will gladly show you how.

(1) *The three main groups.*—Grasp the rifle with the left hand so that the base of the trigger housing is included in the grip of the fingers. (See fig. 8.) Place the butt of the rifle against the left thigh. Grasp the rear portion of the trigger guard with the thumb and forefinger of the right hand and exert sufficient downward pressure to unlatch the trigger guard from the trigger housing. Then swing the trigger guard away from the trigger housing to the extreme opened position as shown in figure 8. Pull out the trigger housing group. Place this group on a smooth, clean surface. Grasp the rifle over the rear sight with the left hand, muzzle down and barrel to your left. (See fig. 9.) Strike and grasp the small of the stock with the right hand so as to separate the stock group from the barrel and receiver group as shown in figure 9.

(2) *Barrel and receiver group.*—(a) Place the group on a smooth surface, barrel down, and pointing to your left. Grasp the follower rod with the left thumb and forefinger at the knurled portion and disengage it from the follower arm by pressure toward the muzzle. Withdraw the follower rod (with compensating spring attached) to the right. (See fig. 10.) If necessary, remove the compensating spring from the follower rod by grasping the compensating spring with the left hand and twisting the follower rod toward your body with the right hand, exerting a slight pull to the right. Withdraw the operating rod spring.

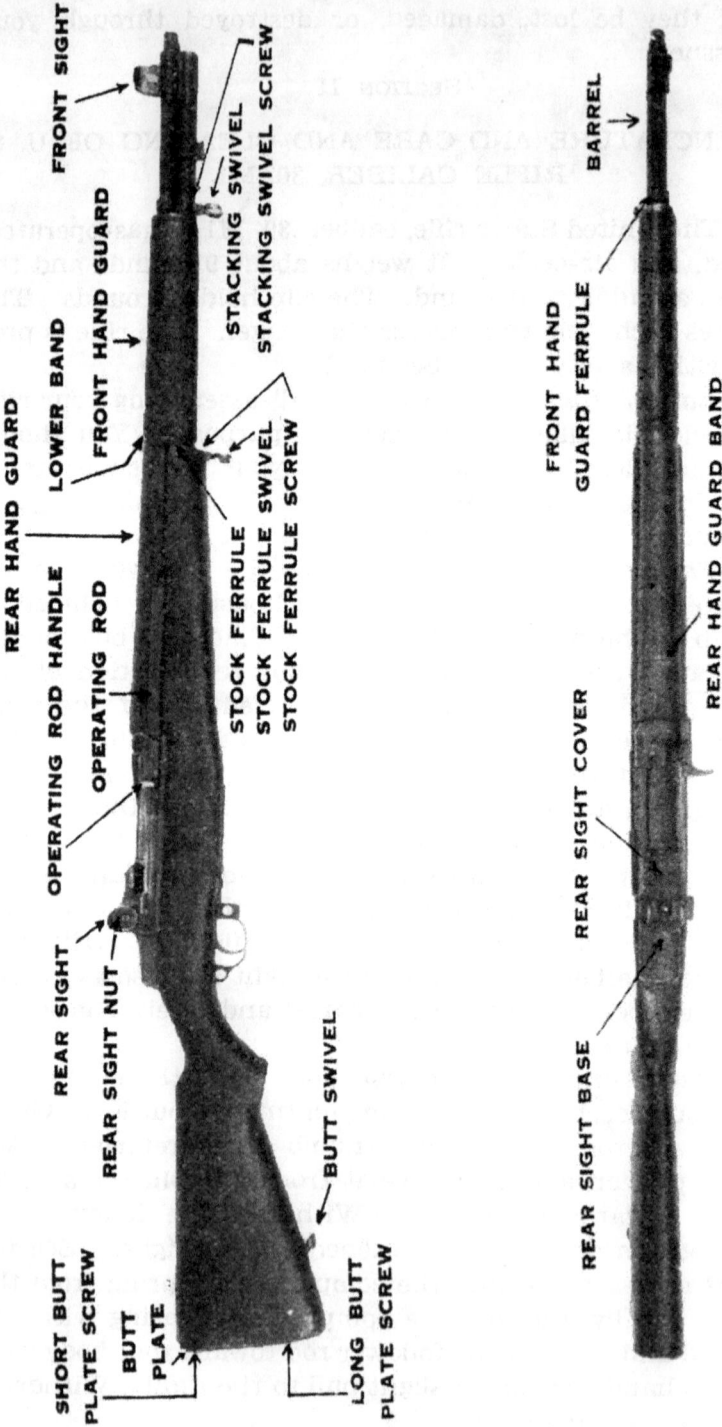

FIGURE 7.—U. S. rifle, caliber .30, M1.

FIGURE 8.

FIGURE 9.

(*b*) Drift the follower arm pin from its seat by starting it with the point of a bullet (or with the drift of the combination tool) held in the right hand and applied on the side of the receiver farthest from your body. Pull out the pin from the near side with the left hand. Grasp the bullet guide, the follower arm, and the operating rod catch assembly and pull to the left until these parts are disengaged. Lift out and separate these three parts. Do not remove the accelerator from the operating rod catch assembly, as the accelerator

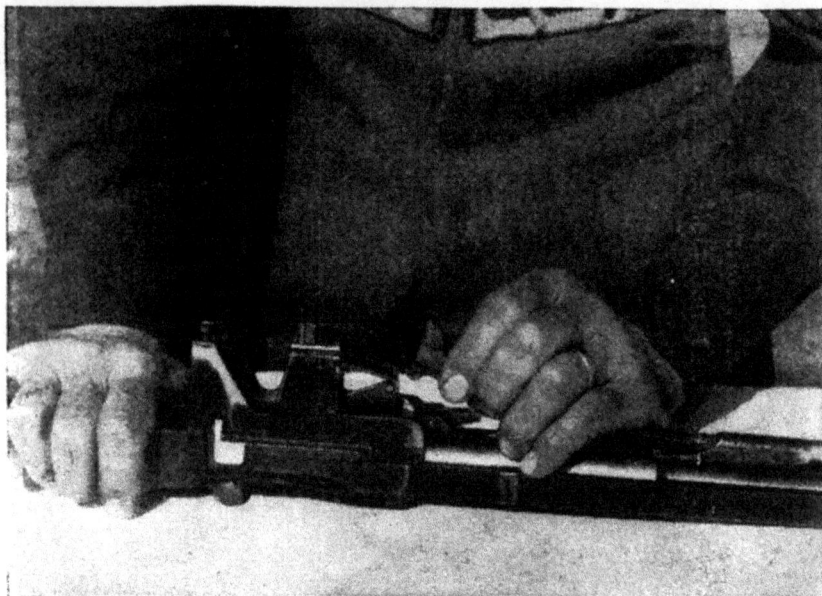

FIGURE 10.

pin is riveted in its seat. Lift out the follower with the follower slide attached. Do not separate the follower from the follower slide.

(*c*) Grasp the barrel and receiver assembly with the left hand and the operating rod handle with the right hand as shown in figure 11. Move the operating rod slowly to the rear, *pulling the operating rod handle upward and away from the receiver*. This will disengage the operating rod from the bolt when the lug on the operating rod slides up into the dismount notch of the operating rod guide groove. When the operating rod is thus disengaged, remove it with a downward and rearward movement.

NOTE.—The operating rod has been intentionally bent. Do not try to straighten it.

(d) Grasp the bolt by the operating lug, slide it from rear to front, and lift it up and out to the right front with a slight rotary motion. (See fig. 12.)

(3) *Gas cylinder.*—(a) There are now in existence two types of gas cylinders and front sight assemblies for the M1

FIGURE 11.

rifle. In the newer or spline type the barrel protrudes beyond the gas cylinder, and the front sight screw enters from the front and is sealed to prevent tampering. In the older or screw-on type the barrel does not protrude and the front sight screw enters from the side.

(b) In order to prevent undue wear, to insure proper maintenance of gas port adjustment, and to avoid improper assembly, the gas cylinder assembly should not be removed except when necessary to replace the front hand guard assembly. Before such removal be sure the operating rod has been removed. To remove the gas cylinder, proceed as follows:

       1. Spline type.—Unscrew gas cylinder lock screw, using combination tool. Unscrew gas cylinder lock. Tap gas cylinder lightly toward muzzle to remove it from barrel. The front sight will not

FIGURE 12.

       be dismounted from the gas cylinder assembly. Do not attempt to adjust the front sight.

       2. Screw-on type.—Remove front sight screw and lift out front sight. Unscrew gas cylinder assembly from barrel.

b. Assembling.—(1) *Gas cylinder.*—Replace the gas cylinder reversing the procedure of the preceding paragraph.

   (2) *Barrel and receiver group.*—(a) Incline the barrel and receiver assembly at an angle of approximately 45°, sights

up, muzzle up and to the front. Hold the bolt by the right locking lug so that the front end of the bolt is slightly above and to the right of its extreme forward position in the receiver. Insert the rear end in its *bearing on the bridge of the receiver*, rotating it in a counterclockwise direction sufficiently to permit the tang of the firing pin to clear the top of the bridge. Then guide the left locking lug of the bolt into its groove at a point just to the rear of the lug on the left side of the receiver, and the right locking lug onto its bearing in the receiver, and slide the bolt back to its extreme rear position.

(b) Turn the barrel and receiver assembly, in the left hand, until the barrel is down. With the right hand, grasp the operating rod at the handle. Hold the handle up and insert the piston head into the gas cylinder about three-eighths of an inch, making sure that the operating rod handle is to the left of the receiver. Hold the barrel and receiver assembly in the left hand and rotate it to the right until the barrel is uppermost. With the right hand, adjust the operating rod so that the camming recess on its rear end fits over the operating lug of the bolt. Press the operating rod forward and downward until the bolt is seated in its forward position.

(c) Place the barrel and receiver assembly on a smooth surface, barrel down and muzzle to your left. Replace the follower (with the follower slide attached) so that its guide ribs fit into their grooves in the receiver, the *square hole* in the follower to the right. Follower slide will rest on bottom surface of the bolt when the follower is in position correctly.

(d) With the left hand replace the bullet guide so that the shoulders of the bullet guide fit in their slots in the receiver and the hole in the projecting lug is in line with the holes in the receiver.

(e) With the left hand replace the follower arm by passing its studded end through the slot in the bullet guide and inserting the studs in their grooves in the front end of the follower. Place the forked end of the follower arm in position astride the projecting lug on the bullet guide with the pin holes in alinement. Insert the rear arm of the operating rod catch through the clearance cut in the bullet guide, *making sure that its rear end is underneath the forward stud on the clip latch* which projects into the receiver opening. Aline the holes in the operating rod catch, the follower arm, and the bullet guide with those in the receiver. Insert the follower arm pin in the side of the receiver which is toward your body and press the pin home.

(*f*) If separated, insert the operating rod spring into the operating rod. Assemble the follower rod and the compensating spring by grasping the spring in the left hand and inserting the follower rod with the right hand, twisting the two together so that the compensating spring is fully seated on the follower rod. Grasp the knurled portion of the follower rod with the thumb and forefinger of the left hand, forked end to the right, hump down. Insert the left end of the follower rod into the operating rod spring, push to the left, and seat the forked end against the studs on the follower arm. The hump on the follower rod must be in the slot in the operating rod catch.

(3) *The three main groups.*—(*a*) Insert the U-shaped flange of the stock ferrule in its seat in the lower band. Pivoting about this point, guide and press the barrel and receiver group into position in the stock. Insert the trigger housing group, with the trigger guard in its open position, into the opening in the stock. Press it into position and close and latch the trigger guard.

(*b*) Test the assembly as follows: Pull back the operating handle to its rearmost position; press down on the follower and allow the bolt to go fully home; set the safety in its rearmost position; pull the trigger; hammer should *not* fall; set the safety in its foremost position; pull trigger; hammer *should fall.*

c. Model 1903 rifle.—This rifle is sometimes called the *Springfield rifle.* It is a breech-loading magazine rifle of the bolt type. The magazine holds 5 rounds which are ordinarily put up in brass clips of 5 for easy loading. The rifle weighs about 8½ pounds and the bayonet an additional pound. If you are equipped with this rifle, learn to disassemble the bolt and floor plate as soon as practicable. Your squad leader will gladly show you how.

d. Care of the rifle.—(1) *General.*—Your rifle is a machine. It gives the best results when it is clean and properly lubricated. A dirty, poorly lubricated rifle may have stoppages which will make it useless in battle. Inspect your rifle daily and see that it is clean and properly lubricated. Neglect of your rifle may cost you your life on the battlefield.

(2) *Cleaning the bore.*—Powder fouling in the bore contains salts. Salts rust steel. To remove these salts, run a clean patch which has been saturated with hot water and issue soap through the bore a number of times. Plain, clean water, hot or cold, should be used when soap is lacking. While still wet, the metal brush should be run through the bore several times to loosen up any material which has not been dissolved by the water. The bore should then be thoroughly dried and coated with a light issue gun oil. The chamber is included in this process, the chamber cleaning tool being used.

(3) *Cleaning gas cylinder, M1 rifle.*—Carbon will accumulate from firing. The frequency of carbon removal is a factor peculiar to individual rifles. Excess deposits of carbon in the rifle show themselves by sluggishness in action and failure to feed.

(a) *Spline type.*—To remove accumulated deposits of carbon from the gas cylinder, remove the lock screw and remove carbon, using the screw driver blade of the combination tool. The gas cylinder lock may be removed and the lock screw reinserted in the gas cylinder and threaded in enough to break loose the carbon. The inside of the gas cylinder should be thoroughly wiped clean and oiled at the conclusion of firing. (A few drops of oil placed between the rear gas cylinder lug and the operating rod, with the muzzle tipped down, will be sufficient if firing is contemplated on the next day. Hand operate the rod through a few cycles to distribute the oil properly.) The exterior finish should be cleaned and lightly oiled. The sight should be kept free from dust and dirt.

(b) *Screw-on type.*—Scrape the carbon from the exposed surface of the front of the gas cylinder and gas cylinder plug and piston head after extensive firing. Clean the gas cylinder plug and the grooves in the gas cylinder to insure correct seating of the plug. The frequency of this cleaning depends on the amount of firing. A sharp-bladed instrument similar to a mess kit knife should be used to remove the carbon from the gas cylinder plug and piston head. If an abrasive cloth is used care should be taken that the corners of the plug or piston head are not rounded. *Do not remove the gas cylinder for cleaning.* The gas cylinder is cleaned by using the cleaning rod and a patch in the same manner followed in cleaning the bore.

(4) *Miscellaneous.*—(a) All metal parts should be cleaned and covered with a uniform light coat of oil. The following parts are excepted. They should be lubricated with a thin, uniform coating of graphite cup grease issued for that purpose.

1. Bolt lugs (locking and operating).

2. Bolt guides.

3. Cocking cam on bolt.

4. Compensating spring.

5. Contact surfaces of barrel and operating rod.

6. Operating rod cam.

7. Operating rod groove in receiver.

8. Operating rod spring.

(b) Wooden parts should be treated with a light coat of raw linseed oil not oftener than once a month.

(c) Screw heads should be kept clean or they will collect rust.

(d) Clips should be kept clean.

(e) Leather sling should be washed, dried with a rag, and lightly oiled with neat's-foot oil while still damp. You should do this whenever the sling shows signs of stiffening or drying.

(f) To remove rust from metal parts, rub the spot with a piece of soft wood and oil.

(5) *Don'ts.*—(a) Do not apply graphite cup grease to the follower slide or under surface of the bolt. It might get into the chamber and cause excessive pressures.

(b) Do not use sandpaper, metal polish, or other like meterials on your rifle. They may remove the antirust finish on your rifle; then you have a job on your hands to keep it free from rust.

(c) Do not put a plug in the muzzle. It will cause the bore to rust. You may forget it is in there and fire the rifle, causing it to blow up.

(d) Do not put off until tomorow cleaning a rifle that has been fired. The rifle will rust overnight and your job will be that much harder.

(*e*) Do not over-oil your rifle. Heavy coats of oil will collect dirt.

SECTION III

NOMENCLATURE, CARE AND CLEANING, AND SAFETY DEVICES OF AUTOMATIC PISTOL, CALIBER .45, M1911

■ 65. The automatic pistol, caliber .45, M1911, is a recoil-operated, magazine-fed, self-loading, hand weapon. The magazine holds 7 rounds. The pistol weighs about 2½ pounds. (See fig. 13.)

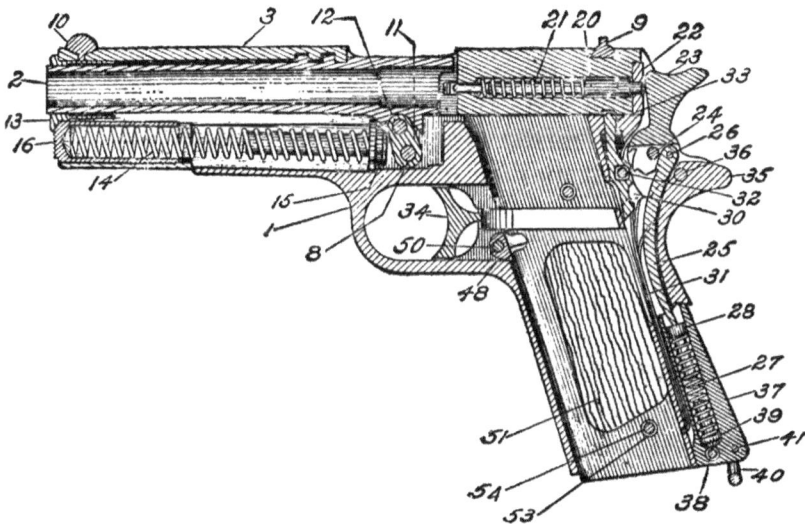

FIGURE 13.—Longitudinal section of pistol, showing component parts in assembled position.

a. The method of disassembling your pistol given below is sufficient for cleaning purposes. You should not attempt more detailed disassembling until you have received instruction from your officers or noncommissioned officers.

(1) Remove the magazine by pressing the magazine catch (**48**).

(2) Press the plug (**16**) inward and turn the barrel bushing (**13**) to the right until the plug (**16**) and the end of the recoil spring (**14**) protrude from their seat, releasing the tension of the spring (**14**). As the plug (**16**) is allowed to protrude from its seat, keep your finger or thumb over it so that it will not jump away and be lost, or strike you in the

face. Draw the slide (3) rearward until the smaller rear recess in its lower left edge stands above the projection on the thumbpiece of the slide stop (8); press gently against the end of the pin of the slide stop (8) which protrudes from the right side of the receiver (1) above the trigger guard and remove the slide stop (8).

(3) This releases the link (11), allowing the barrel (2), with the link (11) and the slide (3), to be drawn forward together from the receiver (1), carrying with them the barrel bushing (13), recoil spring (14), plug (16), and recoil-spring guide (15).

(4) Remove these parts from the slide (3) by withdrawing the recoil-spring guide (15) from the rear of the recoil spring (14), and drawing the plug (16) and the recoil spring (14) forward from the slide (3). Turn plug (16) to right to remove from recoil spring (14). Turn the barrel bushing (13) to the left until it may be drawn forward from the slide (3). This releases the barrel (2), which, with the link (11), may be drawn forward from the slide (3), and by pushing out the link pin (12) the link (11) is released from the barrel (2).

b. To assemble, proceed in the reverse order. When replacing the slide (3) and barrel (2) on the receiver (1), care must be taken that the link (11) is tilted forward as far as possible and that the link pin (12) is in place.

c. The pistol is provided with a number of safety devices which you should test frequently. A safety device is a dangerous device if it does not work when expected. The following tests will determine whether the safety devices are working or not.

(1) *Safety lock.*—Cock the hammer and then press the safety lock upward into the "safe" position. Grasp the stock so that the grip safety is depressed and squeeze the trigger three or four times. If the hammer falls, the safety lock is not safe and must be repaired.

(2) *Grip safety.*—Cock the hammer and, being careful not to depress the grip safety, point pistol downward and squeeze the trigger three or four times. If the hammer falls, or the grip safety is depressed by its own weight, the grip safety is not safe and must be repaired.

(3) *Half-cock notch.*—Draw back the hammer until the sear engages the half-cock notch and squeeze the trigger. If

the hammer falls, the hammer or sear must be replaced or repaired. Draw the hammer back nearly to full cock, and then let it slip. It should fall only to half cock.

(4) *Disconnector.*—Cock the hammer. Shove the slide one-quarter inch to the rear; hold slide in that position and squeeze the trigger. Let the slide go forward, maintaining the pressure on the trigger. If the hammer falls, the disconnector is worn on top and must be replaced. Pull the slide all the way to the rear and engage the slide stop. Squeeze the trigger and at the same time release the slide. The hammer should not fall. Release the pressure on the trigger and then squeeze it. The hammer should then fall. The disconnector prevents the release of the hammer unless the slide and barrel are in the forward position safely interlocked. It also prevents more than one shot following each squeeze of the trigger.

d. Care of pistol.—(1) *General.*—To prevent wear and tear on the working parts of your pistol, keep it clean and properly lubricated. A dirty, dry pistol, or one which has been over-oiled and allowed to gather dirt will have stoppages that may make it useless in battle. A failure of your pistol in battle may cost you your life.

(2) *Cleaning the bore.*—Powder fouling in the bore contains salts. Salts rust steel. To remove these salts, run a cleaning patch soaked in hot water and issue soap through the bore a number of times. Plain, clean water, hot or cold, should be used when soap is lacking. While still wet, the metal brush should be run through the bore several times. This will loosen up any material which has not been dissolved by the water. The bore should then be thoroughly dried and coated with a thin, uniform coat of issue gun oil.

(3) *Miscellaneous.*—(a) All metal parts should be cleaned and covered with a thin, uniform coat of oil.

(b) Screw heads should be kept clean or they will collect rust.

(c) The magazine should be cleaned with an oily rag. If dirt and grit have gotten into it, remove the follower and spring and clean the inside.

(d) Remove rust spots by rubbing with a soft stick and oil.

(4) *Don'ts.*—(a) Do not use sandpaper, metal polish, or like materials on your pistol. They may remove the antirust

finish from your pistol, then you will have a job keeping it free from rust.

(*b*) Do not put a plug in the muzzle of the bore. It will cause the bore to rust. You may forget it is in there and fire your pistol, causing it to explode.

(*c*) Do not lay your pistol down where dirt can get into it.

(*d*) Do not fail to inspect your pistol daily in the field. Your life may depend on its functioning at the proper moment.

SECTION IV

SAFETY PRECAUTIONS

■ 66. All weapons used in the Army are designed to kill. Remember this and handle them with care. Observe the following rules at all times:

a. Treat all weapons as though they were loaded until you, *yourself,* have inspected them to see that they are not loaded.

b. Do not take someone else's word that the weapon is empty. Inspect it.

c. Each time you pick up a weapon find out if it is loaded by inspecting it yourself.

d. Do not leave a loaded weapon around where someone else may unknowingly pick it up.

e. When you put your weapons away, inspect them to see that they are unloaded.

f. Do not point a weapon at anyone unless you intend to kill him.

g. Load only when you receive orders to.

h. Learn how to use the safety locks before you ever load a weapon.

i. When your weapon is loaded and you are not firing, keep the safety lock on, particularly when advancing, as you may catch your trigger in brush and kill yourself or comrade.

j. Do not pick up shells, bombs, hand grenades, and the like, until you have been instructed in the handling of such ammunition and then only when you receive orders to do so.

k. Do not pick up any shell or other metal object which you may see on the battlefield or firing range. It may be a "dud" (an unexploded shell), which may go off when you disturb it.

44

l. Be careful what you pick up on the battlefield. A magazine, newspaper, can of food, and other apparently innocent articles may be "bait" for a "fool's trap," or "booby" mine which will explode when you pick it up.

SECTION V

THE GAS MASK

■ 67. The American Army service gas mask which is issued to you is the best all around military gas mask known. It is the main device for protecting your face, eyes, lungs, and throat from the effects of gases, smokes, fumes, dusts, and chemical fogs, and is made to take care of all the known chemical warfare agents. However, it will *not* protect against carbon monoxide or ammonia gas and is not suitable for use in fighting fires or in industrial accidents where ammonia gas is present.

■ 68. *a.* The gas mask consists essentially of a facepiece, a hose, and a can containing a filter. This can, called the canister, is connected by the hose to the facepiece, which fits tightly to your face. Air is drawn in through the canister, where the objectionable gases, vapors, fogs, dusts, or smokes are removed, either mechanically or by chemical action. The cleaned air then passes on to the facepiece where it is breathed and then expelled through a valve. The drawing (fig. 14) illustrates how your gas mask works.

b. The facepiece is made of rubber or a similar fabric and is held to your face by means of an elastic head harness. These materials may easily be damaged by carelessness and improper use. For example, if a facepiece is not properly placed in the carrier, or if it is distorted, a crease might be formed which would prevent a positive seal between the facepiece and your face. Unless the rim of the facepiece fits snugly to your face, gas-laden air may leak in. The elastic straps may also become damaged by excessive stretching.

■ 69. Inexperienced persons often make the mistake of pulling up the head harnesses too tight, or of pulling up one strap more than its mate. If you adjust the harness too tightly, you will soon get a headache. If you adjust the head harness

45

unevenly, a channel and consequent leak between the facepiece and your face is often formed. (Fig. 15.) This also
often happens if you put the facepiece on carelessly.

■ 70. The canister is the most important part of your mask,
for it is here that the air is cleaned and made safe for breathing. It contains chemicals which will be damaged if water

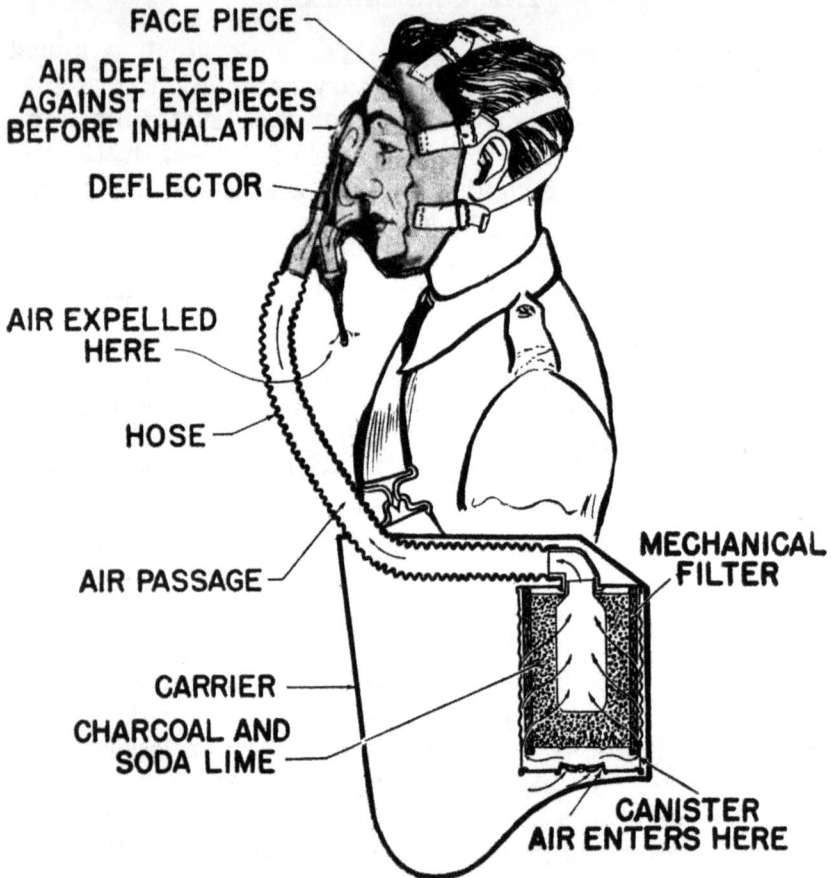

FACE PIECE

AIR DEFLECTED
AGAINST EYEPIECES
BEFORE INHALATION

DEFLECTOR

AIR EXPELLED
HERE

HOSE

AIR PASSAGE

CARRIER

CHARCOAL AND
SODA LIME

MECHANICAL
FILTER

CANISTER
AIR ENTERS HERE

FIGURE 14.—How your gas mask works.

gets inside. You must always guard your gas mask canister
from excess moisture.

■ 71. You should always be careful of your gas mask.
Never use it as a seat or pillow. Although it is pretty strong
and rugged, it will not stand abuse. You should never
carry anything but the gas mask and antidim can in the

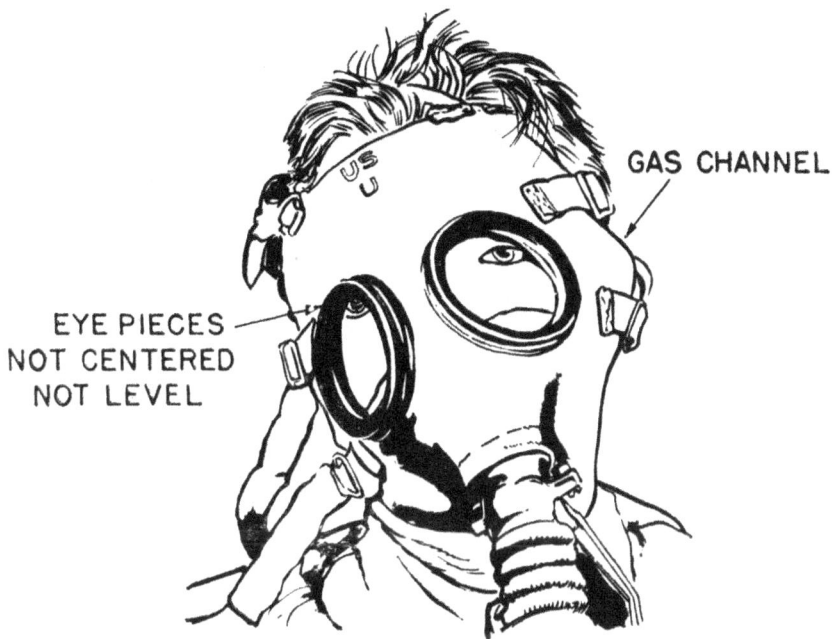

GAS CHANNEL

EYE PIECES
NOT CENTERED
NOT LEVEL

① Faulty—front view.

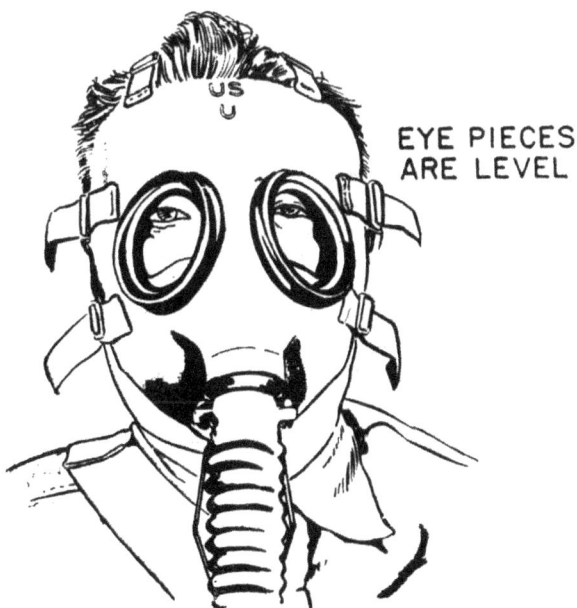

EYE PIECES
ARE LEVEL

② Correct—front view.

FIGURE 15.—Mask adjustment.

HEAD PAD
NOT CENTERED

GAS
CHANNEL

STRAPS
NOT
ADJUSTED
EVENLY

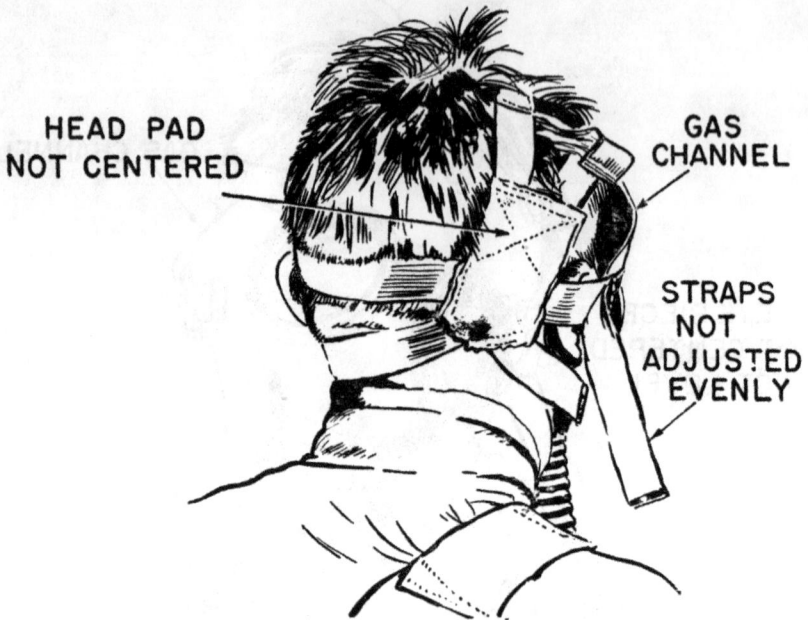

③ Faulty—rear view.

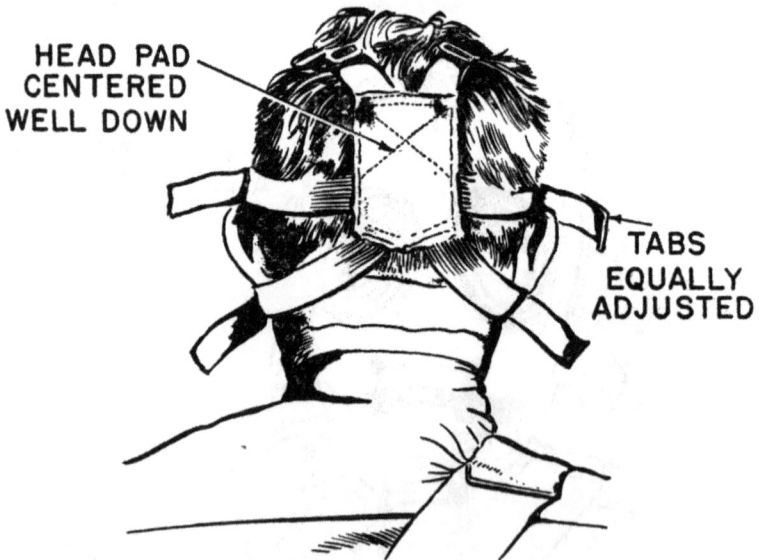

HEAD PAD
CENTERED
WELL DOWN

TABS
EQUALLY
ADJUSTED

④ Correct—rear view.

FIGURE 15.—Mask adjustment—Continued.

carrier. Socks, tobacco, apples, or other objects may choke up the mask, or otherwise injure it. Such objects also prevent quick removal of the facepiece from the carrier. The wise soldier quickly learns how to inspect his gas mask and makes a daily inspection of it as a matter of habit.

■ 72. Before you become accustomed to it you may find your gas mask uncomfortable. But as you become more used to wearing it, and as you habitually train yourself to work and exercise with it properly adjusted, such discomfort disappears. It is only by wearing the mask daily and performing some sort of work, or drill, while masked that you can train your chest and lung muscles to the unaccustomed extra work and strain. You also become accustomed to your decreased ability to move and see. When adjusting the gas mask at the command GAS, care in putting it on is more important than great speed. However, with practice, you should be able to stop breathing for 30 seconds, and in this time the mask can be securely and carefully adjusted to your face.

■ 73. An enemy will try to attack troops who are known to be inexperienced or careless in gas mask drill and gas discipline. If he suspects that your battalion as a whole is liable to go out without gas masks, or that it cannot do a reasonable amount of work while masked, or that it fails to post gas sentries, he will very likely make a gas attack. To beat him, you should always keep your gas mask with you, keep it in good condition, and not abuse it. You should know how to put it on, and be able to wear it for several hours at a stretch while fighting or working, and, finally, you should always be on the lookout for a gas attack.

SECTION VI

FIELD EQUIPMENT

■ 74. The articles of field equipment issued to you have been developed and manufactured after careful study and experiment by the War Department. You must keep them in proper condition for field service and not remove or change the finish of any article. If it becomes necessary to renew any worn surfaces your company, troop, or battery commander will explain how it is to be done and supervise the work. By following the instructions given below you will find that your equipment will always be in first class condition for inspections and field service.

■ 75. All cloth equipment should be well brushed frequently with a stiff-bristled brush. A dry scrub brush will serve this purpose. During ordinary garrison duty it should seldom be necessary to wash the equipment. Soiled spots can usually be removed by a light local washing. During field service, equipment becomes soiled much more rapidly. Dirty equipment should be given a thorough washing, otherwise it will become insanitary and liable to rot.

■ 76. A white soap is issued for the washing of cloth equipment, but any good grade of white laundry soap will serve the purpose. Strong soap, such as yellow kitchen soap, should never be used for washing equipment because it usually contains a large amount of free alkali and it will fade or bleach the material.

a. Before being washed, the equipment should be thoroughly brushed to remove all dust and mud.

b. Spread the belt, haversack, pack carrier, or other article on a clean board or rock and apply the soap solution with a scrub brush. After working up a good lather, wash off with clear water. A bad grease spot can ordinarily be removed by the direct application of soap with the brush, followed by a good scrubbing.

c. Always dry washed equipment in the shade. The bleaching action of the sun on damp fabric is strong. Equipment wet from a march in the rain should also be dried in the shade if practicable. Excessive fading of equipment can thus be reduced.

■ 77. Such articles as the canteen and the different parts of the mess outfit should be kept clean. Water and food should not be kept in them longer than necessary. Aluminumware should be cleaned with soap and water, although a little sand will sometimes assist in the cleaning of canteens. Sometimes small white particles will be found in canteens which have been filled with hard water. These particles are harmless. When not actually in use, the canteen should be emptied and the cup left off to dry.

■ 78. The knife blade is made of tempered steel and when put away for long periods should be covered with a light film of oil to prevent rust.

■ 79. Bits, curb chains, and all metal parts issued unpainted will be oiled lightly when not in use. When in use they will be kept clean and free from rust. Removing paint from metal parts which are issued painted is prohibited except under the direction of your company, troop, or battery commander.

■ 80. *a.* Leather equipment is expensive, and its proper care is important because of its value and the fact that if neglected it soon becomes unserviceable.

b. Two agents are necessary to the proper care of leather equipment—a cleaning agent and an oiling agent. The cleaning agent issued is castile or similar type soap; the oiling agents are neat's-foot oil substitute, saddle soap, and harness soap.

c. Neat's-foot oil is the most satisfactory oiling agent for leather. It penetrates the pores and saturates the fibers, making them pliable and elastic. Dry leather is brittle, but leather oiled excessively will soil the clothing and accumulate dirt.

d. Leather should be treated with enough oil to make it soft and pliable, but should not be given so much oil that it will squeeze out.

e. When leather is washed with any soap, some of the surface oil is always removed. This leaves the surface, after drying, hard and liable to crack. If this surface oil is replaced by direct application of neat's-foot oil, it is very difficult not to apply too much. This has led to the development of saddle soaps, which contain a small amount of neat's-foot oil, so that the surface of the leather after washing is not deprived of its oil.

f. Leather equipment in use should be wiped off daily with a damp cloth to remove mud, dust, or other dirt. Under no conditions should it be cleansed by immersion in water or in running water. This daily care is necessary to maintain the appearance of the equipment, but is insufficient alone to preserve it properly.   At intervals of from 1 to 4 weeks, depending upon circumstances, it is essential that the equipment be thoroughly cleaned in accordance with the following instructions:

(1) Separate all parts, unbuckle straps, remove all buckles, loops, etc., where possible.

(2) Wipe off all surface dust and mud with a damp (not wet) sponge. Rinse out the sponge and make a lather by rubbing it vigorously on white soap. The sponge must not contain an excess of water if a thick lather is desired. When a creamy lather is obtained, clean each piece of equipment, taking care that no part is neglected. Each strap should be drawn its entire length through the lathered sponge to remove the dirt and sweat from the leather.

(3) Rinse the sponge again and make a thick lather with saddle soap; go over each separate piece with the same care as before.

(4) Allow the leather to become partially dry and then rub it vigorously with a soft cloth. The equipment should now have a neat, healthy appearance.

g. If the foregoing instructions have been carefully followed, the leather should now be soft and pliable and no further treatment should be necessary. At certain intervals, however, it is necessary to apply a small amount of neat's-foot oil. No general rule in regard to the frequency of oiling can be given because different conditions of climate and service have to be taken into consideration. Experience has shown that during the first few months of use a set of new equipment should be given at least two applications of neat's-foot oil per month. Thereafter need for oiling is indicated by the appearance and pliability of the leather. Frequent light applications of oil are much better than infrequent heavy applications.

h. New leather equipment should always be given a light application of neat's-foot oil before it is put into use; cleaning with soap is unnecessary because the equipment is clean.

i. Whenever leather becomes wet from any cause whatever, it should be slowly dried in the shade. Leather should never be dried in the sun or close to a radiator, fire, or other heat.

■ 81. Soon after your equipment is issued to you, you will receive instructions from your officers and noncommissioned officers as to how the different parts should be assembled so that it can be carried or worn. The following table will help you in remembering the different items of your equipment and how they will be carried. This table includes the basic equipment common to the greater portion of our military service. Should special equipment be issued to you for particular conditions, or should you belong to an arm or service which has its own special equipment, you will receive instructions as to how it will be carried.

Field equipment, enlisted men (other than clothing worn on person)

Article	Dismounted	Mounted on horse (artillery drivers, see next column)	Driver, horse (artillery only)	Driver, vehicle	Men mounted in vehicle*
Bag, canvas, field, with carrying strap.	On right side, slung by a strap passing over left shoulder to right side.			On right side, slung by a strap passing over left shoulder to right side or in/on vehicle.	On right side, slung by a strap passing over left shoulder to right side or in/on vehicle.
Bags, feed and grain		On pommel under raincoat.	On seat of saddle, off horse, or on limber.		
Belt, pistol, revolver, cartridge, or magazine.	Worn.	Worn.	Worn.	Worn.	Worn.
Blankets, wool	In pack carrier. Carried on back or in cargo vehicle.	In cantle or blanket roll.	In cantle or blanket roll.	In pack carrier or in blanket roll. Carried on back or in/on vehicle.	In pack carrier or in blanket roll. Carried on back or in/on vehicle.
Canteen, cup and cover.	On belt, left rear.	Slung from off (right) cantle ring and attached to off saddlebag.	Slung from near (left) cantle ring, off horse and attached to saddlebag.	On belt, left rear or in/on vehicle.	On belt, left rear or in/on vehicle.
Glasses, field	On right side, slung by strap passing over left shoulder.	On right side, slung by strap passing over left shoulder.		On right side, slung by strap passing over left shoulder.	On right side, slung by strap passing over left shoulder.

Handkerchiefs	In blanket roll	Near (left) saddle bag.	Near (left) saddlebag, off horse.	In blanket roll, or in saddle bag.	In blanket roll.
Haversack	On back, attached to belt.		On back, attached to belt.	On back, attached to belt.	On back, attached to belt.
Helmet, steel	Attached to rear of haversack.	Attached to near (left) saddlebag.	Attached to off (right) saddlebag, off horse.	Attached to bag, canvas, field, near saddlebag, or to rear of haversack.	Attached to haversack, or bag, canvas, field.
Holster, pistol	Attached to belt, opposite right hip.	Attached to belt, opposite right hip.	Attached to belt, opposite right hip.	Attached to belt, opposite right hip.	Attached to belt, opposite right hip.
Horseshoes, 2 extra, with nails.		In off (right) saddlebag.	In off (right) saddlebag, off horse.		
Intrenching tool (machete or bolo).	Attached to rear of haversack.		In off (right) saddlebag, off horse.		Attached to rear of haversack.
Kit, grooming, complete, and saddle soap and sponge.		In off (right) saddlebag.	In near (left) saddlebag, off horse.		
Kit, mess, complete.	In haversack	In near (left) saddlebag.	In near (left) saddlebag, off horse.	In bag, canvas, field, in haversack, or in saddlebag.	In haversack or in bag, canvas, field.
Laces, shoe, extra.	In haversack	In near (left) saddlebag.	In near (left) saddlebag, off horse.	In bag, canvas, field, in haversack, or in left saddlebag.	In haversack or in bag, canvas, field.

*Alternative methods for carrying equipment of men mounted in vehicles are prescribed for the reason that types of vehicles, nature and lengths of march, etc., vary so greatly that the description of only one method for one vehicle will not suffice.

Field equipment, enlisted men (other than clothing worn on person)—Continued

Article	Dismounted	Mounted on horse (artillery drivers, see next column)	Driver, horse (artillery only)	Driver, vehicle	Men mounted in vehicle*
Mask, gas, horse		Strapped to halter under throat latch.	Strapped to halter under throat latch.		
Mask, gas, service	Slung under left arm by strap passing over right shoulder.	Slung under left arm by strap passing over right shoulder.	Slung under left arm by strap passing over right shoulder.	Slung under left arm by strap passing over right shoulder.	Slung under left arm by strap passing over right shoulder.
Overcoat	Attached to haversack.	Strapped to pommel over feed bag.	Strapped across seat of saddle, off horse.	Attached to haversack, to bag, canvas, field, or in/on vehicle.	Attached to haversack, to bag, canvas, field, or in/on vehicle.
Pocket, magazine, web, double.	Left front of belt.	Left front of belt.	Left front of belt.	Left front of belt.	Left front of belt.
Pouch, first-aid packet.	Right rear of belt.	Right rear of belt.	Right rear of belt.	Right rear of belt.	Right rear of belt.
Raincoat	In haversack.	Attached to pommel over feed bag.	Strapped across seat of saddle, off horse.	In haversack, in bag, canvas, field, or in/on vehicle.	In haversack, in bag, canvas, field, or in/on vehicle.
Rations	In haversack.	Distributed between the two saddlebags to balance load.	Distributed between the two saddlebags of horse to balance load.	In haversack, in bag, canvas, field, or in saddlebags.	In haversack or in bag, canvas, field.

Item					
Saddlebags, pair	---	On bars of saddle in rear of cantle.	Across seat off saddle or on bars of saddle in rear of cantle, off horse.	Motorcyclists—in rear of seat.	---
Scabbard, bayonet	Attached to left side of haversack.	---	---	---	Attached to left side of haversack.
Scabbard, rifle	---	Attached to near (left) side of saddle, under skirt.	---	Attached to vehicle.	---
Set, toilet	In haversack	In near (left) saddlebag.	In near (left) saddlebag, off horse.	In blanket roll or in saddlebag.	In blanket roll.
Socks, pair	In blanket roll	In near (left) saddlebag.	In near (left) saddlebag, off horse.	In blanket roll or in saddlebag.	In blanket roll.
Surcingle	---	In off (right) saddlebag, or over saddle blanket.	Attached, one to each saddlebag, off horse.	Attached, one to each saddlebag, off horse.	---
Suspenders	---	Attached to belt.	Attached to belt.	Attached to belt.	Attached to belt.
Tag, identification, with tape.	Around neck, under shirt.	Around neck, under shirt.	Around neck, under shirt.	Around neck, under shirt.	Around neck, under shirt.
Tent, shelter half, complete with pole, rope, and pins.	In pack carrier, carried on back, or in vehicle.	Covering (pole, rope, and pins within) blanket roll, on cantle or in/on vehicle.	Covering (pole, rope, and pins within) blanket roll, carried on seat of saddle, off horse or on limber.	Covering (pole, rope, and pins within) blanket roll, carried in/on vehicle.	Covering (pole, rope, and pins within) blanket roll, carried on back or in/on vehicle.
Towel, face	In haversack	In near (left) saddlebag.	In near (left) saddlebag, off horse.	In haversack, in bag, canvas, field, or in saddlebag.	In haversack or in bag, canvas, field.

*See note on page 55.

Field equipment, enlisted men (other than clothing worn on person)—Continued

Article	Dismounted	Mounted on horse (artillery drivers, see next column)	Driver, horse (artillery only)	Driver, vehicle	Men mounted in vehicle*
Trumpet	Suspended on right side by strap passing over left shoulder.	Suspended on right side by strap passing over left shoulder.			Suspended on right side by strap passing over left shoulder.
Underclothing	In blanket roll. Carried on back or in cargo vehicle.	In near (left) saddlebag, or blanket roll.	In near (left) saddlebag, off horse, or in blanket roll.	In blanket roll, in bag, canvas, field, or in saddlebag.	In blanket roll. Carried on back or in cargo vehicle.
Whistle (chain, hooked to left shoulder loop buttonhole).	In left pocket, shirt or coat.	In left pocket, shirt or coat.	In left pocket, shirt or coat.	In left pocket, shirt or coat.	In left pocket, shirt or coat.

*See note on page 55.

SECTION VII

THE INFANTRY PACK

■ 82. THE INFANTRY PACK.—The normal way in which you
will carry your basic equipment is given in the table in paragraph 81. In this section is described and illustrated the
proper way for you to assemble your pack with full field
equipment, to adjust it, and to discard the roll without
removing the remainder of the equipment from your body.

■ 83. METHOD OF ASSEMBLING HAVERSACK AND PACK CARRIER.—
a. Belt.—(1) *Pistol or revolver belt* (fig. 16).—Place belt on the
ground, outer side of belt down. Insert hook end of belt
through sliding keeper, then through unattached male buckle

FIGURE 16.—Pistol belt.

with stud down, double belt back through sliding keeper and
secure end hook in the particular center eyelet required to
give proper length. Slide magazine pouch over attached
female buckle end and attach it to the fastener provided. The
belt is put on with male buckle on the man's right.

(2) *Cartridge or magazine belt* (fig. 17).—Place adjusting
strap on the ground, eyeleted edge to the front; place pocket
sections on the ground in prolongation of adjusting strap,
pockets down, tops of pockets to the front; insert end of
adjusting strap in outer loop of metal guide from the upper
side, carry it under middle bar and up through inner loop;
engage hooks on the end of adjusting strap in eyelets provided
on inner surface of belt. The belt is adjusted to fit the
individual. It should fit loosely about the waist so that when
buckled it may rest well down over hip bones and below the
pit of the abdomen. Care should be taken that adjustments
are made equally from both ends of adjusting strap so that
center eyelet will be in the middle of belt. The proper position of the belt is the same, whether filled or empty.

b. To attach pack carrier to haversack (figs. 18 and 19).— Spread haversack on the ground, inner side down, outer flap and meat can pouch to the front. Place buttonholed edge

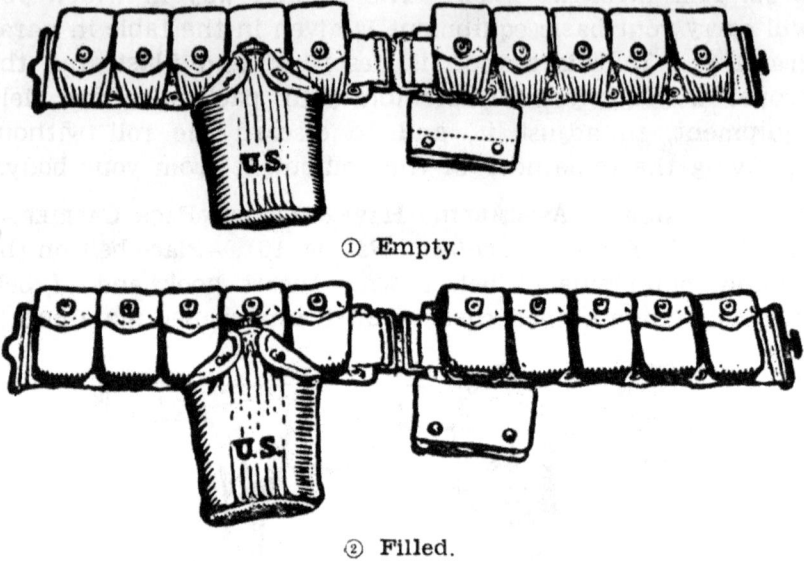

① Empty.

② Filled.

FIGURE 17.—Belt, cartridge, or magazine.

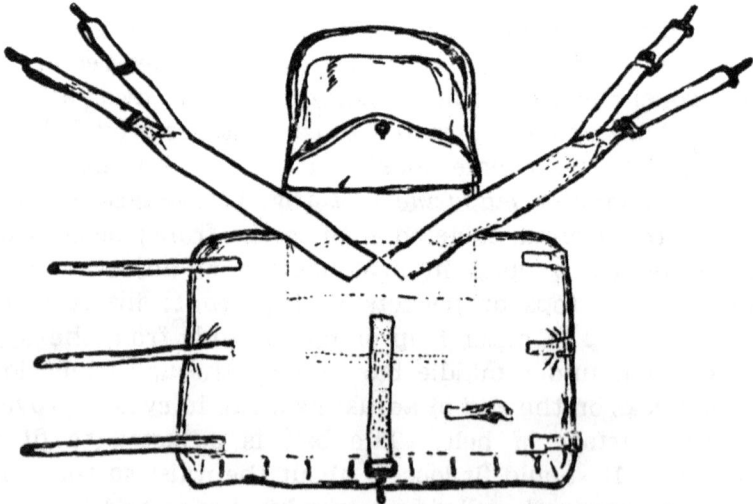

FIGURE 18.—Haversack without pack carrier.

of pack carrier, lettered side of pack carrier up, under buttonholed edge of haversack. Superimpose buttonholes of

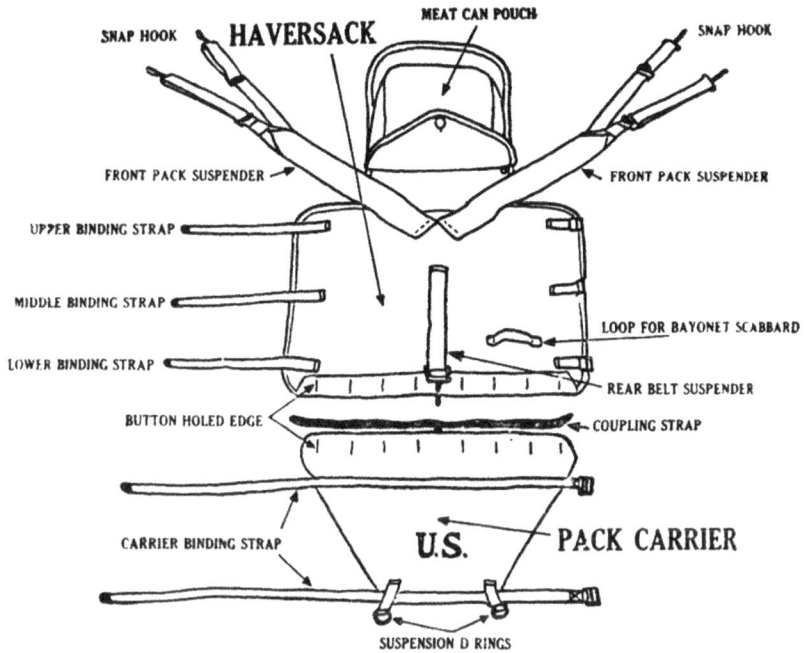

① Before joining (outside view).

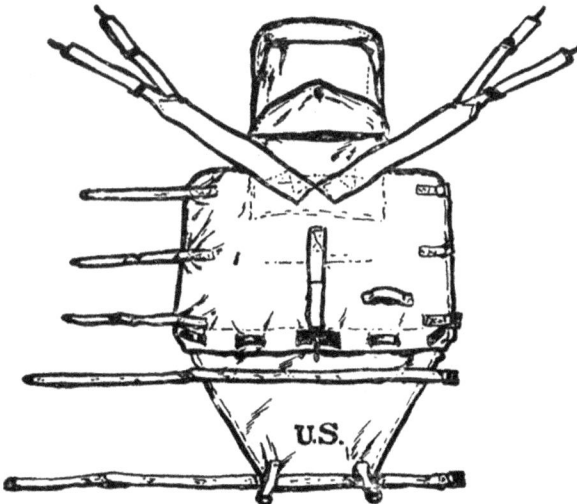

② After joining (outside view).

FIGURE 19.—Haversack and pack carrier.

haversack upon corresponding ones of pack carrier. Lace
the pack carrier to haversack by passing the ends of coupling strap down through corresponding buttonholes of
haversack and pack carrier nearest the center, bringing the
ends up through next buttonholes and continuing to the
right and left, respectively, to the sides.

c. *To attach haversack.*—(1) *To cartridge or magazine
belt.*—Place haversack and pack carrier (assembled) on the

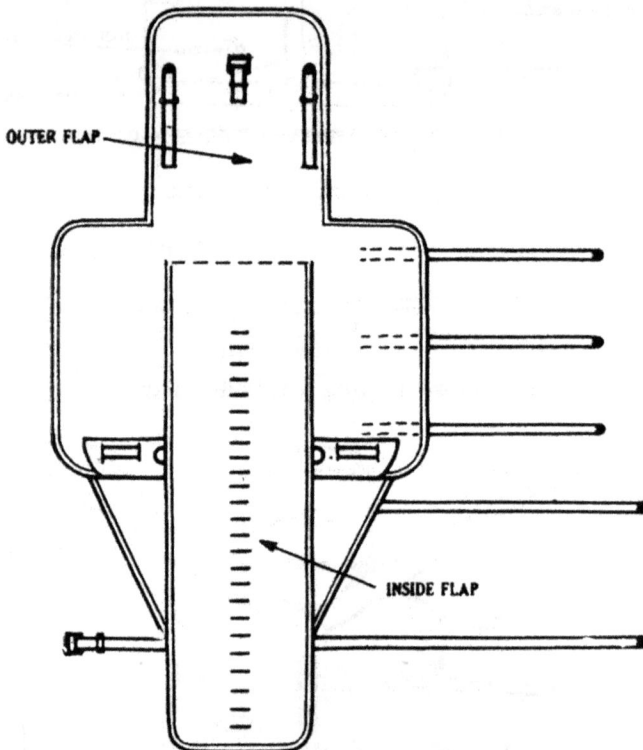

③ Inside view.

FIGURE 19.—Haversack and pack carrier—Continued.

ground, inner side down; place belt along the junction of
haversack and carrier, pockets down, tops toward the haversack; insert hooks on rear belt suspenders in upper rear eyelets of each belt section so that point of hooks will be on
the outside of belt; twist from belt suspenders toward the
ends of belt and insert snap hooks in eyelets between first
and second pockets from each end of belt so that the points

of the snap hooks will be on the outside of belt and suspenders will be flat on the body.

(2) *To pistol or revolver belt.*—Proceed as with the cartridge belt, the hooks on the end of front belt suspenders being inserted in the third eyelets from the buckle, and hooks on rear belt suspenders in two of the upper eyelets respectively to right and left of center of belt.

d. To attach bayonet scabbard.—(1) *To haversack.*—Attach scabbard by passing its lower end through loops provided on the side of haversack body; then engage double hook attachment in eyelets on outer flap of haversack, inserting hook from the under side. Place bayonet in scabbard, ring to the rear. (See fig. 25③.)

(2) *To cartridge belt.*—When the haversack is not carried, attach scabbard to left side of cartridge belt over left hip. Place bayonet in scabbard, ring to the front.

e. To attach intrenching tool or machete carrier to haversack.—Fold outer flap of haversack over so that meat can pouch is uppermost; pass intrenching tool carrier underneath meat can pouch and engage double hook attachment in eyelets in flap provided, inserting hooks from the under side. Secure intrenching tool to roll by means of third haversack binding strap. (See fig. 25③.)

f. To make the roll (fig. 20).—Spread shelter half on the ground and fold in triangular end so that shelter half forms a rectangle. Make a second fold by carrying folded edge to opposite edge. Fold the blanket twice parallel to its longer axis so that blanket is now one-fourth its previous width, and then fold once at the middle so as to bring the ends together. Place blanket symmetrically in center of folded shelter half; place underwear, socks, and handkerchief between folds of blanket. Place tent pole on that end of the blanket from which the rolling is to begin. Place pins as shown in figure 20②. (An alternate method is to place pins next to and parallel with pole.) Fold sides and then the near end of shelter half snugly over the blanket; fold 10 inches of far end of shelter half toward the blanket and, beginning at near end, roll tightly into folded end of shelter half, thus making an envelope roll.

g. To pack the haversack (fig. 21).—(1) Place equipment on the ground, inside of haversack up, pockets of belt up, haversack spread out, inside flap and pack carrier extended to their full length. Place rations in the center of haversack in front of and touching line of attachment of inside flap. Place toilet articles in front of rations. Fold inside flap of haversack over these articles. Fold sides of haversack over rations and toilet articles. Pass upper two binding straps through loop opposite point of attachment of the strap to haversack body. Fasten each strap by passing end of strap through the opening of its opposite buckle next to the buckle attachment, over center bar and back through opening of buckle away from attachment. Pull strap tight and make fastening secure. Fold over outer flap of haversack and fasten it by means of the lower haversack binding strap passed through the buckle on inside of outer flap. Pull strap toward the right, drawing outer flap snugly over filled haversack. The haversack is now packed and the carrier is ready for reception of the roll.

(2) When rations are not carried, roll toilet articles in inside flap so that top of toilet articles will be on line with top of haversack body. Then fold up lower haversack strap against the roll thus formed.

① First step.
FIGURE 20.—To make the roll.

h. To assemble the pack (fig. 22).—Place roll in pack carrier and haversack with one end against bottom of packed haversack. Grasp lower suspension rings, one in each hand. Place right knee against bottom of roll. Pull carrier down and force roll up close against bottom of packed haversack. Without removing the knee, fasten lower pack carrier binding strap over the roll and secure it by

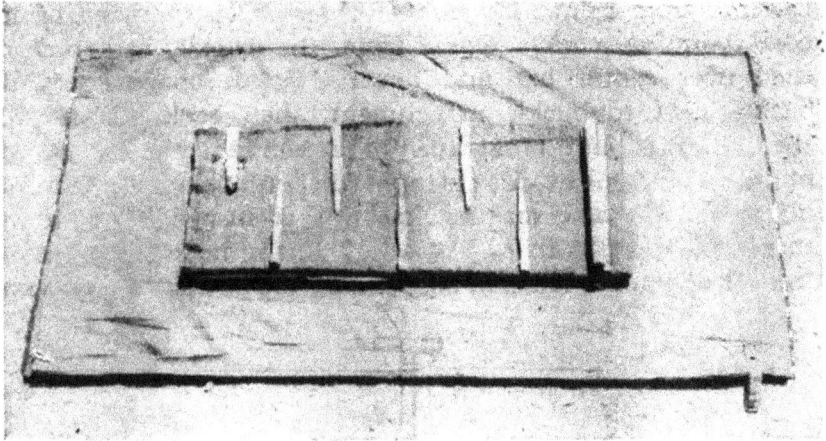

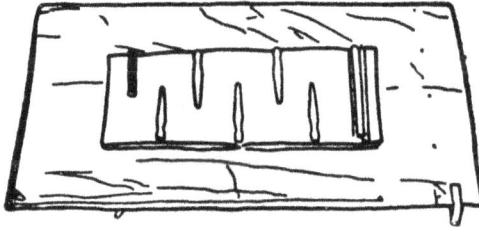

② Second step.

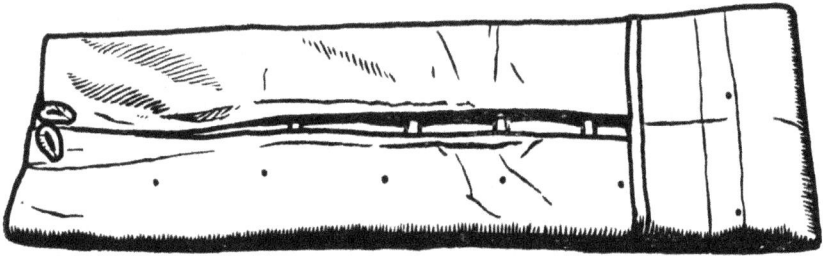

③ Third step.

④ Completed roll.

FIGURE 20.—To make the roll—Continued.

passing, from below, its end up through the opening of its corresponding buckle away from the buckle attachment, then over center bar and down through opening of the buckle next to buckle attachment, then back underneath the standing end of strap. In a similar manner secure middle haversack binding strap and then upper carrier binding strap. Engage snap hooks on pack suspenders in lower suspension rings. In order to obtain the maximum benefit from the shoulder loops in suspending the pack on the wearer,

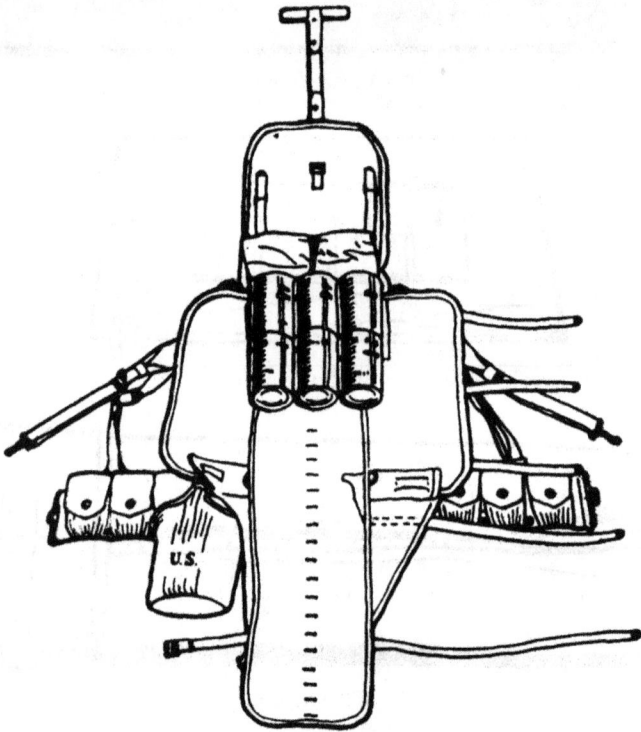

① First step.

FIGURE 21.—To pack the haversack.

each pack should be so assembled that when the roll is carried the length of the assembled haversack and pack carrier is at least 27 inches. This may be done by placing clothing or equipment ordinarily carried elsewhere in the ration space in the haversack so that the assembled pack will be the same length as when rations are carried. When this method is used, the pack carrier will not be folded under.

i. To fold and attach the overcoat (figs. 23 and 24).—Turn sleeves inside out, place overcoat on the ground, outside down, coat smooth, collar extended, sleeves smooth and extended toward pockets; move inside flap of tail under outside flap about 6 inches and gather the slack in the coat thus caused in one fold along middle seam, tapering toward the collar. Fold bottom of front edges of coat about 12 inches toward center seam, forming an approximate parallelogram, the side of

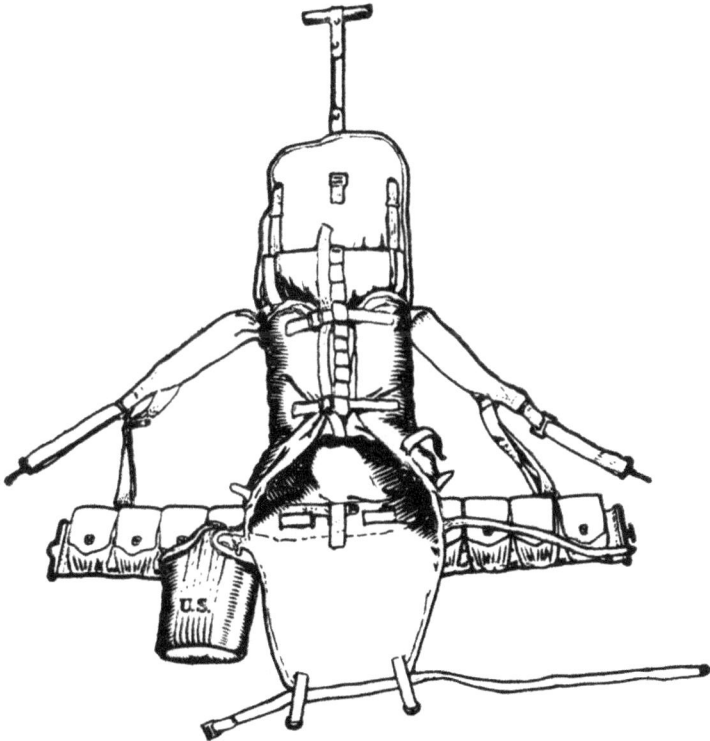

② Second step.

FIGURE 21.—To pack the haversack—Continued.

which across the coat will be 42 inches. Fold collar end down about 15 inches at the top and roll smoothly and tightly toward the tail; turn tail up to a depth of about 9 inches, and roll entire coat into this pocket. Place the overcoat thus rolled, open side of roll down, on top of haversack, in rear of bayonet handle so that center back seam is over center of top of haversack. Secure coat at the top with a shelter half rope. Bind the ends of overcoat down and along the sides of haversack. Lash the ends of roll to haversack with the rope, using a half hitch near each end of overcoat and passing the rope around haversack over outside flap.

j. To attach the raincoat.—Fold raincoat neatly into a rectangle about 10½ inches long by 8½ inches wide, with outside of raincoat out. Place raincoat between inner and outer haversack flaps. Secure it with lower haversack bind-

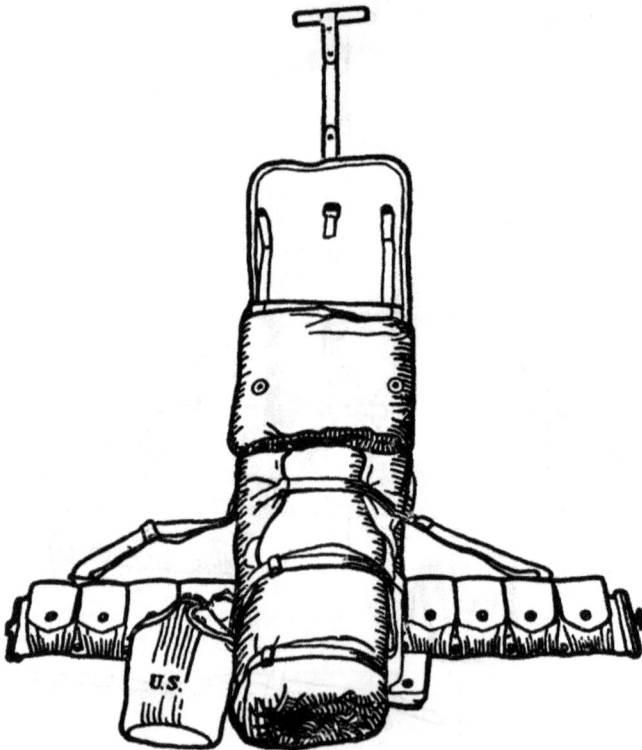

FIGURE 22.—Pack assembled.

ing strap by passing the latter under bottom haversack binding strap and fastening it tightly to the buckle on under side of outer haversack flap.

k. To attach the helmet.—Attach and secure the helmet by placing chin strap over meat can pouch.

l. To adjust full equipment.—Put on equipment, slipping the arms through pack suspenders as through sleeves of a coat. By means of adjusting buckles on belt suspenders,

raise or lower the belt until it rests well down over hip bones
and below pit of abdomen. Raise or lower it in rear until
adjusting strap lies smoothly across small of the back. By
means of adjusting straps on pack suspenders, raise or lower
the load on the back until the top of haversack is on a
level with top of shoulders, so that pack suspenders from
their point of attachment on the haversack to the shoulders
will be horizontal. The latter is essential to proper adjustment of the load. (See fig. 25.)

*m. To discard the roll without removing equipment from
the body.*—Unsnap pack suspenders from suspension rings

① First step.
FIGURE 23.—To fold the overcoat.

and snap them into eyelets on top of belt and in rear of
rear pockets of right and left pocket sections. Support bottom of pack with left hand, with right hand grasp coupling
strap at its middle and withdraw first one side and then the
other. Pull down on the roll with both hands and remove
it. When the roll has been removed, lace coupling strap
through buttonholes along upper edge of carrier.

② Second step.

③ Completed fold.

FIGURE 23.—To fold the overcoat—Continued.

SECTION VIII

PACKING INDIVIDUAL EQUIPMENT ON HORSE

■ 84. The method of packing your saddle is very important in keeping your mount in top condition and able to withstand hard work. You must distribute the weight evenly on your horse's back. Pressure resulting from an uneven distribution of arms and equipment may result in sores or cause injury to withers and back. Consequently, *balance* the weight of articles attached to one side of the saddle as

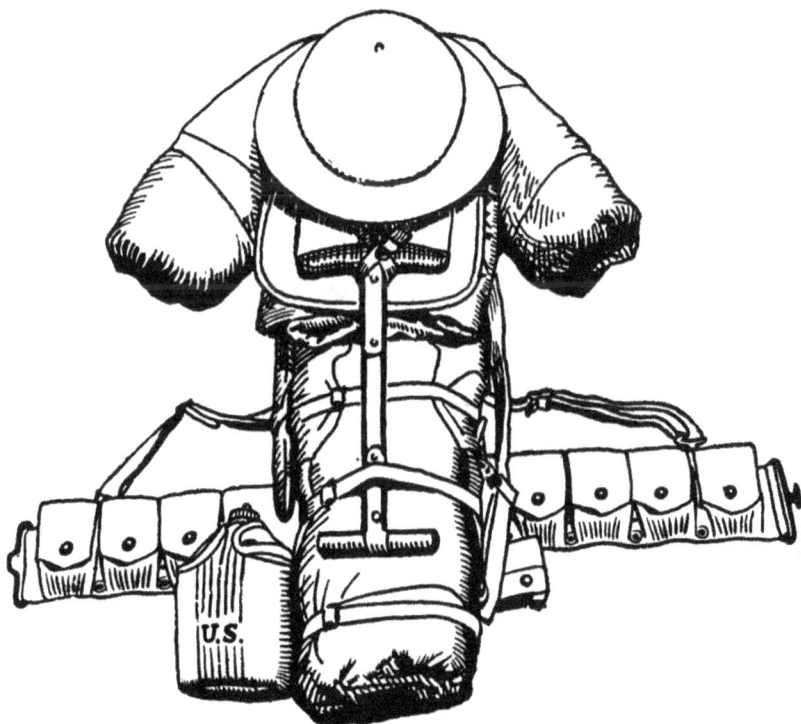

FIGURE 24.—Full equipment with overcoat and raincoat.

nearly as possible by the weight of articles attached to the other side. Weight is carried better by the pommel than by the cantle.

■ 85. *a.* In this paragraph the method of packing individual equipment on horse is described and illustrated.

b. To assemble and pack the cantle or blanket roll.—(1) The shelter tent half is spread flat on the ground, buttons up. The triangular flap is folded over shelter tent half,

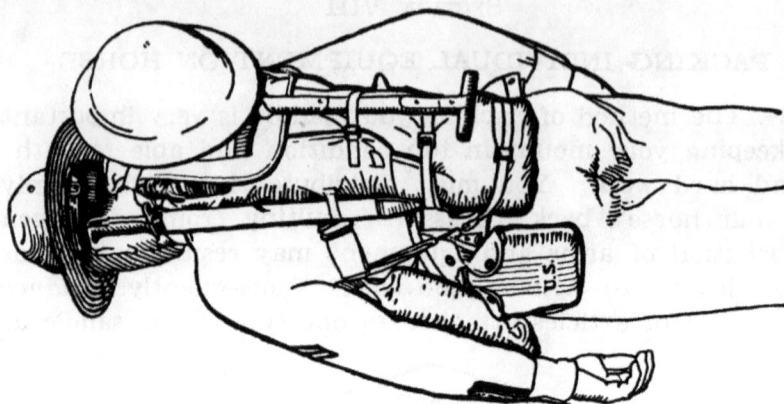

③ Left rear view.

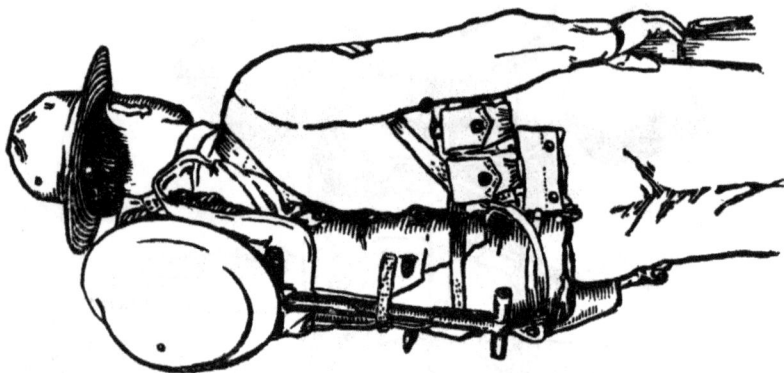

② Right rear view.

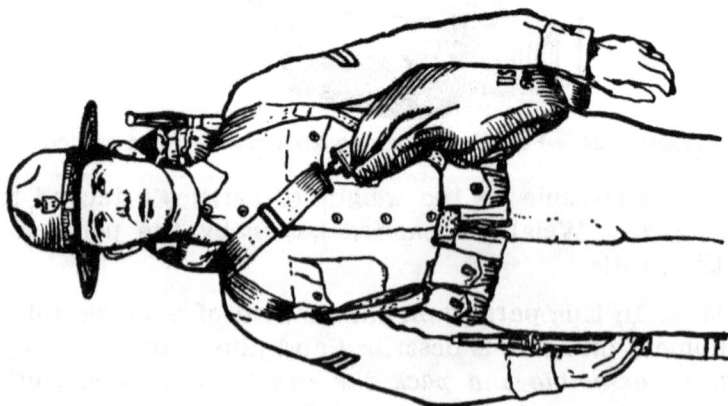

① Front view.

FIGURE 25.—Full equipment (less overcoat).

making the latter a rectangle. The blanket is folded once through the center, parallel to short side, and again through the center perpendicular to short sides. The blanket is then laid on shelter tent half, the longer folded edge parallel to and 1 inch from long side of shelter tent half, opposite the buttons, the shorter folded edge toward triangular flap, the blanket equidistant from ends of shelter tent half.

(2) The tent pole, folded, is inserted in double fold of blanket, end of pole flush with shorter folded edges, the pole parallel to and fitting snugly into the double fold. The tent pins are inserted in double fold of blanket, near loose edges, placed alternately head and point and overlapping each other so as to occupy about the same space as the tent pole, the pins parallel to and fitting snugly into double fold of blanket. This leaves a "break" at center of completed roll which allows it to fit the saddle.

(3) The free ends of shelter tent half are folded over corresponding portions of the blanket, the ends of shelter half throughout their length being parallel to its center line. As a prevention against the ends of completed roll pulling out, the free (loop) end of tent rope is passed several times through tent pin loops on the two opposite corners of button side of shelter tent half, stretched flat, and tied with a single bowknot. The button side of roll is folded back about 6 inches (as far as second button) in order to form a pocket when roll is completed, edge of pocket being parallel to edge of blanket.

(4) Using the hands and knees, the blanket and shelter tent half are rolled tightly from side opposite buttons into pocket at button side, making a tightly bound roll. The roll is then "broken" or curved to fit the cantle of saddle, with free edge of pocket uppermost and to the rear, so that this edge fits snugly against the roll and prevents entrance of rain or snow when roll is on the saddle. It is advisable for two men to work together in making up the roll.

c. *To fold the raincoat or overcoat.*—The raincoat, inside out, with collar extended is folded once lengthwise. It is rolled tightly from folded edge toward buttons, making length of roll the same as full length of garment. If the overcoat is carried, it is rolled in the same manner as the raincoat.

d. *Feed and grain bag.*—The grain bag, with or without grain, is secured inside the feed bag.

e. To pack the saddle (fig. 26).—(1) The saddle, off the horse, is placed on the ground or otherwise as is most convenient for packing. The saddlebags are placed on the cantle and secured thereto by the attachments provided. The cantle roll is strapped to the cantle by means of the cantle straps which are wrapped three times around the roll. The straps are securely buckled and the loose ends, falling to the front, are tucked under the straps. The buckles should be far enough to the rear to prevent injury or discomfort to the

① Near side.

FIGURE 26.—Saddle, packed.

trooper. The ends of the roll are pressed forward and down toward the saddlebags. The two outside straps should pass over the roll well down toward its ends in order to keep the roll curved to the shape of the cantle.

(2) The feed bag and grain bag are strapped on top of the pommel bar (under the raincoat or overcoat), regardless of whether grain is carried. The loose ends of the straps, falling

to the rear, are tucked under the straps. The raincoat, and/or overcoat, collar to the left, is placed on top of feed and grain bag and strapped on by means of the pommel straps. The ends of the roll are pressed in toward the horse's shoulders. All buckles should be far enough forward to prevent injury or discomfort to the trooper.

(3) The canteen and cup, in their cover, are snapped to the right cantle ring. The cover is fastened tight to the saddlebag by buckling the two rear saddlebag cover straps over the canteen cover strap where it passes under the bottom of the canteen cover.

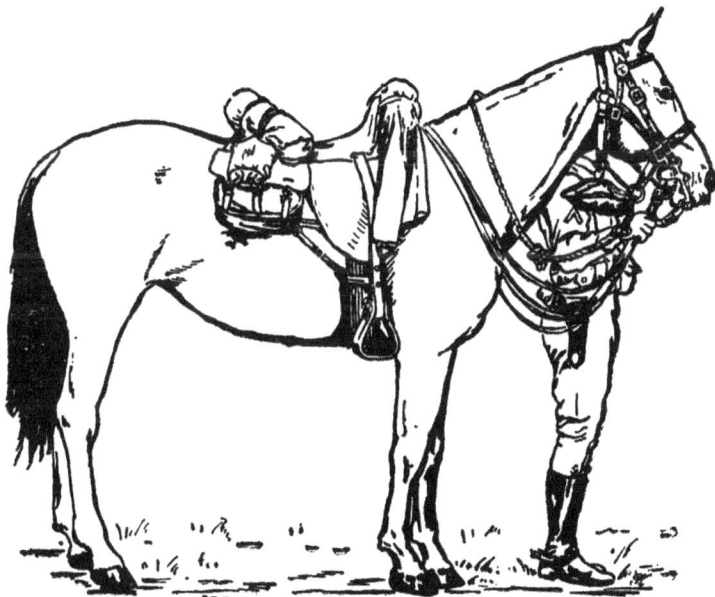

② Off side.

FIGURE 26.—Saddle, packed—Continued.

(4) Attach helmet to near (left) saddlebag by buckling the three straps of saddlebag flap through the chin strap.

(5) The rifle scabbard is secured to left side of saddle, attached to the pommel ring by the upper strap of scabbard and to cantle ring by lower strap. Both straps are so adjusted that the scabbard will hang at an angle of 30° with the vertical. The rifle is not inserted in the scabbard until after the horse is saddled.

(6) Wherever possible, two men work together in placing the packed saddle on the horse's back. In case only one man

is available, it may be found advisable to attach saddlebags, canteen, cup and cover, and rifle scabbard after the horse has been saddled.

f. Drivers (artillery).—(1) *General.*—In order to equalize loads on the two horses, certain articles, as prescribed by the table shown in paragraph 81 may be placed on saddle of the off horse instead of on riding horse.

(2) *To pack feed bags.*—To pack feed bags, fill the grain bags; tie mouths securely and place a filled grain bag in each feed bag, mouths of grain bags down. Roll feed bags, securing closed ends by means of web straps at ends of feed bags. The snap ends of the straps are either snapped in the rings on feed bags or tucked under turns in straps. The open ends of the two feed bags are closely secured together to prevent lower ends from rubbing against traces. When grain is not carried, fold empty grain bags and place them inside feed bags. Roll feed bags along their longer edges and secure as above.

(3) *To pack saddle.*—To pack the saddle of the off horse, the near stirrup being passed over seat of saddle, the procedure is as follows:

(*a*) The saddlebags are placed on cantle and secured by attachments provided.

(*b*) Place surcingles under straps of saddlebag flaps above the loops in saddlebag flaps through which the straps pass.

(*c*) Attach mounted canteen cover to left rear cantle ring by the snap of canteen strap.

(*d*) Attach helmet to off (right) saddlebag by buckling the three straps of saddlebag flap through the chin strap.

(*e*) Extend center cantle strap. Place roll on top of buckle end of cantle strap in the center of seat of saddle so that open edge will be down. Place the two feed bags, secured together at their open ends, across seat of saddle in front of roll. Bring tongue end of cantle strap to the front over center of roll and junction of the two feed bags; take one turn around the junction of the two feed bags; pass strap to rear under roll, bring it forward over center of roll, and buckle it. Each coat strap is passed under rear quarter strap and once around feed bag about 4 inches from the lower end, punching a throat in feed bag to prevent strap from slipping; pass each strap to rear and once around roll about 6 inches from end of roll; bring strap from under roll, over itself at the interval between feed bags, roll and buckle. The ends of roll are drawn close to ends of feed bags before being secured. The coat straps are attached to saddlebag side—strap rings about saddlebag side straps to avoid twisting the rings.

(*f*) Place overcoat, collar, to the left, across seat of saddle in front of feed bags and secure by two pommel coat straps. When raincoat and overcoat are both carried, place raincoat on top of overcoat. When overcoat is not carried, raincoat is packed as provided for overcoat. (See fig. 27.)

FIGURE 27.—Driver's (artillery) off horse

(4) *To pack saddle of the off horse when blanket rolls and feed bags are carried on limber.*—To pack the saddle of the off horse, the near stirrup being passed over seat of saddle, the procedure is as follows:

(*a*) Place the saddlebags on the seat of the saddle and secure them by passing the saddlebag straps through the cinch rings and drawing them tight.

(*b*) Place the overcoat on top of the saddlebags, collar to the left; place the raincoat on top of the overcoat. Take a couple of turns with the middle cantle strap around the two coats. Then take several turns around each end of the coats, using a coat strap on each end. Place the free end of each strap through the cinch ring on each side and pull the coats down firmly against the saddle.

(c) Secure end of halter tie rope of off horse to off pommel ring of off saddle, and that of near horse to near pommel ring of near saddle.

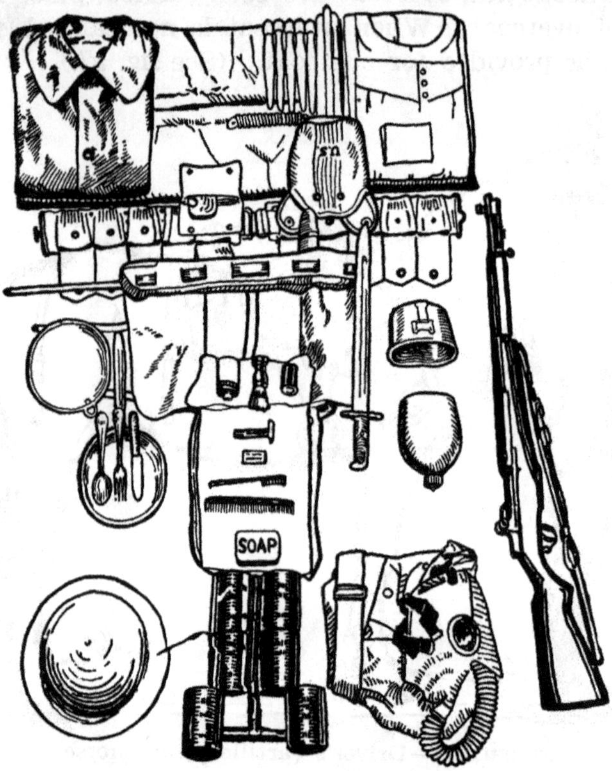

FIGURE 28.—Display of equipment, dismounted.

SECTION IX

DISPLAY OF EQUIPMENT

■ 86. *a.* As mentioned in paragraph 61, you will attend inspections at which you will be required to display your field equipment. At these inspections your officers will check your field equipment to see that no items are missing and that all items are clean and in condition for immediate field service. Figure 28 shows how your equipment should be displayed if you are a dismounted soldier or equipped with a haversack and pack carrier.

b. Figure 29 shows how your equipment should be displayed if you are a mounted soldier.

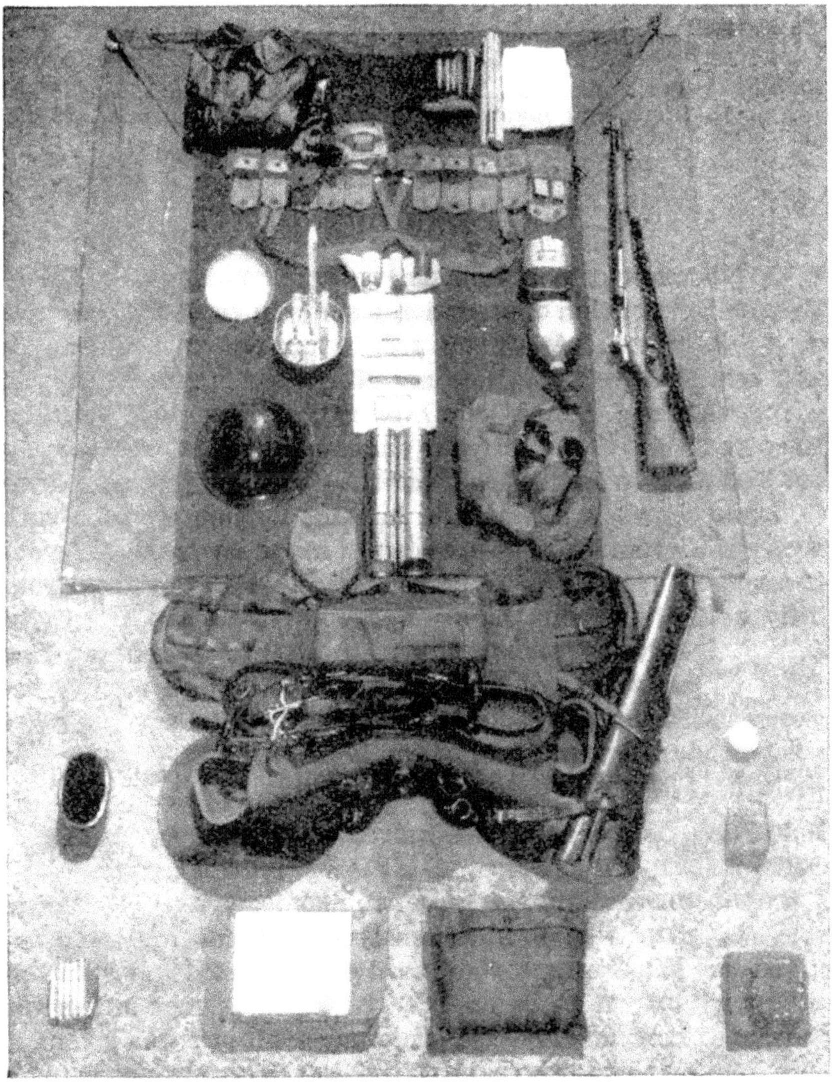

FIGURE 29.—Display of equipment, mounted.

CHAPTER 7

SCHOOL OF THE SOLDIER WITHOUT ARMS
(DISMOUNTED)

SECTION I

POSITIONS

■ 87. Position of the Soldier, or of Attention (fig. 30).— To take the position of attention place your heels together and on the same line. Allow your feet to turn out equally, forming an angle of 45° with each other. Keep your knees straight but without stiffness. Draw your hips up under your body slightly. Keep your chest up and your shoulders back. Do not allow one shoulder to be higher than the other. Keep your arms straight without stiffness, and hanging at your sides, in such a way that your thumbs are always along the seams of your trousers. Turn the backs of your hands out away from your body and allow your hands and fingers to cup naturally. Always keep your eyes straight to the front. When standing properly the weight of your body will be divided equally between the heels and balls of both feet. When assuming the position of attention, bring your heels together smartly and audibly.

■ 88. Rests.—Being at the halt the commands are: FALL OUT; REST; AT EASE; and 1. parade, 2. REST.

a. At the command FALL OUT, you may leave your position in ranks but must remain in the immediate vicinity. At the command FALL IN, resume your position in ranks and stand at attention. When on the march, you fall in AT EASE unless you were at attention when the command FALL OUT was given.

b. While at rest it is required that you keep one foot in place in ranks. At the command REST, except for keeping one foot in place, you may move around and talk.

c. At the command AT EASE, you are authorized to move around but must keep your right foot in place in ranks. Silence is always maintained while at ease.

d. PARADE REST is a movement that is executed in unison by all soldiers in ranks. At the command of execution (REST) of 1. PARADE, 2. REST, move your left foot smartly 12 inches to the left of your right foot. As at attention, your knees are kept straight without stiffness, and the weight of your body rests equally on both feet. At the same time your foot is moved, clasp your hands behind your back, palms to the rear, the thumb and fingers of your right hand clasping your left thumb. As at attention, you are required to maintain both silence and immobility.

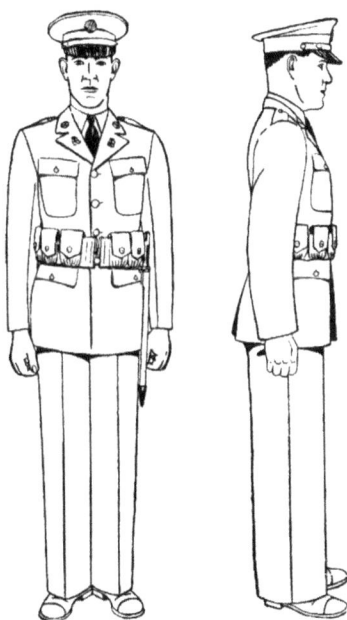

FIGURE 30.—Position of the soldier, or of attention.

e. Being at any of the rests, except FALL OUT, you resume the position of attention at the command of execution (ATTEN-TION) of 1. SQUAD, 2. ATTENTION.

■ 89. EYES RIGHT OR LEFT.—The commands are: 1. EYES, 2. RIGHT (LEFT), 3. READY, 4. FRONT.

a. At the command RIGHT, turn your head and eyes to the right.

b. At the command LEFT, turn your head and eyes to the left.

c. At the command FRONT, turn your head and eyes to the front.

■ 90. FACINGS.—All facings are executed from the halt and in the cadence of quick time. The commands are: 1. RIGHT (LEFT), 2. FACE; and 1. ABOUT, 2. FACE.

a. At the command FACE of 1. RIGHT, 2. FACE, slightly raise your left heel and your right toe; turn 90° to the right by pivoting on the right heel. This movement is assisted by pushing slightly with the ball of your left foot. Hold your left leg straight without stiffness. The second part of this movement consists in placing your left foot alongside of your right and assuming the position of attention.

b. At the command FACE of 1. LEFT, 2. FACE, you execute the above movement in a corresponding manner to the left and on your left heel.

c. At the command FACE of 1. ABOUT, 2. FACE, place the toe of your right foot a half-foot length in rear and slightly to the left of your left heel. Do not move your left foot. Keep the weight of your body mainly on your left heel. Keep your right leg straight without stiffness. The second part of this movement consists in turning your body 180° to the right on your left heel and the ball of your right foot. Now place your right heel beside your left. If you do this movement properly you will find you have turned exactly 180° and your heels come together on the same line without the necessity of moving either foot forward or backward.

■ 91. SALUTE WITH THE HAND (fig. 31).—*a.* The commands are: 1. HAND, 2. SALUTE. At the command SALUTE, raise your right hand smartly until the tip of your forefinger (index finger) touches the brim of your headdress, above and slightly to the right of your right eye. If you are without cap or hat, the tip of your forefinger touches your forehead above and slightly to the right of your right eye. In either case you keep your thumbs and fingers extended and joined, palm to the left, and the hand and wrist straight. You also keep your upper arm horizontal and the forearm inclined at an angle of 45°. At the same time, you turn your head and eyes toward the person you are saluting. The second part of this movement consists in dropping your arm to your side and turning your head and eyes to the front.

b. You execute the first position of the hand salute when the person you are saluting is six paces from you or at his nearest point of approach if more than six paces. You hold that position until your salute has been returned or until the person saluted has passed you if he does not return the salute. You then execute the second movement of the hand salute.

FIGURE 31.—Hand salute.

SECTION II

STEPS AND MARCHINGS

■ 92. *a.* All steps and marchings that are executed from the halt, except right step, begin with the left foot.

b. Whenever necessary your instructor will indicate the cadence to you by calling "One," "Two," "Three," "Four," as your left and right foot, respectively, touch the ground.

c. All steps and marchings are executed at attention except 1. ROUTE STEP, 2. MARCH and 1. AT EASE, 2. MARCH.

■ **93. QUICK TIME.**—Being at the halt the commands to move forward in quick time are: 1. FORWARD, 2. MARCH. At the command FORWARD, you shift the weight of your body to the right leg without making any noticeable movement. Do not start to move forward. At the command MARCH, step off smartly with your left foot and continue to march with 30-inch steps straight to the front, at the rate of 120 steps per minute. You do this without stiffness and without exaggerating any of the movements. Swing your arms easily and in their natural arcs, 6 inches to the front and 3 inches to the rear of your body.

■ **94. DOUBLE TIME.**—*a.* Being at the halt, or in march in quick time, to march in double time the commands are: 1. DOUBLE TIME, 2. MARCH.

(1) If you are at the halt and the command DOUBLE TIME is given, shift your weight to your right leg without noticeable movement just as you did at the command FORWARD. At the command MARCH, step out and take up an easy running step in the cadence of double time (180 steps, 36 inches each, per minute). At the double time you raise your forearms to a horizontal position at your side, close your fingers, with knuckles out, and allow your arms to swing naturally. Remember to keep your lower arms (forearms) horizontal along your waistline.

(2) If you are already marching at quick time you continue the march at the command DOUBLE TIME. At the command MARCH you take one more step in the cadence of quick time and then step out at the double. You swing your arms the same as you did in (1) above.

b. Being at the double time, to resume the cadence of quick time the commands are: 1. QUICK TIME, 2. MARCH. At the command MARCH you take one step in double time and then commence marching in the cadence of quick time. Allow your arms to drop to your sides and then swing as they should in the cadence of quick time.

■ **95. To HALT.**—*a.* The halt may be executed as either foot strikes the ground. To halt when marching in quick time, the commands are: 1. SQUAD, 2. HALT. At the command HALT, given as either foot strikes the ground, take one step in quick time and then place your rear foot alongside the leading foot and assume the position of attention.

b. To halt when marching at the double time, the commands are: 1. SQUAD, 2. HALT. At the command HALT, take one step in double time, then one step in quick time and then place your rear foot alongside the leading foot and assume the position of attention.

■ 96. To MARK TIME.—Mark time may be given either while you are marching or while you are at a halt. Mark time may be executed either at quick time or at double time. The commands are: 1. MARK TIME, 2. MARCH.

a. If you are marching when the command MARCH is given, you take one more step forward and then bring up your rear foot and plant it beside your leading foot with your heels on the same line. You then continue the cadence by alternately raising and planting each foot. You raise your feet 2 inches in marking time. The command MARCH may be given as either foot is on the ground.

b. If you are at a halt when the command MARCH is given, you alternately raise and plant each foot beginning with your left just as you did in *a* above.

c. You execute the halt from mark time just as you did from quick time or from double time, except that a 2-inch vertical step is substituted for the 30-inch forward step.

d. FORWARD, HALT, OR MARK TIME may each be executed one from the other either in quick or double time.

■ 97. HALF STEP.—*a.* The commands are: 1. HALF STEP, 2. MARCH. If you are marching, when the command MARCH is given, you take one more 30-inch step, then begin taking 15-inch steps. The cadence does not change. The half step is executed in quick time only.

b. If you are marching at the half step, the commands to take up the full step will be: 1. FORWARD, 2. MARCH.

c. If you are marking time, the same commands are given to take up the full step, that is: 1. FORWARD, 2. MARCH.

■ 98. SIDE STEP.—*a.* The commands to take up the side step are: 1. RIGHT (LEFT) STEP, 2. MARCH. These commands are given only from the halt.

(1) 1. RIGHT STEP, 2. MARCH.—At the command MARCH, you move the right foot 12 inches to the right and plant it. You then move the left foot and place it beside the right, left knee straight. You now continue in the cadence of quick time by starting again with the right foot.

(2) 1. LEFT STEP, 2. MARCH.—Left step is executed in the corresponding manner, starting with the left foot instead of the right.

b. The side steps are used for short distances only. The side step is never executed in double time.

c. To halt from the side step the commands are: 1. SQUAD, 2. HALT. The command HALT is always given when the heels are together. At the command HALT you take one more 12-inch step to the flank and then bring your feet together and halt.

■ 99. BACK STEP.—The commands to take up the back step are: 1. BACKWARD, 2. MARCH. These commands are given only while at the halt.

a. At the command MARCH you take a 15-inch step straight to the rear.

b. The back step, like the side step, is used for short distances only and is never executed at double time.

■ 100. TO FACE IN MARCHING.—The facings in marching are an important part of movements such as COLUMN RIGHT, CLOSE, TAKE INTERVAL, EXTEND, etc. Facings in marching may be executed either from the halt or while marching.

a. (1) Assume you are at a halt and are required to face to the right and commence marching in that direction. At the command of execution you turn to the right on the ball of your right foot and at the same time you step off with your left foot in the new direction. The length of this step will vary with the movement being executed. It may be a full step or a half step. It may be executed at either quick time or at double time.

(2) Assume you are at the halt and are required to face to the left and commence marching in that direction. At the command of execution you face to the left on the ball of the right foot and at the same time step off with your left foot in the new direction.

b. (1) Assume you are now marching and are required to face to the right and continue marching in the new direction. The command of execution will be given as your right foot strikes the ground. At that command you advance and plant your left foot. You then face to the right in marching and at the same time step off in the new direction with your right foot. Again the length of this step will depend on whether you are marching at the half step, quick time, or double time.

(2) Assume you are now marching and are required to face to the left and continue marching in the new direction. This time the command of execution will be given as your left foot strikes the ground. At the command you advance and plant your right foot. You then face to the left in marching and at the same time step off in the new direction with your left foot.

c. To face to the rear while marching the commands are: 1. TO THE REAR, 2. MARCH. This command will be given as your right foot strikes the ground. At the command of execution, advance and plant your left foot. You then turn to the right about on the balls of both feet and immediately step off in the new direction with your left foot.

■ 101. To MARCH BY THE FLANK.—Being in march, the commands are: 1. BY THE RIGHT (LEFT) FLANK, 2. MARCH.

a. 1. BY THE RIGHT FLANK, 2. MARCH.—This command will be given as your right foot strikes the ground. At the command MARCH, advance and plant your left foot and face to the right in marching. You then step off in the new direction with the right foot.

b. 1. BY THE LEFT FLANK, 2. MARCH.—This command will be given as your left foot strikes the ground. At the command MARCH advance and plant your right foot, face to the left in marching, and move off in the new direction with your left foot.

■ 102. To CHANGE STEP.—The commands are: 1. CHANGE STEP, 2. MARCH. This command may be given as either foot strikes the ground. The command is used only while marching.

a. If the command of execution (MARCH) is given as your right foot strikes the ground, you advance and plant your left foot. You then place the toe of your right foot near the heel of your left foot and immediately step off with your left foot.

b. If the command of execution is given as your left foot strikes the ground, you change step on the right foot.

■ 103. To March Other Than at Attention.—The commands are: 1. ROUTE STEP, 2. MARCH; or 1. AT EASE, 2. MARCH.

a. 1. ROUTE STEP, 2. MARCH.—At the command MARCH you are not required to march at attention, in cadence, or to maintain silence.

b. 1. AT EASE, 2. MARCH.—At the command of execution you are not required to march at attention or in cadence. You are, however, required to maintain silence.

CHAPTER 8

SCHOOL OF THE SOLDIER WITH ARMS (DISMOUNTED)

SECTION I

GENERAL

■ 104. RULES GOVERNING CARRYING OF RIFLES.—Except where otherwise indicated, these rules will be applicable alike to the U. S. rifle, caliber .30, M1903, and to the U. S. rifle, caliber .30, M1.

a. (1) The U. S. rifle, caliber .30, M1903, is not carried with cartridges in either the chamber or the magazine except when specifically ordered. When so loaded or when supposed to be loaded, it is habitually carried locked; that is, with the safety lock turned to the "safe." At all other times it is carried unlocked with the trigger pulled. The cut-off is kept turned off except when cartridges are actually used.

(2) Whenever troops equipped with the U. S. rifle, caliber .30, M1903, are formed under arms, pieces are immediately inspected at the commands: 1. INSPECTION, 2. ARMS. A similar inspection is made before dismissal. If cartridges are found in the chamber or magazine they are removed and placed in the belt.

b. (1) The U. S. rifle, caliber .30, M1, is not carried with cartridges in either the chamber or the receiver except when specifically ordered. When so loaded or when supposed to be loaded, it is habitually carried locked; that is, with the safety in its rearmost position, inside the trigger guard.

(2) Whenever troops equipped with the U. S. rifle, caliber .30, M1, are formed under arms, pieces are immediately inspected at the commands: 1. INSPECTION, 2. ARMS, 3. LOCK PIECES. At the command LOCK PIECES, each man in ranks closes the bolt, sets the safety of his piece in its rearmost position, and resumes PORT ARMS. Rifles are again inspected

at dismissal by the commands: 1. INSPECTION, 2. ARMS, 3. UNLOCK PIECES. At the command UNLOCK PIECES, each man in ranks closes the bolt, sets the safety of his piece in its foremost position, pulls the trigger, and resumes PORT ARMS. If cartridges are found in the chamber or receiver, they are removed and placed in the belt. The procedure prescribed for these inspections is intended first, to insure that U. S. rifles, caliber .30, M1, in the hands of troops are carried cocked and locked; second, to insure that hammers are released on unloaded pieces not in use to prevent damage from long continued compression of the hammer springs.

c. The bayonet is fixed only when so ordered.

d. FALL IN is executed with the rifle at the ORDER ARMS.

e. (1) Before starting any movement for troops armed with rifles, the commands, 1. RIGHT SHOULDER (SLING), 2. ARMS, are given *before* the command for movement.

(2) Movements for short distances may be executed AT THE TRAIL by prefacing the preparatory command with the words "at trail," as 1. AT TRAIL, FORWARD, 2. MARCH. The trail is taken at the command MARCH.

(3) Weapons such as the automatic rifle, light machine gun, light mortar, etc., which have no manual of arms are slung from the right shoulder at the command of execution, ARMS, of 1. RIGHT SHOULDER, 2. ARMS. They are kept slung until the command REST or AT EASE. In long halts at attention, the men carrying such equipment may be directed to "unsling arms,"

f. When the facings, alinements, open and close ranks, side step, back step, forming for shelter tents, extending and closing are executed from the order, the weapon is brought to the trail while in motion and the order resumed on halting. The position of TRAIL ARMS is taken at the command of execution in each case.

g. At the command HALT, men armed with the rifle remain at the position of right (left) shoulder arms until the command: 1. ORDER, 2. ARMS, is given.

h. In double time under arms, a disengaged hand is held as when without arms.

SECTION II

MANUAL OF ARMS FOR THE RIFLE

■ 105. RULES GOVERNING EXECUTION OF THE MANUAL OF ARMS.—Except where otherwise indicated, these rules will be applicable alike to the U. S. rifle, caliber .30, M1903, and to the U. S. rifle, caliber .30, M1.

a. In all positions of the left hand at the balance, the thumb clasps the rifle; the sling is included in the grasp of the hand (fig. 32). In describing the manual of arms, the term "at the balance" refers to points on rifles as follows:

(1) *U. S. rifle, caliber .30, M1903.*—The center of the rear sight leaf.

(2) *U. S. rifle, caliber .30, M1.*—A point just forward of the trigger housing.

b. In all positions of the rifle, diagonally across the body, the barrel is up, butt in front of the right hip, barrel crossing opposite the junction of the neck with the left shoulder. The rifle is grasped at the balance with the left hand, palm toward the body, wrist straight.

c. The cadence of the motions is that of quick time. Soldiers are first required to give their whole attention to the details of the motions, the cadence being gradually acquired as they become accustomed to handling their rifles. The instructor may require them to count aloud in cadence with the motions.

d. (1) The manual is not executed in marching except to pass from right shoulder to left shoulder or port arms and the reverse in marching at attention. These movements may be used to add interest to the drill or to prevent fatigue in long marches at attention.

(2) The manual is taught at a halt and the movements may, for the purpose of instruction, be divided into motions and executed in detail. In this case, the command of execution determines the prompt execution of the first motion, and the commands TWO, THREE, FOUR, that of the other motions.

(3) To execute the movement in detail, the instructor first cautions, "By the numbers." All movements divided into

91

motions are then executed as above explained until he cautions, "Without the numbers."

e. (1) Any appropriate position of the manual of arms may be ordered from a previous position by giving the suitable commands.

FIGURE 32.—Left hand at the balance.

(2) Under exceptional conditions of weather and fatigue, the rifle may be carried as directed.

■ 106. POSITION OF ORDER ARMS.—The butt of the rifle rests on the ground, barrel to the rear, toe of the butt on line with the toe of, and touching the right shoe, right hand holding the rifle between the thumb and fingers, left hand as in position of the soldier without arms.

■ 107. BEING AT ORDER ARMS.—1. TRAIL, 2. ARMS. At the command ARMS, raise the rifle and incline the muzzle forward so that the barrel makes an angle of about 15° with the vertical, the right arm slightly bent.

■ 108. BEING AT TRAIL ARMS.—1. ORDER, 2. ARMS. At the command ARMS, lower the rifle with the right hand and resume the order.

FIGURE 33.—Position of ORDER ARMS.

FIGURE 34.—Position of TRAIL ARMS.

■ 109. Being at Order Arms to Sling Arms, and Being at Sling Arms to Unsling Arms.—*a.* sling arms. This movement is not executed in cadence and applies to any rifle, automatic rifle, light machine gun, light mortar, etc. Loosen the sling, if not already loosened, and in the most convenient manner assume the position shown in figure 35. This position is authorized for long parades, long reviews, and for occasions when the prolonged holding of the rifle becomes a hardship on the troops. When used in ceremonies the bayonet may be fixed.

Figure 35.—Position of sling arms.

b. 1. unsling, 2. ARMS, 3. adjust, 4. SLINGS. At the command ARMS, pieces are unslung. At the command slings, slings are adjusted to the drill position. This adjustment of the sling will be made before precise movements of the manual are to be executed.

■ 110. Being at Order Arms.—1. port, 2. ARMS. At the command ARMS, raise the rifle with the right hand and carry it diagonally across the front of the body until the right hand is in front of and slightly to the left of the chin (fig. 36①), so that the barrel is up, butt in front of the right hip, barrel crossing opposite the junction of the neck with the left shoulder. At the same time, grasp the rifle at the balance with the left hand, palm toward the body, wrist straight. (TWO) Carry the right hand to the small of the stock, grasping it, palm down, holding right forearm horizontal, left elbow resting against the body; the rifle in a vertical plane parallel to the front (fig. 36②).

① First position.   ② Second position.

FIGURE 36.—Position of PORT ARMS.

■ 111. BEING AT ORDER ARMS.—1. PRESENT, 2. ARMS. At the command ARMS, with the right hand carry the rifle in front of the center of the body, barrel to the rear and vertical, grasp it with the left hand at the balance, forearm horizontal and resting against the body. (TWO) Grasp the small of the stock with the right hand.

■ 112. BEING AT PRESENT OR PORT ARMS.—1. ORDER, 2. ARMS. At the command ARMS, let go of the rifle with the right hand and regrasp the piece between the upper sling swivel and stacking swivel. (TWO) Let go of the rifle with the left hand, lower the piece to the right so that the butt is 3 inches from the ground, barrel to the rear, left hand with the fingers extended and joined steadying the rifle, forearm and wrist straight and inclining downward. (THREE) Complete the order by lowering the rifle gently to the ground with the right hand. Cut away the left hand smartly to the side. Allowing the rifle to drop to the ground forcibly injures the rifle and is prohibited.

■ 113. BEING AT ORDER ARMS.—*a. U. S. rifle, caliber .30, M1903.*—1. INSPECTION, 2. ARMS. At the command ARMS, take the position of PORT ARMS. Seize the bolt handle with the thumb and forefinger of the right hand, turn the handle up, draw the bolt back, lower the head and eyes sufficiently to glance into the magazine. Having found the magazine empty, or having emptied it, raise the head and eyes to the front.

b. U. S. rifle, caliber .30, M1.—1. INSPECTION, 2. ARMS. At the command ARMS, take the position of PORT ARMS. With the fingers of the left hand closed, place the left thumb on the operating rod handle and push it smartly to the rear until it is caught by the operating rod catch; at the same time lower the head and eyes sufficiently to glance into the receiver. Having found the receiver empty, or having emptied it, raise the head and eyes to the front; at the same time regrasp the piece with the left hand at the balance.

■ 114. BEING AT INSPECTION ARMS.—*a. U. S. rifle, caliber .30, M1903.*—1. ORDER (RIGHT SHOULDER, PORT), 2. ARMS. At the preparatory command, push the bolt forward, turn the handle down, pull the trigger, and resume PORT ARMS. At the command ARMS, complete the movement ordered.

b. U. S. rifle, caliber .30, M1.—1. LOCK PIECES, 2. ORDER (RIGHT SHOULDER), 3. ARMS, or 1. UNLOCK PIECES, 2. DISMISSED. At the command LOCK (or UNLOCK) PIECES, place the right side of the right hand against the operating rod handle with the fingers extended and joined and the thumb on the follower. (TWO) Force the operating rod handle slightly to the rear, depress the follower with the right thumb, and permit the bolt to ride forward about 1 inch over the follower. (THREE) Remove the thumb from the follower

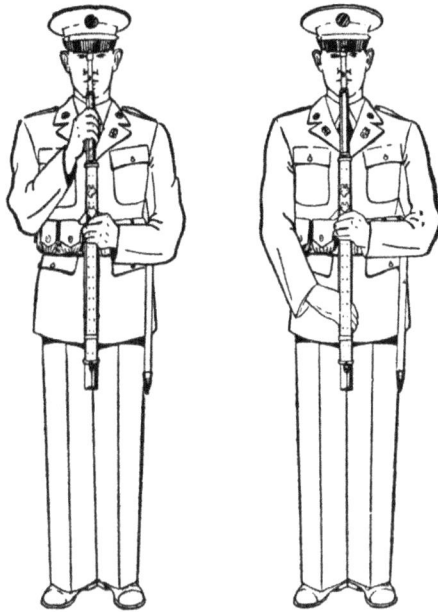

FIGURE 37.—Execution of PRESENT ARMS.

FIGURE 38.—Next to last position of ORDER ARMS.

and release the operating rod handle. (FOUR) Lock the piece, or unlock the piece and pull the trigger as the case may be (par. 104*b*(2)) and resume the position of PORT ARMS. After the pieces have been locked or unlocked, as prescribed above, ORDER or RIGHT SHOULDER ARMS is given or the unit is dismissed.

■ 115. BEING AT ORDER ARMS.—1. RIGHT SHOULDER, 2. ARMS. At the command ARMS, raise and carry the rifle diagonally across the body with the right hand as shown in figure 39, at the same time grasp it at the balance with the left hand. (TWO) Regrasp it with the right hand on the butt, the heel between the first two fingers, thumb and fingers closed on the stock. (THREE) Without changing the grasp of the right hand, place the rifle on the right shoulder, barrel up and inclined at an angle of about 45° from the horizontal, trigger guard in the hollow of the shoulder, right elbow against the side, forearm horizontal, the rifle in a vertical plane perpendicular to the front; carry the left hand, thumb and fingers extended and joined, to the small of the stock, first joint of the forefinger touching the cocking piece (or, for the M1 rifle, touching the rear end of the receiver), wrist straight, and elbow down. (FOUR) Cut away the left hand smartly to the side.

■ 116. BEING AT RIGHT SHOULDER ARMS.—1. PORT, 2. ARMS. At the command ARMS, press the butt down quickly and throw the rifle diagonally across the body, at the same time turning it to the left so as to bring the barrel up, the right hand retaining its grasp on the butt, the left grasping the rifle at the balance. (TWO) Change the right hand to the small of the stock.

■ 117. BEING AT RIGHT SHOULDER ARMS.—1. ORDER, 2. ARMS. At the command ARMS, press the butt down quickly and throw the rifle diagonally across the body, the right hand retaining the grasp on the butt, the left hand grasping the rifle at the balance. Then execute ORDER ARMS as described in paragraph 112.

■ 118. BEING AT PORT ARMS.—1. RIGHT SHOULDER, 2. ARMS. At the command ARMS, change the right hand to the butt as described in paragraph 115. (TWO), (THREE) Execute the last two movements as in RIGHT SHOULDER ARMS from ORDER ARMS.

■ 119. BEING AT ORDER ARMS.—1. PARADE, 2. REST. At the command REST, move the left foot smartly 12 inches to the left of the right foot, keeping the legs straight, so that the weight of the body rests equally on both feet. At the same time incline the muzzle of the rifle to the front, the right arm extended, right hand grasping the rifle just below the upper band. Hold the left hand behind the body, resting in the small of the back, palm to the rear.

FIGURE 39.—Execution of RIGHT SHOULDER ARMS.

■ 120. BEING AT PARADE REST.—1. SQUAD, 2. ATTENTION. At the command ATTENTION, resume the position of ORDER ARMS.

■ 121. BEING AT RIGHT SHOULDER ARMS.—LEFT SHOULDER, 2. ARMS. At the command ARMS, execute PORT ARMS in two counts as described in paragraph 116. (THREE) Let go of the rifle with the left hand and with the right hand still grasping the small of the stock place it on the left shoulder, barrel up, trigger guard in the hollow of the shoulder; at the same time grasp the butt with the left hand; heel between the first and second fingers, thumb and fingers closed on the stock, left forearm horizontal, left elbow against the side, the rifle in a vertical plane perpendicular to the front. (FOUR) Drop the right hand quickly to the right side.

■ 122. BEING AT LEFT SHOULDER ARMS.—*a*. 1. PORT, 2. ARMS. At the command ARMS, grasp the rifle with the right hand at the small of the stock. (TWO) Let go with the left hand and at the same time carry the piece with the right hand to the position of PORT ARMS and then regrasp it with the left.

b. LEFT SHOULDER ARMS may be ordered directly from the ORDER, RIGHT SHOULDER, or PRESENT. At the command ARMS, execute PORT ARMS and continue in cadence to the position ordered.

■ 123. BEING AT LEFT SHOULDER ARMS.—1. RIGHT SHOULDER, 2. ARMS. At the command ARMS, execute PORT ARMS as described in paragraph 122, and then RIGHT SHOULDER ARMS as described in paragraph 118.

■ 124. BEING AT LEFT SHOULDER ARMS.—1. ORDER, 2. ARMS. At the command ARMS, execute PORT ARMS as described in paragraph 122 and complete the movement of ORDER ARMS as described in paragraph 112.

■ 125. BEING AT ORDER OR TRAIL ARMS.—1. RIFLE, 2. SALUTE. At the command SALUTE, carry the left hand smartly to the right side, palm of the hand down, thumb and fingers extended and joined, forearm and wrist straight, first joint of forefinger between the stacking swivel and the muzzle as the conformation of the man permits, and look toward the person saluted. (TWO) Cut away the left hand smartly to the side; turn the head and eyes to the front.

■ 126. BEING AT RIGHT SHOULDER ARMS.—1. RIFLE, 2. SALUTE. At the command SALUTE, carry the left hand smartly to small of the stock, forearm horizontal, palm of the hand down, thumb and fingers extended and joined, first joint of the forefinger touching end of cocking piece (or, for the M1 rifle, touching the rear end of the receiver); look toward the person saluted. (TWO) Cut away the left hand smartly to the side; turn the head and eyes to the front.

■ **127.** Being at Order Arms.—1. FIX, 2. BAYONETS.   At the command BAYONETS—

a. If the bayonet scabbard is carried on the belt, move the muzzle of the rifle to the left front and grasp the rifle below the stacking swivel with the left hand; grasp the bayonet with the right hand, back of the hand toward the body; pressing the spring with the forefinger, draw the bayonet from the scabbard and fix it on the barrel, glancing at the muzzle; resume the order.

b. If the bayonet is carried on the haversack, draw and fix the bayonet in the most convenient manner.

c. These movements are not executed in cadence.

FIGURE 40.—Position of PARADE REST.

■ **128.** Being at Order Arms.—1. UNFIX, 2. BAYONETS. At the command BAYONETS—

a. If the bayonet scabbard is carried on the belt, take the position for fixing bayonets; grasp the handle of the bayonet with the right hand, pressing the spring, raise the bayonet until the handle is about 12 inches above the muzzle of the rifle; drop the point to the left, back of the hand toward the body and, glancing at the scabbard, return the

FIGURE 41.—Rifle salute at RIGHT SHOULDER ARMS and at ORDER ARMS.

FIGURE 42.—To fix bayonets.

bayonet, the blade passing between the left arm and the body; regrasp the rifle with the right hand and resume the order.

b. If the bayonet scabbard is carried on the haversack, take the bayonet from the rifle as described above and return it to the scabbard in the most convenient manner.

c. These movements are not executed in cadence.

SECTION III

LOADINGS AND FIRINGS

■ 129. GENERAL RULES.—Except where otherwise indicated, these rules will be applicable alike to the U. S. rifle, caliber .30, M1903, and the U. S. rifle, caliber .30, M1.

a. For ceremonial firing, the front rank only of units larger than a squad executes the loading and firing. A squad is always formed in line preliminary to such firing.

b. Rifles, caliber .30, M1903, are loaded and locked before any orders for firing are given. Rifles, caliber .30, M1, are loaded while locked. (See par. 104*b*(2).)

c. Except during firing, if rifles have been ordered loaded and locked, they are kept loaded and locked without command until the command UNLOAD, or 1. INSPECTION, 2. ARMS. During firing, fresh clips will be inserted when the magazine or clip is exhausted.

d. Except when used as a single loader, the U. S. rifle, caliber .30, M1, is habitually loaded by placing a full clip of eight cartridges in the receiver.

■ 130. TO LOAD.—*a.* The unit being in any formation, standing at a halt, the commands are: 1. WITH BALL (BLANK, DUMMY, GUARD) CARTRIDGES, 2. LOAD.

(1) *U. S. rifle, caliber .30, M1903.*—At the command LOAD, each front rank rifleman faces half right and carries the right foot 12 inches to the right and to such position as will insure the greatest firmness and steadiness of the body; raises or lowers the rifle and drops it into the left hand at the balance, left thumb extending along the stock, muzzle pointed into the air at an angle of 45°, and turns the cutoff up. With the right hand he turns up the bolt and draws it back; takes a loaded clip and inserts the end in the clip slots; places his thumb on the powder space of the top

103

cartridge, the fingers extending around the rifle and tips resting on the magazine floor plate; forces the cartridges into the magazine by pressing down with the thumb; removes the clip; thrusts the bolt home, turning down the handle; turns the safety lock to the "safe" and carries the hand to the small of the stock. Automatic riflemen do not execute the ceremonial loadings or firings.

(2) *U. S. rifle, caliber .30, M1.*—At the command LOAD, each front rank rifleman faces half right and carries his right foot 12 inches to the right and to such position as will secure the greatest firmness and steadiness of the body, raises or lowers the rifle and drops it into the left hand at the balance, right hand at the small of the stock, muzzle in the air at an angle of 45°. With the forefinger of the right hand, he pulls the operating rod handle smartly to the rear until the operating rod is caught by the operating rod catch. With his right hand he takes a fully loaded clip and places it on top of the follower. He places the right side of his right hand against the operating rod handle and with his thumb presses the clip down into the receiver until it engages the clip latch. He swings his thumb to the right so as to clear the bolt in its forward movement. He releases the operating rod handle. He then pushes forward on the operating rod handle with the heel of his right hand to make certain of complete closing of the bolt and carries his right hand to the small of the stock. Automatic riflemen do not execute the ceremonial loadings and firings.

b. For instruction in loading, the commands are: 1. SIMULATE, 2. LOAD.

(1) *U. S. rifle, caliber .30, M1903.*—At the command LOAD, execute loading as described in *a*(1) above, except that the cut-off remains "off" and the handling of the cartridge is simulated.

(2) *U. S. rifle, caliber .30, M1.*—At the command LOAD, execute loading as described in *a*(2) above except that the handling of cartridges is simulated.

c. (1) The U. S. rifle, caliber .30, M1903, may be used as a single loader by turning the cut-off to "off." At the command LOAD, the magazine may be filled in whole or in part by pressing cartridges singly down and back until they are in the proper place. The use of the rifle as a single loader is, however, to be regarded as exceptional.

(2) To use the U. S. rifle, caliber .30, M1, as a single loader, at the command LOAD, take the position of LOAD and open the bolt. With the right hand, place one round in the chamber, seating it in place with the thumb. With the side of the right hand against the operating rod handle and the fingers extended and joined, force the operating rod handle slightly to the rear, depress the follower with the right thumb, and permit the bolt to ride forward about 1 inch over the follower. Then remove the thumb from the follower, release the operating rod handle, and push forward on the operating rod handle with the heel of the hand to be certain that the bolt is completely closed. Carry the right hand to the small of the stock.

■ 131. To UNLOAD.—Being in any formation, the command is: UNLOAD.

a. U. S. rifle, caliber .30, M1903.—At the command UNLOAD, take the position of LOAD, turn the safety lock up, and move the bolt alternately backward and forward until all the cartridges are ejected. After the last cartridge is ejected, the chamber is closed by first thrusting the bolt forward slightly to free it from the stud holding it in place when the chamber is opened, pressing the follower down and back to engage it under the bolt, and then thrusting the bolt home. The trigger is then pulled, the cartridges are picked up, cleaned, and returned to the belt. and the rifle is brought to the order.

b. U. S. rifle, caliber .30, M1.—At the command UNLOAD, take the position of LOAD. Hook the right thumb over the operating rod handle, pull and hold the operating rod in the extreme rear position. Hold the rifle with the right hand, thumb on operating rod handle, fingers around trigger guard. Steady the rifle by pressing the stock against the right hip. Place the left hand over the receiver and release the clip latch with the left thumb. Catch the ejected clip in the left hand, return the clip to the belt, return the left hand to the balance. Place the right side of the right hand against the operating rod handle and force the operating rod slightly to the rear. Depress the follower with the right thumb and permit the bolt to ride forward about 1 inch over the follower. Remove the thumb from the follower and release the operating rod handle. Bring the rifle to the order.

① To execute position of LOAD.

② To execute position of FIRE.

FIGURE 43.—Platoon in ceremonial firing.

■ 132. To FIRE THE RIFLE.—*a. U. S. rifle, caliber .30, M1903, fully loaded with ball (blank or guard) ammunition.*—Squeeze the trigger for each shot. After each shot draw back and thrust home the bolt with the right hand, leaving the safety lock turned up to the "ready."

b. U. S. rifle, caliber .30, M1.—(1) *Fully loaded with clips of ball ammunition.*—Squeeze the trigger for each shot. When the eighth shot has been fired, the clip will be ejected automatically and the bolt will remain open for the insertion of a new clip.

(2) *Fully loaded with clips of blank or guard ammunition.*—Squeeze the trigger for each shot. After each shot, pull the operating rod handle to the rear with the right forefinger and release it. Push forward on the operating rod handle with the heel of the right hand to insure that the bolt is fully closed.

■ 133. To FIRE BY VOLLEY.—*a.* Being in firing formation with rifles loaded, the commands are: 1. FRONT RANK, 2. READY, 3. AIM, 4. SQUAD, 5. FIRE. (For ceremonial purposes, blank ammunition is used and only the front rank executes the commands.)

(1) *U. S. rifle, caliber .30, M1903.*—At the command READY, take the position of LOAD, if not already in that position, and turn the safety lock to the "ready." At the command AIM, raise the rifle with both hands, butt placed and held firmly against the shoulder, left hand well under the rifle grasping it at or in front of the balance, rifle resting in the palm of the left hand, right elbow at the height of the shoulder, right cheek held firmly against the stock as far forward as it can be placed without straining. The rifle is raised 45° from the horizontal or, if ordered, at the horizontal. The left eye is closed, right eye looking through the notch of the rear sight. At the command FIRE, the trigger is squeezed rapidly; the rifle is then lowered to the position of LOAD and loaded.

(2) *U. S. rifle, caliber .30, M1.*—At the command READY, take the position of LOAD, if not already in that position. At the command AIM, raise the rifle with both hands, butt placed and held firmly against the shoulder, left hand well under the rifle grasping it at or in front of the balance, rifle resting in the palm of the left hand, right elbow at the height of the

shoulder, right cheek held firmly against the stock as far forward as it can be placed without straining, and press the safety lock to its forward position with the trigger finger. The rifle is raised 45° from the horizontal or, if ordered, at the horizontal. The left eye is closed, right eye looking over the rear sight. At the command FIRE, the trigger is squeezed rapidly; the rifle is then lowered to the position of LOAD and loaded.

b. To continue the firing, the commands are: 1. AIM, 2. SQUAD, 3. FIRE.

(1) *U. S. rifle, caliber .30, M1903.*—Each command is executed as previously explained. LOAD (from the magazine) is executed by drawing back and thrusting home the bolt with the right hand, leaving the safety lock turned up to the "ready".

(2) *U. S. rifle, caliber .30, M1.*—Each command is executed as previously explained. LOAD (from the clip) is executed by pulling the operating rod handle fully to the rear with the right forefinger and releasing it, leaving the "safety" in its forward position.

■ 134. To CEASE FIRING.—The command is: CEASE FIRING. At the command CEASE FIRING, firing stops; rifles not already at the position of LOAD are brought to that position.

SECTION IV

CARRYING THE AUTOMATIC RIFLE

■ 135. GENERAL RULES.—*a.* Except as otherwise prescribed, the automatic rifle is habitually carried slung over the right shoulder, butt down, barrel to the rear, right hand grasping the sling, hand in front of armpit.

b. For marches and field exercises, the automatic rifle may be carried slung over either shoulder.

c. When troops are at ease, the automatic rifle is kept slung unless otherwise ordered.

d. When troops are at rest, the automatic rifle may be unslung and the position of ORDER ARMS taken.

e. Only the following movements of the manual are executed by the automatic rifleman:

(1) *Parade rest.*—If at SLING ARMS, execute as without arms keeping the right hand on the sling.

(2) *Inspection arms.*—At the command of execution, grasp the magazine with the left hand; at the same time press the magazine release with the right hand. Withdraw the magazine with the left hand and place it in the belt. Pull back the operating handle with the left hand.

(3) *Being at inspection arms.*—1. ORDER (PORT, RIGHT SHOULDER), 2. ARMS. At the command of execution, pull

FIGURE 44.—Position of automatic rifle slung over right shoulder.

the trigger, replace the magazine, and resume the position of ATTENTION, the automatic rifle being kept slung.

f. Men armed with the automatic rifle execute INSPECTION ARMS when a unit is formed or dismissed at the command: 1. INSPECTION, 2. ARMS.

g. Men armed with the automatic rifle salute with the hand salute when not in ranks. In ranks they do not salute.

h. For instruction, ceremonies, and drill, the organization commander may, at his discretion, substitute rifles for automatic rifles.

SECTION V

MANUAL OF THE PISTOL

■ 136. GENERAL.—*a.* The movements herein described differ in purpose from the manual of arms for the rifle in that they are not designed to be executed in exact unison. Furthermore, with only a few exceptions, there is no real necessity for their simultaneous execution. They are not therefore planned as a disciplinary drill to be executed in cadence with snap and precision, but merely as simple, quick, and safe methods of handling the pistol. Commands are prescribed for such movements only as may be occasionally executed simultaneously by the squad or larger unit.

b. In general movements begin and end at the position of RAISE PISTOL.

c. Commands for firing, when required, are limited to COMMENCE FIRING and CEASE FIRING.

d. Officers and enlisted men armed with the pistol remain at the position of attention during the manual of arms, except when their units are presented to their commanders or are presented during ceremonies, at retreat, and at guard mounting. In such cases they execute the hand salute at the command of execution, ARMS, of 1. PRESENT, 2. ARMS, and resume the position of attention at the command of execution of the next command.

e. Men armed with the pistol execute INSPECTION PISTOL when a unit is formed or dismissed at the command: 1. INSPECTION, 2. ARMS.

f. Whenever the pistol is carried mounted the lanyard will be used. The lanyard should be of such length that the arm may be fully extended without constraint.

DISMOUNTED

■ 137. TO RAISE PISTOL.—The commands are: 1. RAISE, 2. PISTOL. At the command PISTOL, unbutton the flap of the holster with the right hand and grasp the stock, back of the hand outward. Draw the pistol from the holster; reverse it, muzzle up, the thumb and last three fingers holding the stock, the forefinger extended outside the trigger guard, the barrel of the pistol to the rear and inclined to the front at an angle of 30°, the hand as high as, and 6 inches in front of, the point of the right shoulder. This is the position of RAISE PISTOL.

■ 138. To WITHDRAW THE MAGAZINE.—Without lowering the right hand, turn the barrel slightly to the right; press the magazine catch with the right thumb and with the left hand remove the magazine. Place it in the belt or pocket.

■ 139. To OPEN THE CHAMBER.—Withdraw the magazine and resume the position of RAISE PISTOL. Without lowering the right hand, grasp the slide with the thumb and the first two fingers of the left hand (thumb on left side of slide and pointing downward); keeping the muzzle elevated, shift the grip of the right hand so that the right thumb engages with the slide stop. Push the slide downward to its full extent and force the slide stop into its notch with the right thumb without lowering the muzzle of the pistol.

■ 140. To CLOSE THE CHAMBER.—With the right thumb press down the slide stop and let the slide go forward. Squeeze the trigger.

■ 141. To INSERT A MAGAZINE.—Without lowering the right hand, turn the barrel to the right. Grasp a magazine with the first two fingers and thumb of the left hand; withdraw it from the belt and insert it in the pistol. Press it fully home.

■ 142. To LOAD PISTOL.—The commands are: 1. LOAD, 2. PISTOL. At the command PISTOL, if a loaded magazine is not already in the pistol, insert one. Without lowering the right hand, turn the barrel slightly to the left. Grasp the slide with the thumb and fingers of the left hand (thumb on right side of slide and pointing upward). Pull the slide downward to its full extent. Release the slide and engage the safety lock.

■ 143. To UNLOAD PISTOL.—The commands are: 1. UNLOAD, 2. PISTOL. At the command PISTOL, withdraw the magazine. Open the chamber as prescribed in paragraph 142. Glance at the chamber to verify that it is empty. Close the chamber. Take the position of RAISE PISTOL and squeeze the trigger. Then insert an empty magazine.

■ 144. To INSPECT PISTOL.—The commands are: 1. INSPECTION, 2. PISTOL. At the command PISTOL, withdraw the magazine. Open the chamber as prescribed in paragraph

139. Take the position of RAISE PISTOL. The withdrawn magazine is held in the open left hand at the height of the belt. After the pistol has been inspected, or at the command 1. RETURN, 2. PISTOL, close the chamber, take the position of RAISE PISTOL, and squeeze the trigger. Insert an empty magazine and execute RETURN PISTOL.

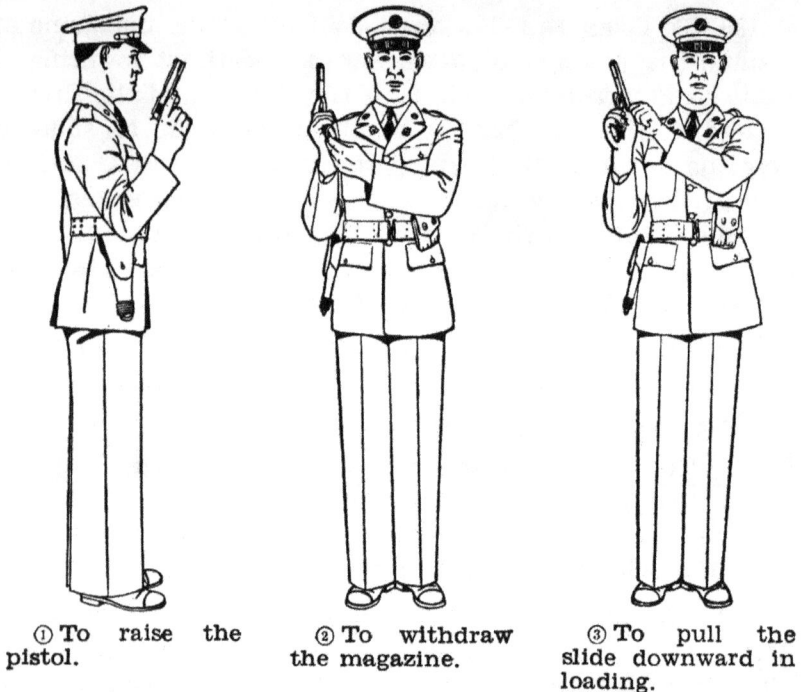

① To raise the pistol.

② To withdraw the magazine.

③ To pull the slide downward in loading.

FIGURE 45.—Manual of the pistol (dismounted).

■ 145. To RETURN PISTOL.—The commands are: 1. RETURN, 2. PISTOL. At the command PISTOL, lower the pistol to the holster, reversing it, muzzle down, back of the hand to the right; raise the flap of the holster with the right thumb; insert the pistol in the holster and thrust it home; button the flap of the holster with the right hand.

MOUNTED

■ 146. GENERAL RULES.—The following movements are executed as when dismounted: RAISE PISTOL, RETURN PISTOL, CLOSE CHAMBER. The mounted movements may be practiced when dismounted by first cautioning, "Mounted position." The

right foot is then carried 20 inches to the right and the left
hand to the position of the bridle hand. Whenever the
pistol is lowered into the bridle hand, the movement is executed by rotating the barrel to the right.   Grasp the slide

④ To open the chamber.   ⑤ To inspect the pistol.

FIGURE 45.—Manual of the pistol (dismounted).

in the full grip of the left hand, thumb extending along the
slide, back of the hand down, barrel down and pointing
upward and to the left front.

■ 147. To WITHDRAW THE MAGAZINE.—Lower the pistol into
the bridle hand.   Press the magazine catch with the forefinger of the right hand, palm of the hand over the base of
the magazine to prevent it from springing out; withdraw the
magazine and place it in the belt or pocket.

■ 148. To OPEN THE CHAMBER.—Withdraw the magazine.
Grasp the stock with the right hand, back of the hand down,
thrust forward and upward with the right hand, and engage
the slide stop by pressure of the right thumb.

■ 149. To INSERT A MAGAZINE.—Lower the pistol into the
bridle hand.   Extra magazines should be carried in the belt

with the projection on the base pointing to the left. Grasp
the magazine with the tip of the right forefinger on the projection, withdraw it from the belt, and insert it in the pistol.
Press it fully home.

■ 150. To Load Pistol.—The commands are: 1. LOAD, 2. PIS-
TOL. At the command PISTOL, lower the pistol into the
bridle hand. If a loaded magazine is not already in the pistol, insert one. Grasp the stock with the right hand, back
of the hand down, and thrust upward and to the left front;
release the slide and engage the safety lock.

■ 151. To Unload Pistol.—The commands are: 1. UNLOAD, 2.
PISTOL. At the command PISTOL, withdraw the magazine.
Open the chamber. Glance at the chamber to verify that it
is empty. Close the chamber. Take the position of RAISE
PISTOL and squeeze the trigger. Then insert an empty maga-
zine.

■ 152. To Inspect Pistol.—The commands are: 1. INSPEC-
TION, 2. PISTOL. (The pistol is inspected mounted only at
mounted guard mounting. The magazine is not withdrawn.)
At the command PISTOL, take the position of RAISE PISTOL.
After the pistol has been inspected, or on command, it is
returned.

CHAPTER 9

SQUAD AND PLATOON DRILL

SECTION I

THE SQUAD

■ **153. GENERAL.**—*a.* The squad is a group of soldiers organized primarily as a combat team. It consists of one squad leader and other personnel as authorized by appropriate Tables of Organization. When the squad leader is absent, he is replaced by the second in command. If the second in command is also absent, the next senior member of the squad acts as leader.

b. As far as practicable, the squad is kept intact. The normal formation of the squad is a single rank or single file. This permits variation in the number of men composing the squad.

c. The squad in line marches to the left or to the front only for minor changes of position.

■ **154. To FORM THE SQUAD.**—*a.* The command is: FALL IN. At the command FALL IN, the squad forms in line as shown in figure 48. On falling in, each man except the one on the left extends his left arm laterally at shoulder height, palm of the hand down, fingers extended and joined. Each man, except the one on the right, turns his head and eyes to the right and places himself in line so that his right shoulder touches lightly the tips of the fingers of the man on his right. As soon as proper intervals have been obtained, each man drops his arm smartly to his side and turns his head to the front.

b. To form at close intervals, the commands are: 1. AT CLOSE INTERVALS, 2. FALL IN. At the command FALL IN, the men fall in as in *a* above, except that close intervals are obtained by placing the left hands on the hips as shown in figure 49. In this position the heel of the palm of the hand

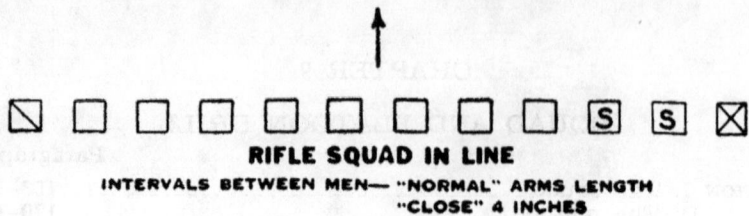

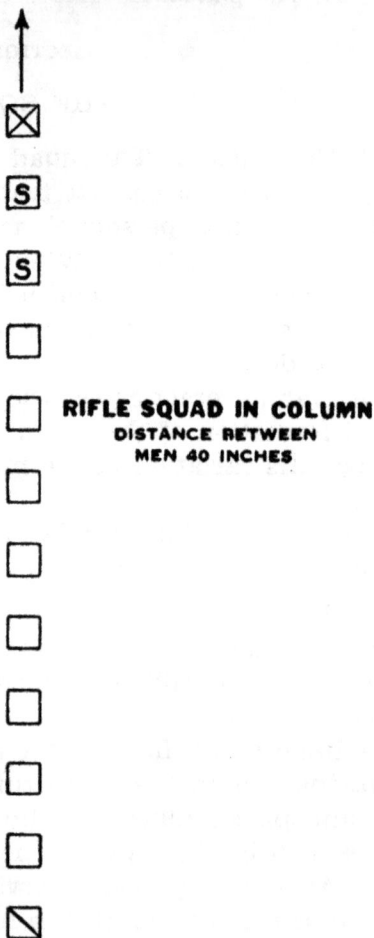

FIGURE 46.—Rifle squad.

RIFLE SQUAD	AUTOMATIC RIFLE SQUAD	LIGHT MACHINE GUN SQUAD	60 MM MORTAR SQUAD
⊠	⊠	⊠	◉
S	◉	◉	A
S	A	A	C
☐	C	C	C
☐	◉	C	C
☐	A		
☐	C		
☐	�णो		
☐			
☐			
☐			
☐			
◹			

⊠ SQUAD LEADER

◹ SECOND IN COMMAND

S SCOUT

☐ RIFLEMAN

◉ AUTOMATIC RIFLEMAN

◉ MACHINE GUNNER

◉ MORTAR GUNNER

A ASSISTANT

C AMMUNITION CARRIER

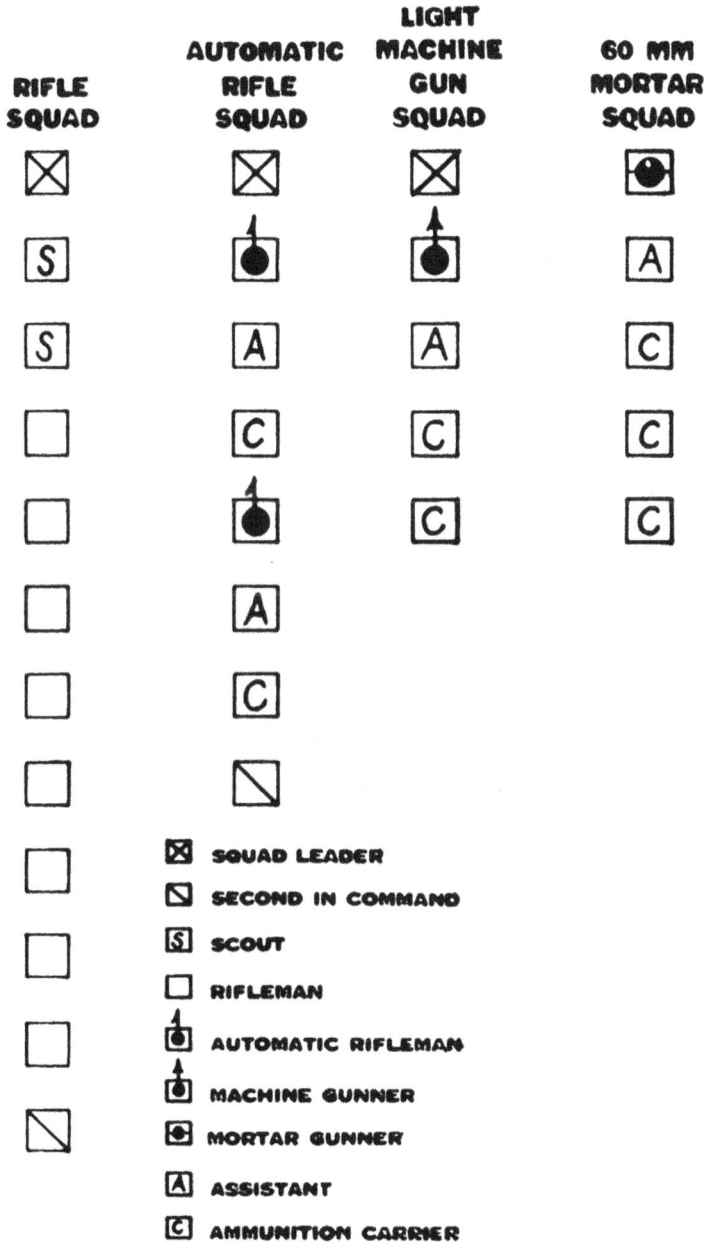

FIGURE 47.—Details of infantry rifle company squads.

117

rests on the hip, the fingers and thumb are extended and joined, and the elbow is in the plane of the body.

c. The squad falls in on the squad leader. If the squad is formed under arms, pieces are at once inspected.

■ 155. PREVIOUS INSTRUCTIONS APPLICABLE.—The squad executes the positions, movements, and manual of arms as prescribed in chapters 7 and 8, all men executing the movements simultaneously.

■ 156. TO DISMISS THE SQUAD.—The commands are: 1. IN-SPECTION, 2. ARMS, 3. PORT, 4. ARMS, 5. DISMISSED, or 3.

FIGURE 48.—FALL IN.

UNLOCK PIECES, 4. DISMISSED (if armed with the M1 rifle).

■ 157. TO COUNT OFF.—a. The command is: COUNT OFF. At the command COUNT OFF, each man of the squad, except the one on the right flank, turns his head and eyes to the right. The right flank man calls out "One." Each man in succession calls out, "Two," "Three," etc., turning his head and eyes to the front as he gives his number.

b. This command may be given whenever it is desired that the men know their relative position in the squad.

■ 158. To ALINE THE SQUAD.—*a.* If in line, the commands are: 1. DRESS RIGHT (LEFT), 2. DRESS, 3. READY, 4. FRONT. At the command DRESS, each man except the one on the left extends his left arm (or if at close interval, places his left hand upon his hip), and all aline themselves to the right. The instructor places himself on the right flank one pace from and in prolongation of the line and facing down the line. From this position he verifies the alinement of the

FIGURE 49.—1. AT CLOSE INTERVAL, 2. FALL IN.

men, ordering individual men to move forward or back as is necessary. Having checked the alinement, he faces to the right in marching and moves three paces forward, halts, faces to the left and commands: 1. READY, 2. FRONT. At the command FRONT, arms are dropped quietly and smartly to the side and heads turned to the front.

b. If in column the command is: COVER. At the command COVER, men cover from front to rear with 40 inches distance between men.

■ **159. Being in Line at Normal Interval, to Obtain Close Interval.**—The commands are: 1. close, 2. MARCH. At the command march, all men except the right flank man face to the right in marching and form at close interval, as prescribed in paragraph 154*b*.

■ **160. Being in Line at Close Interval, to Extend to Normal Interval.**—The commands are: 1. extend, 2. MARCH. At the command march, all men except the right flank man face to the left in marching and form at normal interval as prescribed in paragraph 154*a*.

■ **161. Being in Line, to March to the Flank.**—The commands are: 1. right (left), 2. FACE, 3. forward, 4. MARCH. The movements are executed as explained in paragraphs 90*a* and 93, all men stepping off simultaneously.

■ **162. To March to the Oblique.**—*a.* For the instruction of recruits, the squad being in column or correctly alined, the instructor causes each man to face half right (left), points out his position, and explains that it is to be maintained in the oblique march.

b. The squad being in any formation, the commands are: 1. right (left) oblique, 2. MARCH. At the command march, given as the right foot strikes the ground, each individual advances and plants the left foot, faces half right in marching and steps off in a direction of 45° to the right of his original front. He preserves his relative position, keeping his shoulders parallel to those of the guide (man on right front of line or column), and so regulates his step that the ranks remain parallel to their original front.

c. The command halt is given on the left foot when halting from the right oblique and on the right foot when halting from left oblique. At the command halt, given as the left foot strikes the ground, each individual advances and plants the right foot, turns to the front on the ball of the right foot, and places the left foot by the side of the right foot.

d. To resume the original direction, the commands are: 1. forward, 2. MARCH. At the command march, each individual faces half left in marching and then moves straight to the front.

e. If at HALF STEP or MARK TIME while obliquing, the FULL STEP is resumed by the command: 1. OBLIQUE, 2. MARCH.

f. To give volume to the command the word "oblique" is pronounced to rhyme with "strike."

■ 163. To MARCH TOWARD A FLANK WHILE IN MARCH.—*a.* The commands are: 1. BY THE RIGHT (LEFT) FLANK, 2. MARCH. At the command MARCH, each individual executes the movement as prescribed in paragraph 101.

b. This movement is used when a quick movement to the right or left for a short distance is required. Normally the unit is halted, faced in the desired direction, and started forward again by the commands: 1. FORWARD, 2. MARCH.

■ 164. BEING IN COLUMN, TO CHANGE DIRECTION.—The commands are: 1. COLUMN RIGHT (LEFT) (HALF RIGHT) (HALF LEFT), 2. MARCH. At the command MARCH, the leading man executes the movement as prescribed in paragraph 100*a* and *b*. The other men in the column execute the same movement successively and on the same ground as the leading man.

■ 165. BEING IN LINE, TO TAKE INTERVAL AND ASSEMBLE.—*a.* To take interval, the commands are: 1. TAKE INTERVAL TO THE LEFT (RIGHT), 2. MARCH. At the command MARCH, the right flank man stands fast and extends his left arm at shoulder height, palms of the hand down, fingers extended and joined until the man on his left obtains the proper interval, then he drops his arm. Other men face to the left in marching and step out until they have an interval of two arms' length from the man on their right. Each man, except the one on the left who raises his right arm only, extends both arms laterally at shoulder height. Each man, except the right flank man, then turns his head and eyes to the right and places himself in line so that the finger tips of his right hand touch lightly the finger tips of the left hand of the man on his right. As soon as each man alines himself at two arms' length intervals from the man on his right, he drops his right arm to the side and turns his head and eyes to the front. He drops his left arm to the side when the man on his left has obtained his proper interval. If under arms, rifles will be slung prior to the execution of this movement.

b. To assemble, the commands are: **1.** ASSEMBLE TO THE RIGHT (LEFT), **2.** MARCH. At the command MARCH, the right flank man stands fast. All other men face to the right in marching and form at normal intervals as in paragraph 154*a.*

■ **166. To STACK ARMS.**—*a. Rifle squad.*—The rifle squad being in line at normal or close interval, the commands are: **1.** STACK, **2.** ARMS. Numbers 2, 5, 8, and 11 make the stacks except when no men are on the left of these numbers. The stack is made as follows: At the command ARMS, the man on the left of the stackman regrasps his rifle with the right hand at the balance, carrying it to the horizontal position, barrel up, and passes his rifle to the stackman who grasps it with his left hand between the upper sling swivel and stacking swivel and places the butt between his feet, barrel to the front, muzzle inclined slightly to the front, the thumb and forefinger raising the stacking swivel. The stackman then throws the butt of his own rifle two feet in advance of that of his left file and 6 inches to the right of his right toe; at the same time he allows his right hand to slip to the stacking swivel and engages his rifle with that of his left file. The man on the right of the stackman raises his rifle with his right hand, regrasps it with his right hand at the balance, steps to the left front keeping his right foot in place, and carries his rifle well forward, barrel to the front; the left hand guiding the stacking swivel engages the lower hook of the swivel of his own rifle with the free hook of that of his left file, and then turns the barrel outward into the angle formed by the other two rifles and lowers the butt to the ground so that it will form a uniform stack with the other two rifles. He then assumes the position of attention. Other rifles of the squad are passed toward the nearest stack and laid on the stack by the stackman.

b. Automatic rifle squad.—The automatic rifle squad, rifle company, being in line at normal or close interval, the commands are: **1.** STACK, **2.** ARMS. The second man from the left makes the stack. The stack is made as follows: At the command ARMS, the man on the left of the stackman regrasps his rifle with the right hand at the balance, carrying it to the horizontal position, barrel up, and passes his

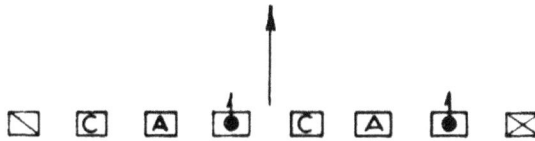

AUTOMATIC RIFLE SQUAD IN LINE
INTERVALS BETWEEN MEN: "NORMAL"—ARMS LENGTH "CLOSE"—4 INCHES

LEGEND

⊠ SQUAD LEADER

◺ SECOND IN COMMAND

◉ AUTOMATIC RIFLEMAN

Ⓐ ASSISTANT AUTOMATIC RIFLEMAN

Ⓒ AMMUNITION CARRIER

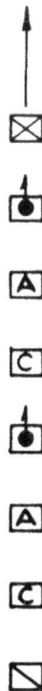

AUTOMATIC RIFLE SQUAD IN COLUMN
DISTANCE BETWEEN MEN:— 40 INCHES

FIGURE 50.—Automatic rifle squad.

rifle to the stackman who grasps it with his left hand between the upper sling swivel and stacking swivel and places the butt between his feet, barrel to the front, muzzle slightly inclined to the front, the thumb and forefinger raising the stacking swivel. The stackman then throws the butt of his own rifle 2 feet in advance of that of his left file and 6 inches to the right of his right toe; at the same time he allows his right hand to slip to the stacking swivel and engages his rifle with that of his left file. The nearest rifle on the right is then passed to the man on the right of the stackman who raises the rifle with his right hand at the balance, steps to the left front keeping his right foot in place, and carries the rifle well forward, barrel to the front; the left hand guiding the stacking swivel engages the lower hook of the swivel of the rifle with the free hook of that of the stackman, and then turns the barrel outward into the angle formed by the other two rifles and lowers the butt to the ground so that it will form a uniform stack with the other two rifles. He then assumes the position of attention. Automatic rifles and the other rifles of the squad are passed toward the stack and laid on the stack by the stackman.

c. Rifle squad of antitank company.—The rifle squad of the antitank company and other types of squads will stack arms in general with the methods prescribed in *a* and *b* above.

■ 167. To TAKE ARMS.—The squad being in line behind the stacks, the commands are: 1. TAKE, 2. ARMS. At the command ARMS, the procedure of stacking arms is reversed. The loose rifles are first passed back. In breaking the stack, the stackman grasps his rifle and that of the man on his left, so that the rifles will not fall when the man on the right raises and disengages his rifle. Each man, as he receives his rifle, resumes the position of ORDER ARMS.

■ 168. COLUMN OF TWOS.—When marching small groups, not at drill, the group may be marched in column of twos by forming it in two ranks and giving the command: 1. RIGHT (LEFT), 2. FACE.

■ 169. To FORM COLUMN OF TWOS FROM SINGLE FILE AND RE-FORM.—*a.* The squad being in column, at a halt, to form

column of twos, the commands are: 1. FORM COLUMN OF
TWOS, 2. MARCH. At the command MARCH, the leading man
stands fast; the second man in the squad moves by the
oblique until he is to the left of and abreast of the corporal
with normal interval, and halts; the third man moves forward until behind the corporal with normal distance and
halts; the fourth man moves by the oblique until he is to
the left of and abreast of the third man with normal interval,
and halts; and so on.

FIGURE 51.—To stack arms (automatic rifle squad).

b. The squad being in column of twos, in marching, to
re-form single file, the squad is first halted. The commands
are: 1. FORM SINGLE FILE FROM THE RIGHT, 2. MARCH. At
the command MARCH, the leading man of the right column
moves forward, the leading man of the left column steps
off to the right oblique, then executes LEFT OBLIQUE so as to
follow the right file at normal distance. Remaining twos
follow successively in like manner.

①

②

FIGURE 52.—To stack arms.

SECTION II

THE PLATOON

■ 170. FORMATIONS OF MORE THAN ONE SQUAD.—*a.* The squads form in line, one behind the other, with 40 inches distance between ranks.

b. Squads are usually arranged to produce a three- or four-rank formation so that by facing to the right the unit will march in column of threes or column of fours depending on the number of squads.

c. A two-squad unit forms in two ranks and marches in column of twos.

d. A three-squad unit forms in three ranks and marches in column of threes.

e. A four-squad unit forms in four ranks and marches in column of fours.

f. A platoon composed of two sections of two squads each forms in four ranks and marches in column of fours.

g. Movements are described herein for COLUMN OF THREES or FOURS and may be executed by either formation.

h. When in line, the platoon is alined as prescribed for the squad in paragraph 158. The alinement of each rank is verified by the platoon leader.

i. The platoon being in line takes interval and assembles as prescribed for the squad in paragraph 165. This movement may be ordered after ranks are opened for the display of field equipment or for other special purpose. It is not utilized in forming for physical training.

■ 171. COMPOSITION AND FORMATION OF THE PLATOON.—The platoon consists of platoon headquarters and several squads. Platoon headquarters consists of a platoon leader and one or more assistants. For purposes of drill and ceremonies, a three-squad or four-squad formation should be arranged and the size of the squads equalized. Figure 53 shows how the platoon formation applies to a rifle platoon.

■ 172. POSITION OF INDIVIDUALS.—*a.* The platoon leader takes position six paces in front of the center of his platoon when in line. In march formation (column of threes or fours), he marches at the head of his platoon as shown in figure 53.

b. The second in command of a platoon takes position on the left of the left man of the rear rank when squads are in line unless otherwise indicated. When squads are in column, he follows the rear man in the right squad of the unit. The second in command observes the conduct of the unit, sees that the proper formation is maintained, and that commands are promptly and properly executed. The platoon guide (a sergeant or other specially designated noncommissioned officer) is posted on the right of the right flank man of the front rank when in line. In column, he takes post in front of the right flank man. He is responsible for maintaining the proper direction and cadence of march of the platoon.

c. Other noncommissioned officers (such as mess and supply sergeants, clerks, etc.) and privates (such as cooks, armorers, etc.), when attached to the platoon, fall in on the left when in line (or in rear when squads are in column) and march as part of regularly organized squads.

■ **173. To Form the Platoon.**—*a.* The command is: FALL IN. At the command FALL IN, the first squad forms in line, as prescribed in paragraph 154*a*, its center opposite and three paces from the platoon sergeant. The other squads form in rear of the first squad and in the same manner, with 40 inches distance between ranks. Members of the rear squads extend their arms to obtain their approximate intervals but cover the corresponding members in the first squad. The guide places himself as shown in figure 53.

b. To form with close interval, the commands are: 1. AT CLOSE INTERVAL, 2. FALL IN. At the command FALL IN, the movement is executed as prescribed in *a* above, except that squads form at close interval (par. 154*b*).

c. The platoon is ordinarily formed and dismissed by the platoon sergeant.

■ **174. To Dismiss the Platoon.**—The commands are: 1. INSPECTION, 2. ARMS, 3. PORT, 4. ARMS, 5. DISMISSED, or 3. UNLOCK PIECES, 4. DISMISSED (if armed with the M1 rifle).

■ **175. To March the Platoon.**—*a.* The normal formation for marching is in column of threes (or fours) with squad columns abreast, squad leaders at the head of their squads.

6 PACES

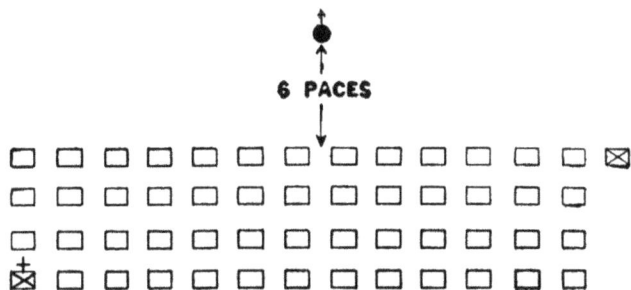

INTERVAL —ARMS LENGTH   DISTANCES-40 INCHES

1. RIFLE PLATOON IN LINE FACED TO THE FRONT.

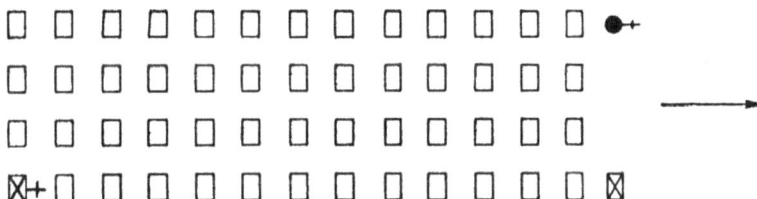

INTERVAL —ARMS LENGTH   DISTANCES-40 INCHES

2. AT THE COMMANDS: 1. RIGHT 2. FACE, THE PLATOON FACES TO THE RIGHT. PLATOON LEADER AND GUIDE CHANGE TO NEW POSITIONS.
AT THE COMMANDS: 1. FORWARD 2. MARCH, IT MOVES OFF.

INTERVAL —4 INCHES   DISTANCE   40 INCHES

3. AT THE COMMANDS: 1. CLOSE 2. MARCH, THE SQUAD COLUMNS CLOSE TO THE CENTER.

LEGEND

● PLATOON LEADER   ⊠ PLATOON GUIDE   ⊞ PLATOON SERGEANT   ☐ ALL OTHERS

FIGURE 53.—Platoon in line, marched to the right.

b. The platoon in line marches to the left or to the front only for minor changes of position.

c. The platoon being in line to march to the right, the commands are: 1. RIGHT, 2. FACE, 3. FORWARD, 4. MARCH. This marches the platoon in column of threes (or fours) to the right.

■ 176. GUIDE IN MARCHING.—Except when otherwise directed, men in ranks keep the proper distance and interval and aline themselves on the men toward the flank on which the guide is marching. When it is desired to guide toward the left, the command is: GUIDE LEFT. The guide and the platoon leader then change their relative positions.

■ 177. BEING IN COLUMN OF THREES (OR FOURS) AT NORMAL INTERVAL BETWEEN SQUADS, TO MARCH (OR FORM) AT CLOSE INTERVAL.—*a.* The commands are: 1. CLOSE, 2. MARCH. At the command MARCH, the squads close to the center by obliquing until the interval between men is 4 inches. The center squad (or squads) take up the half step until the dress has been regained. The distance, 40 inches, remains unchanged.

b. If this movement is executed from the halt, the squads close toward the center by executing RIGHT OR LEFT STEP until 4-inch intervals are reached. If in column of threes, the right and left squads LEFT and RIGHT STEP two steps. If in column of fours, the right center and left center squads LEFT and RIGHT STEP one step, the right and left squads LEFT and RIGHT STEP three steps.

■ 178. BEING IN COLUMN OF THREES (OR FOURS) AT CLOSE INTERVAL BETWEEN SQUADS, TO MARCH, (OR FORM) AT NORMAL INTERVAL.—*a.* The commands are: 1. EXTEND, 2. MARCH. At the command MARCH, the squads open to the right and left from the center by obliquing until the interval between men is one arm's length. The center squad (or squads) will take up the half step until the dress has been regained.

b. If this movement is executed at the halt, the squads execute RIGHT OR LEFT STEP until they have secured the proper interval by reversing the procedure outlined in paragraph 177*b*.

■ 179. BEING IN COLUMN OF THREES (OR FOURS), TO CHANGE DIRECTION.—The commands are: 1. COLUMN RIGHT (LEFT). 2.

MARCH. The right flank man of the leading rank (the guide and the platoon leader excepted) is the pivot of this movement. At the command MARCH, given as the right foot strikes the ground, the right flank man of the leading rank faces to the right in marching as prescribed in paragraph 100a and b, and takes up the half step until the other men of his rank are abreast of him, then he resumes the full step. The other men of the leading rank oblique to the right in marching without changing interval, place themselves abreast of the pivot man and conform to his step. The ranks in rear of the leading rank execute the movement on the same ground, and in the same manner, as the leading rank.

■ 180. BEING IN COLUMN OF THREES (OR FOURS), TO FORM LINE TO THE FRONT.—The commands are: 1. COLUMN RIGHT, 2. MARCH, 3. PLATOON, 4. HALT, 5. LEFT, 6. FACE. Column right is executed as prescribed in paragraph 179. The command HALT is given after the change of direction is completed.

■ 181. BEING IN ANY FORMATION IN MARCH, TO MARCH TO- WARD A FLANK.—The commands are: 1. BY THE RIGHT (LEFT) FLANK, 2. MARCH. This movement is executed as prescribed for the squad in paragraph 163. If the platoon is in column at close (4-inch) intervals, the squads in rear of the squad which becomes the leading squad take up the half step until they each reach 40 inches' distance from the squad ahead. This movement is used only for short distances.

■ 182. STACK ARMS.—Before stacking arms, ranks are opened. Arms are then stacked by each squad as prescribed in para- graph 166.

■ 183. BEING IN LINE, TO OPEN AND CLOSE RANKS.—a. To open ranks the commands are: 1. OPEN RANKS, 2. MARCH, 3. READY, 4. FRONT. At the command MARCH, the front rank takes three steps forward, halts, and executes DRESS RIGHT. The second rank takes two steps forward, halts, and executes DRESS RIGHT. The third rank takes one step forward, halts, and executes DRESS RIGHT. The fourth rank, if any, executes DRESS RIGHT. The platoon leader places himself on the flank of the platoon toward which the dress is to be made, one pace from and in prolongation of the front rank and facing down the line. From this position he alines the front rank. The second and third ranks are alined in the same manner. In moving from one rank to another, the platoon leader faces to the left in marching. After verifying the alinement of the rear rank, he faces to the right in marching, moves three paces beyond the front rank, halts, faces to the left and commands: 1. READY, 2. FRONT.

b. To close ranks, the commands are: 1. CLOSE RANKS, 2. MARCH. At the command MARCH, the front rank stands fast; the second rank takes one step forward and halts; the third rank takes two steps forward and halts; and the fourth rank, if any, takes three steps forward and halts. Each man covers his file leader.

■ 184. TO FORM FOR SHELTER TENTS.—The platoon being in line the commands are: 1. FORM FOR SHELTER TENTS TO THE LEFT (RIGHT), 2. MARCH, 3. DRESS RIGHT (LEFT), 4. DRESS, 5. READY, 6. FRONT, 7. COUNT OFF.

a. At the command FORM FOR SHELTER TENTS TO THE LEFT (RIGHT), the second in command moves to a position on the right of the guide who is on the right of the right man of the front rank. The messenger takes position on the left of the left man of the rear rank.

b. At the command MARCH, all squads except the front squad face to the left in marching and step off. Squad leaders by giving the appropriate commands, 1. BY THE RIGHT (LEFT) FLANK, 2. MARCH, and 1. SQUAD, 2. HALT, move their squads into line abreast of the squad(s) already on line.

c. At the commands 3. DRESS RIGHT (LEFT), 4. DRESS, 5. READY, 6. FRONT, and 7. COUNT OFF, given by the platoon leader the entire rank executes these movements as prescribed in paragraphs 157 and 158.

d. On direction of the platoon leader, the odd numbers draw their bayonets and thrust them into the ground alongside the outside of the left heel near the instep. The bayonet indicates the position of the front tent pole. Men not equipped with bayonets mark the place with the left heel. Odd and even numbers (Nos. 1 and 2; Nos. 3 and 4; etc.) pitch tents together.

e. To assemble, the platoon is faced to the right and reformed from single file into column of threes (or fours) to the right (left) as prescribed in paragraph 185c(2). The platoon sergeant and messenger resume their normal posts.

■ 185. COLUMN OF TWOS AND SINGLE FILE AND RE-FORM.—The platoon may be marched in column of twos or single file by the procedure given below. This is not a precise movement. It is practiced in drill so that when necessary the movement may be executed smoothly and without delay. The change of column is always made from a halt.

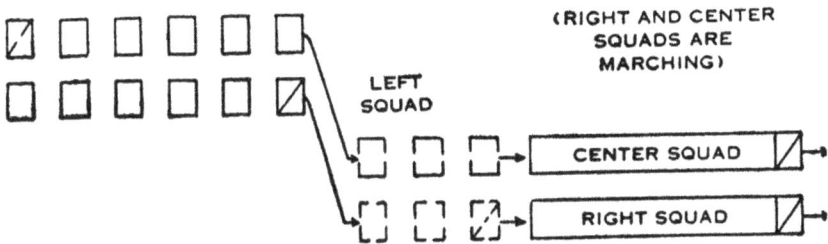

FIGURE 54.—Column of twos from column of threes.

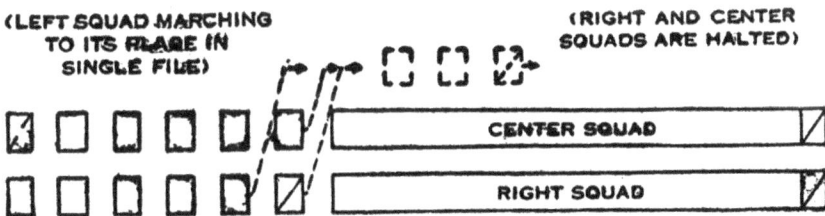

FIGURE 55.—Re-form column of threes from column of twos.

a. (1) The platoon being in column of threes, at a halt, to form column of twos, the commands are: 1. COLUMN OF TWOS FROM THE RIGHT (LEFT), 2. MARCH. At the command MARCH, the right two squads march forward; the left squad forms column of twos as prescribed for the squad and then executes COLUMN HALF RIGHT and COLUMN HALF LEFT so as to follow in column the leading squads. Forty-inch distances are maintained.

(2) The platoon being in column of twos, at a halt, to re-form in column of threes, the commands are: 1. COLUMN OF THREES TO THE LEFT (RIGHT), 2. MARCH. At the command MARCH, the leading two squads stand fast. The rear squad forms single file from the right as prescribed in paragraph 169*b* and moves to its normal place beside the leading squads by executing COLUMN HALF LEFT then COLUMN HALF RIGHT. It is halted when its leading file is on line with the leading rank of the platoon.

b. (1) The platoon being in column of fours, at a halt, to form column of twos, the commands are: 1. COLUMN OF TWOS FROM THE RIGHT (LEFT), 2. MARCH. At the command MARCH, the right two squads march forward; the left two squads initially stand fast, then follow the leading two squads by executing COLUMN HALF RIGHT and COLUMN HALF LEFT. Forty-inch distances are maintained.

(2) The platoon being in column of twos, at a halt, to re-form in column of fours, the commands are: 1. COLUMN OF FOURS TO THE LEFT (RIGHT), 2. MARCH. At the command MARCH, the leading two squads stand fast. The two rear squads move to their normal places by executing COLUMN HALF LEFT then COLUMN HALF RIGHT and are halted when the leading files are on line with the leading rank of the platoon.

c. (1) The platoon being in column of threes (or fours), at a halt, to form single file, the commands are: 1. COLUMN OF FILES FROM THE RIGHT (LEFT), 2. MARCH. At the command MARCH, the right squad of the platoon moves forward. The other squads stand fast initially and then successively follow the leading squad by executing COLUMN HALF RIGHT and COLUMN HALF LEFT. Distances of 40 inches are maintained.

(2) The platoon being in single file, at a halt, to re-form in column of threes (or fours), the commands are: 1. COLUMN OF THREES (OR FOURS) TO THE LEFT (RIGHT), 2. MARCH. At the command MARCH, the leading squad stands fast. The other squads move to their normal places by executing COLUMN HALF LEFT, then, at the proper time, COLUMN HALF RIGHT and are halted when the leading file is on line with the leading rank of the platoon.

d. Whenever commands are given involving movements of squads in which one squad stands fast, takes up the march, continues the march, or changes formation, the squad leader gives the appropriate commands.

CHAPTER 10

INTERIOR GUARD DUTY

■ 186. At each post, camp, or station where troops are present guards are used to preserve order, protect property, and enforce police regulations. The commanding officer of the camp or post determines how large a guard is necessary for these purposes and issues the necessary orders. When your company, troop, or battery commander decides that you have made sufficient progress in your military training, you will probably be detailed for guard duty. The information given in paragraphs below will help you in understanding what this duty will be.

■ 187. The guard consists of—
Officer of the day.
Officer of the guard (except when the guard is small).
Sergeant of the guard.
Corporals of the guard.
Buglers of the guard.
Privates of the guard.
The guard is under the supervision of the officer of the day.

■ 188. The members of the guard may all come from the same company, troop, or battery, or they may be detailed from several different organizations. In either case, when a soldier has served a tour of guard duty he is given credit for it on the guard roster and does not again do guard duty until all other men on the roster have served their tours.

■ 189. The length of a tour of guard duty is 24 hours. At the end of that time the "old guard" is relieved by the "new guard" of the same size. As soon as the new guard relieves the old guard at the guardhouse it is divided into three parts called "reliefs." These reliefs are rotated so that each member of the guard has 2 hours on duty followed by 4 hours off duty. Privates of the guard are assigned to reliefs by the sergeant of the guard, and to posts by the corporals of their reliefs. Privates are not changed from one relief to another during the same tour of duty, except by proper authority.

■ 190. While you are off duty do not remove your clothing or equipment or leave the immediate vicinity of the guardhouse without permission of the commander of the guard. An emergency may occur when you will be needed at once.

■ 191. When you are not posted as a sentinel or on other duty which requires you to carry your rifle, keep it in the arms rack in the guardhouse or in a stack.

■ 192. Orders for sentinels are of two classes: general orders and special orders. *General orders* apply to all sentinels. *Special orders* apply to particular posts and duties. You must know and be able to recite the general orders before you go on guard duty. As soon as you are assigned to a relief and a particular post you must also learn and be able to recite the special orders for that post. Whenever the officer of the day or the commander of the guard considers that a sentinel does not have sufficient instruction or is otherwise unfit for guard duty, he relieves him, sends him back to his organization, and notifies his organization commander.

■ 193. The following are the general orders all sentinels are required to memorize. Learn them as soon as you can.

My general orders are—

1. To take charge of this post and all Government property in view.

2. To walk my post in a military manner, keeping always on the alert and observing everything that takes place within sight or hearing.

3. To report all violations of orders I am instructed to enforce.

4. To repeat all calls from posts more distant from the guardhouse than my own.

5. To quit my post only when properly relieved.

6. To receive, obey, and pass on to the sentinel who relieves me all orders from the commanding officer, officer of the day, and officers and noncommissioned officers of the guard only.

7. To talk to no one except in line of duty.

8. To give the alarm in case of fire or disorder.

9. To call the corporal of the guard in any case not covered by instructions.

10. *To salute all officers and all colors and standards not cased.*

11. *To be especially watchful at night and, during the time for challenging, to challenge all persons on or near my post, and to allow no one to pass without proper authority.*

■ 194. Guard duty is one of your most important duties. Remember that when you are posted as a sentinel you represent the commanding officer whose orders you are required to enforce, on and in the vicinity of your post. Upon the manner in which you perform your duties depends not only the enforcement of military law and orders, but also the security of persons and property under your charge. In time of war your responsibility as a member of the guard is greater than ever, for then the safety of your organization depends upon the manner in which you watch while your comrades rest. This is so important that sleeping on post by a sentinel or other improper performances of duty is punishable by a very severe court-martial sentence.

CHAPTER 11

MARCHES, CAMPS, AND BIVOUACS

SECTION I

MARCHES

■ 195. One of your principal jobs in the field is marching. Battles take place at indefinite intervals, but marches occur daily. To win battles, troops must arrive on the battlefield on time and in good physical condition. To accomplish this they must be able to march.

■ 196. PREPARATIONS.—*a.* When you learn that your organization is to make a march the next day there are certain things you should attend to the evening before. See that your canteen is clean and filled with fresh water as there may be little time for this in the morning. Check your personal equipment and see that you have all the articles necessary for personal cleanliness, and for keeping your clothing in repair. This should include towel, soap, toothbrush, pocket comb, small mirror, needles, thread, safety pins, and spare buttons. Check up on the adjustment of your pack straps and belt. A poorly adjusted pack adds to the discomfort and fatigue of a march. You should have at least two pairs of woolen socks without holes or mends. See that your shoes or boots fit comfortably, are in good repair, and well broken in. Never start a march with a new pair of shoes or boots. If you are in a mounted organization inspect your equipment carefully and replace any missing or doubtful parts. Nose bags should be filled with the morning feed as soon as the animals have finished their evening feed of grain. Grain bags should be filled before dark. If you are on guard, you should know where to find the cooks and when to awaken them.

b. Before dark dispose of any trash or debris that may have collected in or around your tent area. This will save you time and effort in the morning, especially if your organization is to break camp before daylight. Our Army takes pride

138

in always leaving a camp site in better condition than we found it.

c. On the morning of the march turn out promptly at the first call for reveille, perform your toilet, and make up your roll and pack, or pack your saddle. According to the instructions of your commanding officer you will water and feed your animal, if mounted, eat breakfast, and wash and pack your mess kit. After breakfast you will be allowed 10 or 15 minutes to relieve yourself and complete your pack and roll. While drivers warm their motors, or harness and hitch their animals, other soldiers help in packing the kitchen, taking down the officers' tents and picket line, and loading the forage, filling the sink and latrines, and cleaning the camp area. In mounted organizations, after the order to saddle, you must take particular care to see that the blanket is free of sand or cockleburs, and is without wrinkles. You should know your duties and do them promptly and quietly without confusion or noise. At assembly, fall in fully equipped for marching.

■ 197. When you fall in to start the march, do it quietly. One of the indications of a well-trained organization is the absence of noise and confusion when starting a march. When you are close to the enemy it will be necessary to maintain quiet for your own protection as he will be on the alert for noises which will help him locate your position. Even when you are at a distance from the enemy, or making a practice march in peace, loud talking and shouting will disturb civilian communities or troops camped nearby who are trying to rest.

■ 198. CONDUCT OF INDIVIDUALS.—*a.* Drinking water on a march is largely a matter of habit. Drink plentifully before the start of the march, but after that drink sparingly. Drink none at all for the first 3 or 4 hours of the march. After that, take only a few mouthfuls at the end of a rest period to wash out the throat and mouth. A small pebble carried in the mouth keeps it moist and reduces thirst. Do not drink or eat unwholesome foods or beverages. Use only water approved by your commander. The eating of sweets greatly increases thirst and should be avoided. When a cooked meal is carried do not eat it until the proper time. Excessive perspiration causes the loss to the body of necessary salts;

this results in fatigue and heat exhaustion. The eating of common table salt or salt tablets, helps to relieve this condition. Cold coffee or tea will also help.

b. You will remember that in chapter 1 it was stated that civilians will judge your organization and the Army by the conduct and appearance of its members in public. This is especially true of troops on the march. Avoid using profane or obscene language or making remarks to civilians. When you do this, you are not only proving that you are lacking in military discipline but are causing your organization to be considered as poorly trained. This is unfair to your comrades.

c. Halts are made at regular intervals to rest the men and animals, to service motors, to adjust equipment, and for other purposes. A halt of 15 minutes is usually made at the end of the first 45 minutes of marching. After the first halt, columns including foot or mounted troops usually halt for 10 minutes each hour. These halts are for the purpose of permitting men and animals to relieve themselves, adjust equipment, and inspect animals, motors, vehicles, and loading. Attend to these things promptly. Do not wait until the command is ready to march again. A mounted man always attends to the needs of his horse and equipment before satisfying his own wants. You should inspect each foot of your horse to see that no shoes have become loosened, or that no stones have become wedged in the frog or shoe. Remove caked mud or snow with the hoof hook. If you are the driver of a motor vehicle, conduct the general mechanical inspection as you have been instructed, and report promptly the results of your inspection to your chief of section or other designated person.

d. After you have adjusted your own equipment and that of your mount, or completed your vehicle inspection, rest as much as possible during the remainder of the halt. Do not stand or wander about. If the ground is dry, remove your pack and stretch out at full length in as comfortable a position as possible. The next best way is to sit down with a good back rest against a tree, fence, or embankment. Never sit or lie on wet ground. If you find it necessary to answer the calls of nature, dig a small pit and immediately refill it after use.

e. Do not enter private property without permission or take fruit or vegetables from orchards and gardens. These are seriously military offenses.

■ 199. ROAD DISCIPLINE.—*a. General.*—(1) In marching, troops usually keep to the right of the road, leaving the left free for other traffic. If the left of the road has better concealment from air observation, or for other reasons, troops may be directed to march on the left of the road, keeping the right free for traffic. On certain occasions they may march on both sides of the road leaving the middle clear.

(2) In any event, your organization commander will announce how you will march. The important thing for you to remember is that you must stay *at all times* on the side of the road as he has directed, and not straggle back and forth across the road or out into the middle. Before your organization starts its march, other troops, and especially motor units, will be informed which parts of the road will be left free for them. *Acting on this information, motor vehicle units may sometimes move as rapidly as 60 miles an hour past your column.* You can see how easily serious accidents and traffic tie-ups may occur if you do not keep your prescribed distance and place in the column and interfere with the right-of-way of other traffic, both military and civilian. At halts, immediately clear the road by moving off to the side on which you have been marching, unless otherwise directed. At the preparation signal for resuming the march, fall in promptly.

(3) Every march is planned so as to bring troops to a certain place at a definite time, and in such good condition that they can fight immediately, if required. In order to do this a very careful supervision is necessary so that large numbers of troops as well as food, ammunition, and other supplies can move forward without causing traffic jams. To assist in this movement military police are stationed at certain critical places and patrol the roads. They wear a blue arm band with the letters MP in white. They know on which roads it is safe for you to march and at what hours. They are there to help and protect you and their instructions and orders must be obeyed.

(4) If you are marching at night, you must make special efforts to remain alert. Be careful not to ride or walk too

close to the man ahead of you, or to lag behind. When night marches are made to maintain secrecy, you remain silent and smoking and the lighting of matches or flashlights are forbidden.

b. Foot troops.—If you become sick or unable to continue the march, do not fall out until you receive permission from an officer. Then wait beside the road for the medical detachment, which marches at the rear of the column. If you fall out without permission, you are subject to arrest by a police detachment, which follows the column. Your organization will take great pride in the fact that no one has had to fall out. If you have made the proper preparations with respect to your shoes and socks, and do not eat or drink too much, you will have no difficulties with the average march.

c. Mounted troops.—(1) Do not slouch in the saddle or ride with the weight on one buttock. The proper position in the saddle will not only be less tiring to you but will probably prevent your horse from having a sore back.

(2) Keep your head up and remain alert. Increase and decrease your gait *promptly* at the command. Failure to do this, or to maintain the proper gait, will result in a continual stringing out and jamming up of riders in the column. This may not only result in injury to the horse but will soon tire out both horse and man.

(3) Be alert to pass signals down the column, especially warnings of obstacles in the road, such as bottles, wire, holes, and narrow culverts. Failure to do this may result in serious injury to someone in rear of you.

(4) Watch your horse for signs of lameness and ask for permission to fall out if such condition is discovered. He may have picked up a rock or a nail. If necessary, wait for the veterinary officer.

(5) If you have to fall out, regain your position in the column gradually by increasing the length of the trot periods and decreasing the length of the walk periods. If you are delayed more than 10 minutes, join another organization temporarily and rejoin your own organization at one of the hourly halts or in bivouac.

(6) If you are marching at night to maintain secrecy, you should be able to inspect your horse's feet and equipment by feeling, and without the aid of a light.

(7) Select the best possible footing for your horse. A smooth, level surface, even concrete, is to be preferred to rough, sloping shoulders found along many highways.

(8) In removing side loads or equipment at the hourly halts be sure they are placed so that they will not be damaged by horses or be in the way of traffic. Horses moved to the side of the road must be kept clear of wire fences so that bridles or other parts of equipment do not become caught.

(9) In horse-drawn artillery units, the cannoneers usually ride on the vehicles. When walking, they should keep to the right of the column or in the space between vehicles. Under no circumstances should they walk between the front and rear vehicles of limbered vehicles.

d. *Armored and motorized units.*—(1) Since rapid movement is one of the principal advantages of armored and motor units, it is important that every driver and other operating personnel with these units know not only how properly to drive and care for a vehicle but also the fundamentals of successful marching.

(2) Good mechanized and motorized troops can march 180 miles per day on roads at an average speed of 25 miles per hour, or, in an emergency, they can march 450 miles in 24 hours. They can march on roads at night without lights at speeds up to about 15 miles per hour, but marching across country at night is very difficult, except under favorable conditions. In preparing for a march, warning is usually issued ahead of the starting hour so that crews of vehicles can carefully check equipment and vehicles and see to it that everything is ready and in good condition.

(3) If you are the driver of a motor vehicle during the march you must keep on the alert to maintain the ordered speed and the proper distance on the road from the vehicle just ahead in the column. You must also be familiar with arm, hand, and light signals so that these signals may be quickly passed down the column from front to rear. If this is not done it causes vehicles to "jam up" in column, and results in those at the tail having to travel at high speeds at times, in order to keep up and not lose sight of vehicles ahead of them. This often results in accidents, especially when passing through towns, so it can be seen that bad driving on the part of just one driver may spoil the march for an entire unit.

(4) No rule can be given for the distances which should be kept between vehicles in the marching column on the road. This will depend on a number of things, such as the ordered speed of the march, the kind of vehicles in the column, the road conditions and, perhaps most of all, on the possibility of an enemy air attack. To lessen the danger of an air attack, vehicles and organizations must often march at increased distances. When marching at night, speeds are usually reduced and distances lessened so that contact may be maintained in the column.

(5) Halts are usually prescribed in the march order to come at a certain time, and when the time arrives each vehicle either halts in place, or closes up so that the entire unit is closed up when the last vehicle is halted. Whether vehicles halt in place or close up will depend on many factors, but drivers are always told what to do about this before the march starts. Motor vehicles will seldom close up during daylight, because of the danger of an air attack.

(6) Before halting, vehicles always move well off the road so as to keep the road clear. If men dismount, they also move off the road so as not to interfere with other traffic and to avoid accidents. Officers, noncommissioned officers, and drivers proceed with the necessary inspections and servicing. If roads are very narrow, men are usually stationed at the head and tail of each unit to direct civilian traffic and see to it that the road is kept clear.

(7) Halts usually come once every 2 hours and are for 10 minutes' duration, unless a longer halt is made at noon for lunch and servicing. During a march if any vehicle has mechanical trouble, the driver pulls off the road and allows vehicles behind to pass. If the driver or unit mechanic can correct the trouble, he does so and resumes the march. He does not, however, attempt to regain his place in column by picking up high speeds, but falls in at the tail of the nearest unit, and does not pass any vehicles until those ahead have halted, at which time he may go forward to join his unit. If the entire column has passed, he proceeds alone at normal speed into camp.

(8) Every car commander or driver must know the route of the march and where the unit is going to camp for the night and should have a marked road map. Otherwise he

will not know where to go if contact with the vehicle ahead is lost or his vehicle has to stop on account of mechanical trouble.

SECTION II

CAMPS AND BIVOUACS

■ 200. KINDS OF SHELTER.—In the theater of operations, troops are sheltered in billets, bivouac, camp, or cantonment.

a. Troops are in *billets* when they occupy private or public buildings.

b. When troops rest on the ground with no overhead cover, or under shelter tents, or improvised shelter, they are in *bivouac.*

c. When troops are sheltered by heavy tentage (tent camps) they are in *camp;* when quartered in temporary structures, especially constructed for military purposes, they are in *cantonment.*

■ 201. CAMP SITES.—The ideal camp site should have plenty of pure water, tough grass turf, and access to a good road. It should be of ample size and provide concealment from enemy airplanes. It should avoid dusty, polluted, or damp soil, stagnant water, and dry stream beds. In hot weather a shady area free of underbrush is desirable. In war, battle needs may force the use of poor camp sites.

■ 202. PERSONAL CARE AND COMFORT.—a. (1) The shelter tent is a small tent capable of providing shelter for two men. (See fig. 56.)

(2) It may be pitched singly or two tents may be pitched together known as a double shelter tent. (See fig. 57.) Use of double shelter tents conserves space and, being occupied by four men, they are warmer.

(3) (a) The platoon having been formed for shelter tent pitching as described in paragraph 184 (platoon drill), at the command, PITCH TENTS, each man (if armed with the rifle) steps off obliquely with the right foot a full pace to the right front, lays his rifle on the ground, muzzle to the front, barrel to the left, butt near the toe of his right foot. He then steps back into place. All men then unsling equipment and place their packs (or rolls) on the ground in front of them, haversacks (saddle bags or field canvas bags) up and to the front,

FIGURE 56.—Shelter tents.

FIGURE 57.—Double shelter tents.

the packs two paces in front of their positions. They then open their packs and remove their shelter halves, poles, and pins. Each odd-numbered man, when not armed with a bayonet, places a pin in the ground on the spot which he previously marked with his left heel. The men of each pair spread their shelter halves on the ground which the tent is to occupy, triangle to the rear, buttons to the center, the even-numbered man's half on the left.

(b) They then button the halves together. The odd-numbered man adjusts his pole through the eyelets in the front of the tent and holds the pole upright in position beside the bayonet (or pin). The even-numbered man pins down the front corners of the tent in line with the bayonets (or pins). He then drives the front guy pin a rifle length in front of the front pole. If he is not armed with the rifle, he measures this distance with his tent rope by taking the distance from the base of the front tent pole to one of the front tent pins. He places the loop of the guy rope over the front guy pin and runs the other end of the rope through the loops of the shelter halves and ties it, making sure that the pole is vertical when the rope is taut. The even-numbered man then adjusts the rear tent pole through the eyelets in the rear of the tent. The odd-numbered man pins down the rear of the tent and drives the rear guy pin so that it is a bayonet length in rear of the rear pin of the triangle. If he is not armed with the bayonet, he drives the rear guy pin two and a half tent pin lengths from the rear triangle pin. He then adjusts the guy rope. The even-numbered man then drives the remaining pins on the left of the shelter tent and the odd-numbered man drives them on the right.

(c) On maneuvers and in active operations you and your tentmate will normally pitch your tent where you will be concealed from enemy observation. The principles of tent pitching given in (a) and (b) above will apply, but there may be no attempt to aline the tents of your organization.

(4) If possible, pick a dry place on high ground for your tent. As soon as your tent is pitched, ditch it, even though you expect to be there only one night. Dig a ditch about 3 inches deep along each side, with a drainage ditch leading off at the lowest side. If it looks as though water may come

from higher ground, dig a ditch to divert the water before it can reach your tent. In cold or windy weather the dirt should be banked around the tent. If it rains, loosen the guy ropes to prevent the tent pegs from pulling out. Be sure your tent pegs are securely driven in. If the weather is cold, pitch the closed end of the tent into the wind.

(5) Figures 28 and 29 show you in detail how to display your equipment, if it is required.

b. Take time to make a good bed; it will mean better sleeping. First, level the ground. Then place straw, leaves, or branches on the ground. Place your raincoat over this bedding to keep out the damp. In cold weather you need something warm under you as well as over you. A newspaper between blankets and clothing, or straw around the feet, will help. Don't lie down directly on wet ground. Another means for protection against cold is to fold the blanket in such a manner as to form a sleeping bag. Large horse-blanket safety pins or any large safety pins are necessary to keep the folds in position.

c. Take off any wet clothes as soon as you can after reaching camp. Put on dry clothes, or, if that is impossible, dry your clothes before a fire and then put them back on. If you cannot do this wring them out. Dry your shoes by placing warm, not hot, pebbles inside the shoes. Do not place the shoes next to a fire. It is a good idea to oil the shoes while they are dry to make them waterproof and pliable.

d. (1) As soon as possible after reaching camp wash your feet with soap and water. Dry them carefully, especially between the toes. Until your feet are hardened, dust them with foot powder, which you can get from your corporal or the noncommissioned officer in charge of your unit. Put on a clean pair of socks and the extra pair of shoes.

(2) If blisters have appeared on your feet they should be painted with iodine and emptied by pricking them at the lower edge with a pin which has been passed through a flame. Do not remove the skin. The blister should then be covered with zinc oxide plaster which can be obtained at the aid station. If you have serious abrasions on your feet, corns, bunions, or ingrowing nails, have your name put on the sick report and report to the aid station for treatment.

(3) See that your toenails are short and clean. Cut them straight across and not on a curve. This prevents ingrowing nails.

e. Before building a fire, clear away all dry leaves or grass, leaving a bare spot. Dead branches from trees are more apt to burn than wood gathered off the ground. Stones heated red hot and then placed under a bucket in your tent make a good stove. A canteen filled with hot water makes a good hot water bottle for very cold feet.

f. Read instructions for camp sanitation in chapter 14.

■ 203. CAMPS AND BIVOUACS FOR MOUNTED ORGANIZATIONS.—*a.* In campaign your organization will probably be scattered over a large area to take advantage of cover from ground and air. It will often be necessary to tie horses individually to trees or bushes. Soldiers are grouped together by squads or sections, and bivouac close to their mounts to care for them and be able to leave at short notice, or in the dark. Provide good, dry standing ground for your horse, clear of rocks and stubble, and bed him down well. Guard against the possibility of his becoming entangled in the halter rope or picket line.

b. In severe weather protect your horse from cold winds. If woods with heavy undergrowth are not available, protection may be obtained by using the branches of trees. Avoid stream beds in rainy seasons, as a freshet upstream might cause trouble.

c. By taking the precautions mentioned above it will not normally be necessary to use the saddle blanket as a horse cover because the weather is severe. Horses in good condition can withstand severe weather very well. If your horse becomes ill from exhaustion or other causes, even in hot weather, it may be necessary to keep him warm and the saddle blanket is useful for this purpose. You will be well repaid for the care and attention you give your mount.

d. Vehicles should stand on hard ground and be grouped for ease of servicing and to prevent hostile observation by the use of natural cover or camouflage. Space is required for turn-arounds and at least two exits from the bivouac area are desirable.

CHAPTER 12

USE OF COMPASSES AND MAPS

SECTION I

USE OF THE COMPASS

■ 204. As a soldier, you must be thoroughly familiar with the compass and know how to use it by day and by night.

■ 205. Of the several types of compasses issued to the Army, the prismatic compass (see figs. 58 and 59) is the one most generally used. The compass is an instrument which, by means of a magnetized dial-needle, indicates magnetic north. The dial-needle b is graduated into 360 equal subdivisions called degrees, commencing with 0 (zero), or magnetic north, and reading clockwise around the entire circle until 0 (or 360°) is reached again. You will note that with the compass dial-needle at rest the 0 is to the north, the 90° graduation is east, 180° is south, 270° is west. Instead of using the directions north, east, south, and west, we may use the terms magnetic-azimuth 0°; magnetic-azimuth 180°, etc. The magnetic-azimuth of any object is merely the compass reading, expressed in degrees, of a line extending out from the center of the compass toward the object.

■ 206. If a line is drawn from the center of the dial-needle to any object in your view you can find its azimuth by determining which number, or degree of graduation, this line crosses on the compass dial. It is done in this manner: Raise the eyepiece a and the cover d and move the clamp at g releasing the dial b so that it swings freely. Hold the compass as shown in figure 58. Turn about slowly and carefully until the object, the azimuth of which you want, is lined up by the slit on eyepiece a and by the hair-line f on the glass cover. Allow the dial-needle b to come to rest. Then read the azimuth through the eyepiece a.

■ 207. At night you may often depend on your compass almost entirely to keep on a required direction. Assume you are to march at night on a magnetic azimuth of 55°. By daylight, or at night by light in a sheltered place, release the compass box glass by unscrewing the screw at *h*. Move the radiolite marker *c* on the movable index ring to 55, the graduation halfway between the figure 5(50) and 6(60) on the graduated circle around the outside of the compass case.

FIGURE 58.—Prismatic compass, showing compass open and in position for measuring azimuth in daylight.

Then clamp the movable ring with the screw at *h*. Now hold the compass horizontally and carefully turn about until the dial-needle points to the radiolite marker *c* on the movable index ring. The magnetic-azimuth course of 55° is now indicated by the radiolite markers *j*. On a dark night it may be necessary for another soldier to move forward to the limit of visibility while from the rear you use the compass to direct his movement to the right or left in the proper direction. While still in sight of you your comrade halts, waits for you to come abreast, and then repeats as necessary.

■ 208. The compass may be used in a number of ways, all of which can be practiced by you until you are thoroughly proficient in its use.

SECTION II

USE OF MAPS

■ 209. The ability to read a map quickly and accurately is of great importance to you as a soldier. With this ability, and a map in your possession, you will always be able to locate yourself in unfamiliar country. You will be able to accomplish your mission without wasting valuable time in searching for

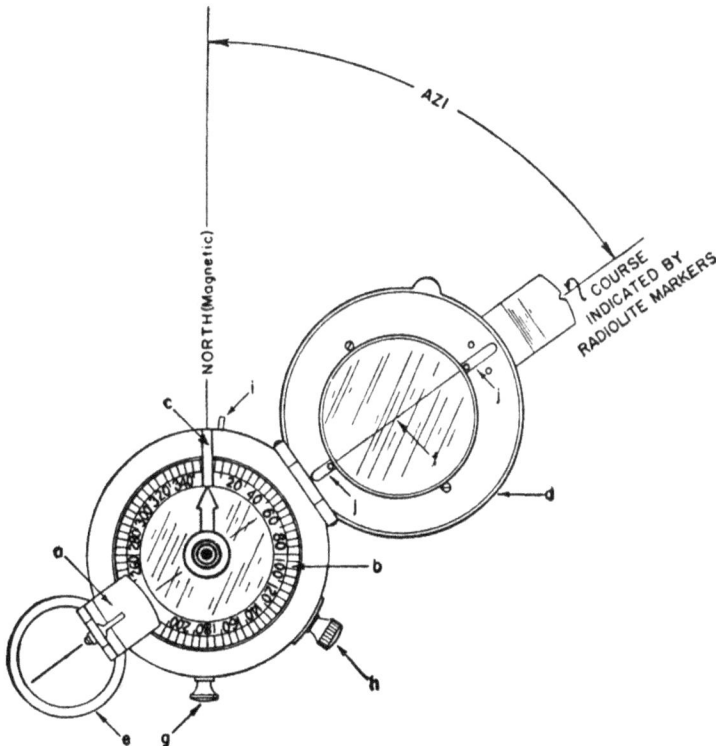

FIGURE 59.—Prismatic compass showing compass open for measurement of azimuth at night by means of radiolite marker.

your destination, and you will be able to return to your commander in time for the information you have obtained to be of value to him.

■ 210. Map reading is not difficult. It is nothing more than the ability to get a clear idea of what the ground looks like from seeing a map of that ground. You will probably receive further instruction from your officers in map reading, but if you have a good grasp of the following simple facts you can feel confident that you know how to understand and use military maps.

■ 211. *a.* A map represents a part of the earth's surface shown on paper. Maps are drawn to scale. This means that a certain distance on a map always represents on that map a certain distance on the ground. For example, suppose the scale of a map is 1 inch equals 1 mile. This means that if, with a ruler, you find that on the map, the distance between two towns, *A* and *B,* is 1 inch, you would actually travel 1 mile if you walked in a straight line from *A* to *B* on the ground. If the distance between towns *C* and *D* on this map is 2 inches then we immediately know that actually these two towns are twice as far apart on the ground as *A* and *B.*

b. Scales are usually shown on a map in one of three ways, as follows:

(1) They may be shown by a single or double line, divided into parts. Each part is marked with the distance which it represents on the ground and may be expressed in feet, yards, or miles. This is the way the scale is shown on automobile road maps, with which you are familiar (fig. 60*A*).

(2) The scale may be stated in words or figures, as 3 inches=1 mile. As explained above, this means that 3 inches on the map equal 1 mile on the ground (fig. 60*B*).

(3) The scale may be expressed as a "representative fraction" (called *RF*), which is merely a fraction in which the numerator (above the line) is a certain distance on the map, and the denominator (below the line) is the corresponding distance on the ground. Suppose the scale of our map is 1 inch equals 1 mile. We could write the fraction $\frac{1 \text{ inch}}{1 \text{ mile}}$. For convenience, however, we always write *RF* with both the numerator and denominator in the same unit. Since we know there are 63,360 inches in a mile, we can write *RF* $\frac{1 \text{ inch}}{63,360 \text{ inches}}$ and, by omitting the word "inches", we have $\frac{1}{63,360}$. So when we see a map with the *RF* $\frac{1}{63,360}$, or written as a ratio 1:63,360, we know that 1 inch on the map equals 1 mile on the ground (fig. 60*C*). In the same way, if we have a map with

the $RF \dfrac{1}{10,560}$, we can change the fraction to $\dfrac{6}{63,360}$ and we see at once that the $RF \dfrac{1}{10,560}$ is the same thing as though it were written 6 inches equal 1 mile.

0   5   10   20   30 miles

A GRAPHIC SCALE

3 INCHES = I MILE

B WORDS & FIGURES

$\dfrac{1}{63,360}$ OR I:63,360

C REPRESENTATIVE FRACTION (R.F.)

FIGURE 60.—Scales.

■ 212. On practically all military maps which you will handle, the north is at the top of the map. On many maps the north is also shown by an arrow, which points in that direction. Sometimes two arrows are used. The arrow with a full barb, or a star at the end, points toward the north pole or true north. The arrow with a half barb points toward what is known as the magnetic pole which attracts the compass needle.

■ 213. *a.* Your map is said to be "oriented" when the north and south arrow on the map points north on the ground.

This makes all lines on the map parallel to corresponding lines on the ground. Your map should always be oriented whenever you use it. It is just as awkward to attempt to use an unoriented map as to read a book with the pages turned upside down or sideways.

b. There are two simple and easy ways of orienting your map:

(1) Suppose there are two points on the ground that you can also locate on the map. Draw a line on the map between these two points which we will call X and Y. Stand at point X. Sight along the line X–Y on the map and turn the map until the line of sight points exactly at Y on the ground. Your map is then oriented.

(2) You may also orient your map by compass. Turn the lid back and down and place the hair-line along the magnetic north-and-south line of the map, the lid lying to the north. Turn both the map and compass, keeping the hair-line over the magnetic north-and-south line on the map, until the compass needle points in exactly the same direction as both lines. Your map is then oriented (fig. 61).

■ 214. You are said to be oriented when you known your own position on an oriented map and the directions on the ground. Suppose you have been proceeding on a mission over unfamiliar ground and you are not now sure of your location on the map. Orient your map. Select a feature of the terrain, such as a hill, and from that feature draw a line on the map toward yourself. Now do the same with reference to another terrain feature. The point where these lines cross or intersect will be your location on the map.

■ 215. a. One of the most important features of map reading will be your ability to determine quickly and accurately the positions of various features on the map. A simple and easily understood method is used in our Army which will help you to do this. It is known as the system of rectangular coordinates or the "grid system." A series of parallel east-and-west and north-and-south lines are placed on the map and divided into a number of squares. This series of lines is called a "grid." The interval between these lines is usually 1,000 yards, that is, each square is 1,000 yards on a side. (See fig. 62.)

b. Beginning at the lower left-hand, or southwest corner,

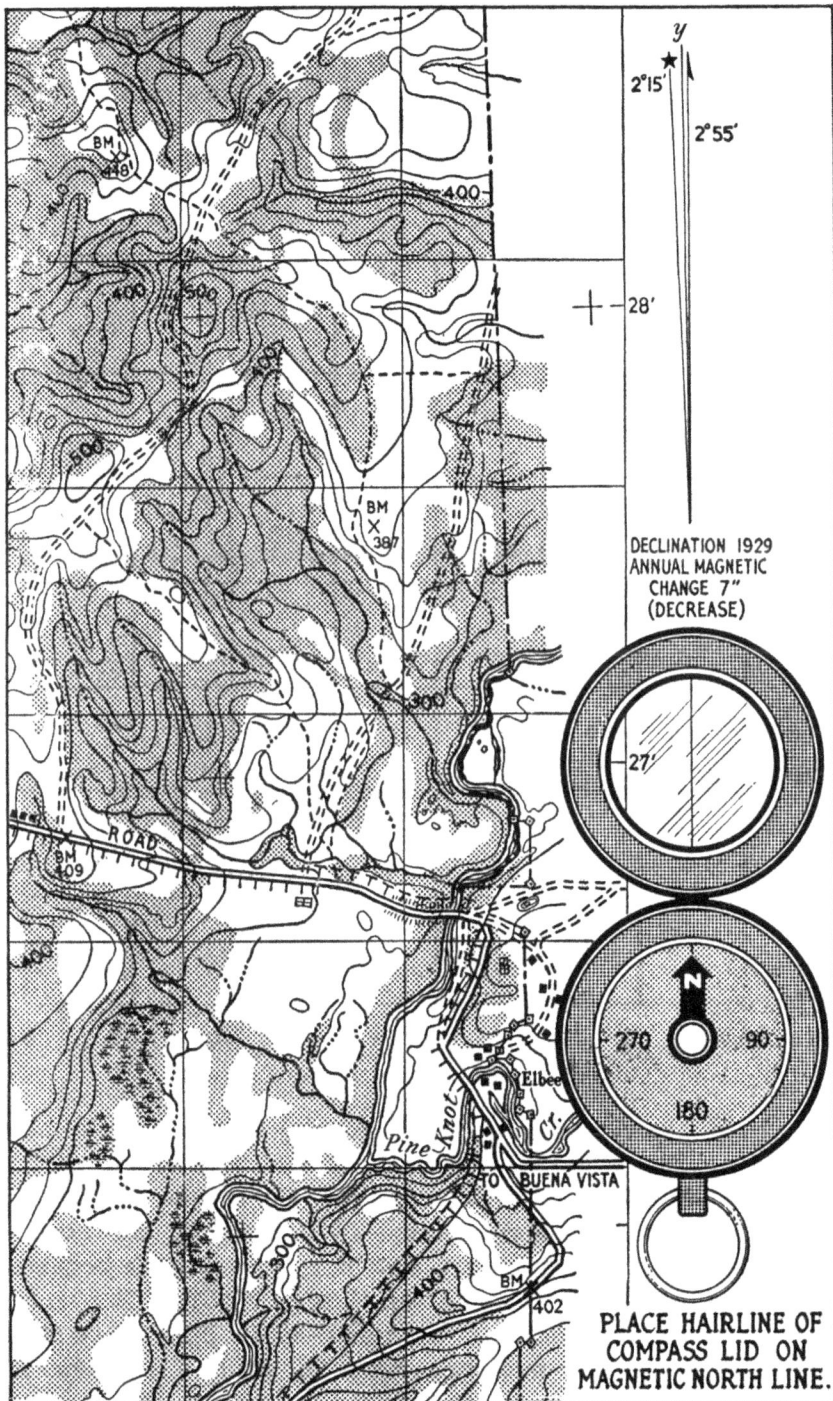

FIGURE 61.—Orientation by compass.

the lines of the grid are numbered. The lines running north
and south are numbered in order from left to right, that is,
from west to east. In the same way, the lines running east
and west are numbered from bottom to top, that is, from
south to north. These numbers are placed on the margins
of the map.

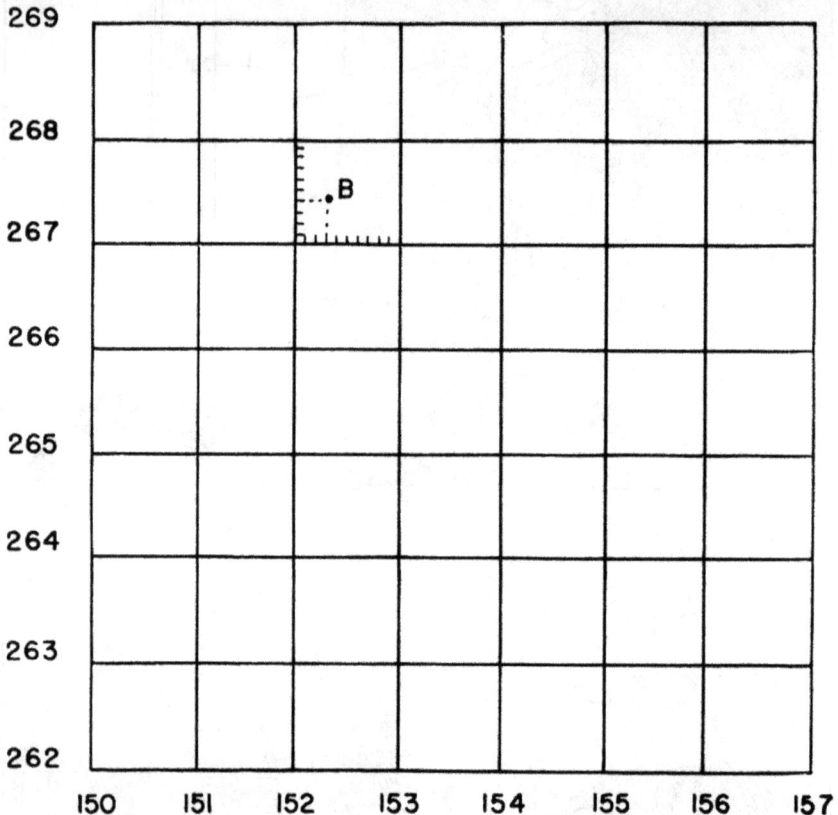

FIGURE 62.—Rectangular coordinates.

c. Now it is very easy to designate any square on the map
by giving the numbers of the lines which intersect at its
lower left-hand corner. For example, the square containing
the point *B* would be designated by giving first the north-
south line and next the east-west line, with a dash between
them and inclosed in parentheses, thus (152–267). But since,
on this particular map, all the north-south lines start with
15, and all the east-west lines with 26, we can omit the 15
and the 26 and designate the square containing the letter *B*

as (2–7). This expression (2–7) is called the rectangular coordinate of the square containing the letter *B*. The principal thing for you to remember is that you read first the number of squares to the right of the southwest corner of the map and next the number of squares up. A simple rule is: *Read right up.*

d. But suppose we wish to designate the point *B* more closely than by just giving the coordinates of the square in which it lies. Divide the sides of the square into ten equal parts as shown by the dots in figure 62. Now we see that *B* is three subdivisions east of the line 152 and four subdivisions north of the line 267. Therefore, the coordinates of *B* are (152.3–267.4) or (2.3–7.4). Become familiar with the system of reading and designating map features by means of coordinates as rapidly as possible.

■ 216. *a*. You will probably remember the maps contained in your school geographies, as well as the common automobile road maps. On these maps certain signs, such as dots, are used to represent cities; other signs, such as wavy lines, represent rivers and the boundaries of states or counties. Signs of this kind which are used to represent cities, rivers, boundaries, mountain ranges, and similar features are known as "conventional signs." Military maps are usually of larger scale and contain many more details than those commonly met with in civil life. Therefore, to represent all the information set forth on them, it is necessary to use many more conventional signs than you knew in your school geography. Some of the most common conventional signs you will find on military maps represent roads, bridges, houses, fences, crops, and form lines.

b. These form lines are called "contours" and represent the variations of the earth's surface caused by hills, ridges, valleys, and the like. The exact shape and condition of the ground has a great influence on all military operations. The map, therefore, must give the person who uses it a clear picture of the shape of the ground. Since the map is flat, special conventional signs are necessary to show these different shapes. A contour line represents an imaginary line on the ground, every part of which is at the same height above sea level. If you walk along a contour line you neither go uphill nor downhill but always stay on a level.

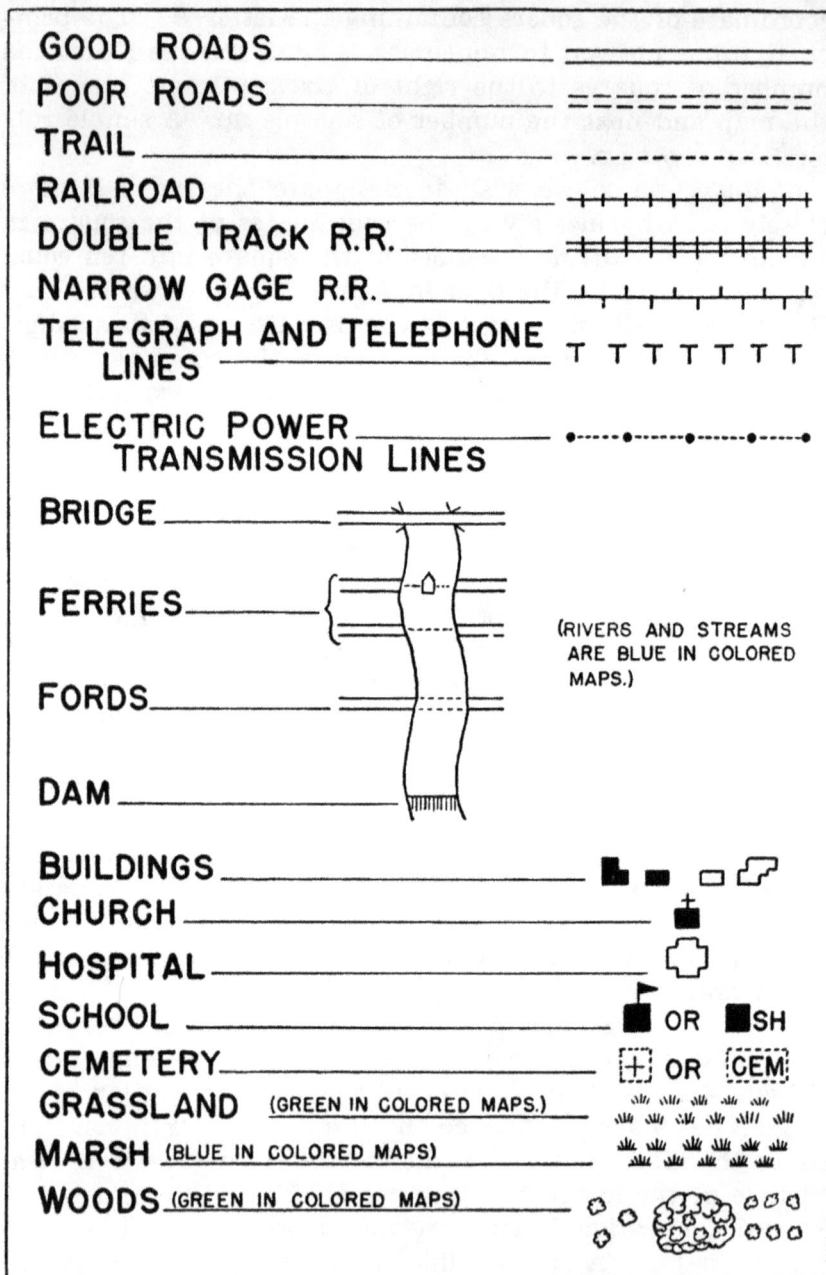

FIGURE 63.—Conventional signs.

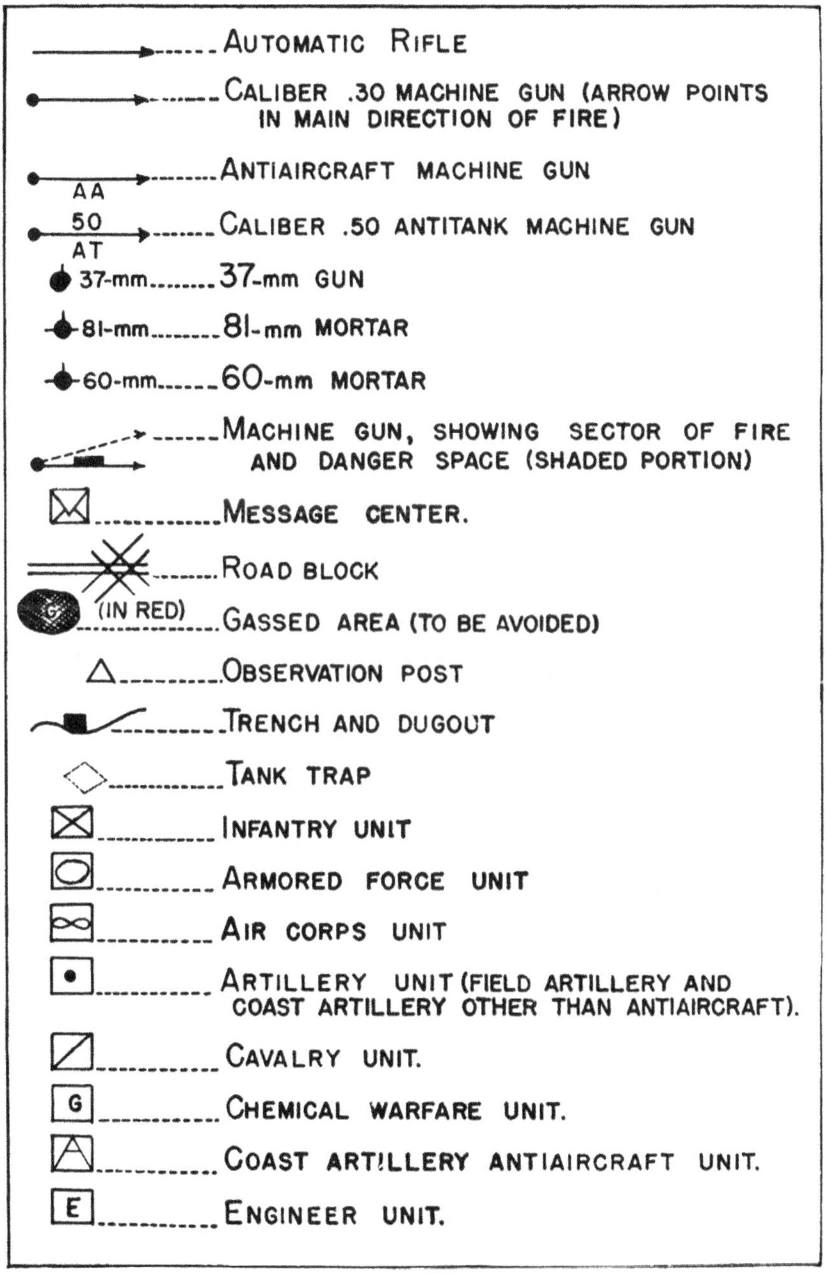
AUTOMATIC RIFLE
CALIBER .30 MACHINE GUN (ARROW POINTS IN MAIN DIRECTION OF FIRE)
AA
ANTIAIRCRAFT MACHINE GUN
50
AT
CALIBER .50 ANTITANK MACHINE GUN
37-mm
37-mm GUN
81-mm
81-mm MORTAR
60-mm
60-mm MORTAR
MACHINE GUN, SHOWING SECTOR OF FIRE AND DANGER SPACE (SHADED PORTION)
MESSAGE CENTER.
ROAD BLOCK
G
(IN RED)
GASSED AREA (TO BE AVOIDED)
OBSERVATION POST
TRENCH AND DUGOUT
TANK TRAP
INFANTRY UNIT
ARMORED FORCE UNIT
AIR CORPS UNIT
ARTILLERY UNIT (FIELD ARTILLERY AND COAST ARTILLERY OTHER THAN ANTIAIRCRAFT).
CAVALRY UNIT.
G
CHEMICAL WARFARE UNIT.
A
COAST ARTILLERY ANTIAIRCRAFT UNIT.
E
ENGINEER UNIT.

FIGURE 64.—Military symbols.

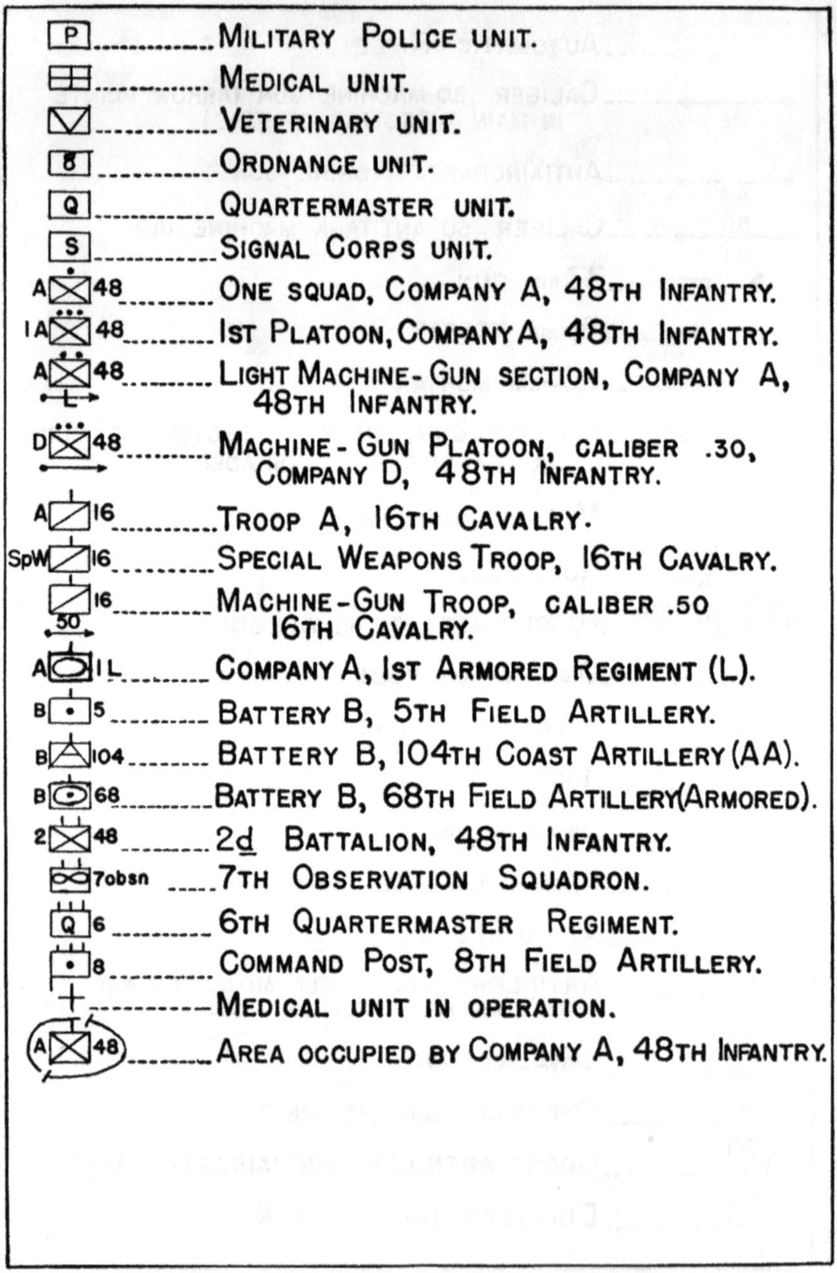

P .... MILITARY POLICE UNIT.

.... MEDICAL UNIT.

.... VETERINARY UNIT.

8 .... ORDNANCE UNIT.

Q .... QUARTERMASTER UNIT.

S .... SIGNAL CORPS UNIT.

A 48 .... ONE SQUAD, COMPANY A, 48TH INFANTRY.

1A 48 .... 1ST PLATOON, COMPANY A, 48TH INFANTRY.

A 48 .... LIGHT MACHINE-GUN SECTION, COMPANY A, 48TH INFANTRY.

D 48 .... MACHINE-GUN PLATOON, CALIBER .30, COMPANY D, 48TH INFANTRY.

A 16 .... TROOP A, 16TH CAVALRY.

SpW 16 .... SPECIAL WEAPONS TROOP, 16TH CAVALRY.

16 .... MACHINE-GUN TROOP, CALIBER .50 16TH CAVALRY.

A 1L .... COMPANY A, 1ST ARMORED REGIMENT (L).

B 5 .... BATTERY B, 5TH FIELD ARTILLERY.

B 104 .... BATTERY B, 104TH COAST ARTILLERY (AA).

B 68 .... BATTERY B, 68TH FIELD ARTILLERY (ARMORED).

2 48 .... 2d BATTALION, 48TH INFANTRY.

7obsn .... 7TH OBSERVATION SQUADRON.

Q 6 .... 6TH QUARTERMASTER REGIMENT.

8 .... COMMAND POST, 8TH FIELD ARTILLERY.

.... MEDICAL UNIT IN OPERATION.

A 48 .... AREA OCCUPIED BY COMPANY A, 48TH INFANTRY.

FIGURE 64.—Military symbols—Continued.

c. You should be able to identify at any time the conventional signs shown in figure 63.

■ 217. It often becomes necessary to put on a map either the location of various bodies of troops, such as companies, battalions, or regiments; or command posts, observation posts, trenches, machine guns, boundaries, or other important data. To do this a special list of conventional signs has been prepared called military symbols. When put on a map, blue is used to designate our own forces and red the enemy. A few of the commonest are shown in figure 64.

CHAPTER 13

SECURITY AND PROTECTION

SECTION I

GENERAL

■ 218. Most of the people you know in civil life probably make an effort at some time or other to save money. They may do this in various ways, such as putting it in the bank, investing in stocks or real estate, or buying different kinds of insurance. With money in the bank and insurance against accident, fire, or death they are relieved of worry as to what will happen to them or their families in case they should lose their jobs or suffer other misfortune. Their savings, investments, or insurance are their protection against the uncertainties of the future.

■ 219. You are also familiar with the police and fire departments in your city or town. They are provided to protect you and your fellow citizens from the dangers of fire or the acts of dishonest persons. In many homes or farms that are beyond the city limits, watch dogs serve the same purpose.

■ 220. All of these things give you, your family, and friends a feeling of safety. They relieve you of anxiety or worry and make you feel secure in the knowledge that misfortune cannot take you by surprise, for you are prepared to meet it.

■ 221. Security in the Army is exactly the same thing except that instead of protection against fire, theft, or loss of a job, we protect ourselves against the actions of the enemy. Each individual soldier and each organization take measures to prevent the enemy from taking them by surprise. No matter how thorough these measures seem to be, however, no individual or organization can ever afford to dismiss completely the possibility of unforeseen action by the enemy. On the other hand, if the security measures have been as carefully planned as possible, we are relieved of a great deal of anxiety and worry. We feel confident that we will be warned in sufficient time to take the necessary action before the enemy can seriously annoy us or interfere with our movements. Thus we are able to give the greater part of our efforts to the main job. When we can do this we are providing for our "freedom of action."

Section II

SECURITY OF INDIVIDUALS

■ 222. *a.* The first thing for you to remember is that in a campaign security is *always* necessary. This is true whether you are resting, marching, or actually fighting. You must always be on the alert for the movements or actions of the enemy, for the sooner you see them and give a warning the better chance you and your commander will have to protect yourselves and retain your freedom of action.

b. During combat you may be required to serve as a scout, observer, sentinel, listener, sniper, messenger, or a member of a patrol. You may have to move about on the battlefield and work your way close to the enemy both by daylight and by darkness. In order to follow directions and report what you see, you must be able to recognize and use the military terms for different features of the terrain, such as valley, gentle slope, ravine, cut, and others. The terms which you will use most often are shown in figure 65.

c. Before you can be expected to help provide security for your organization, however, you must first know how to provide for your own security and protection. There are two ways in which you do this: the first is by learning how to move and remain concealed, or protected, from enemy observation and fire by making use of the ground; the second way is by the proper use of your weapons and equipment.

■ 223. CONDUCT OF INDIVIDUALS.—*a.* In whatever arm or service you may be you must have a knowledge of the proper use of cover and concealment. You can never know when you may find yourself in a situation where you will have to apply this knowledge in order to save your life. In the military sense, to be "concealed" means to be hidden from view, but not necessarily protected from enemy fire. Concealment affords protection only when the enemy does not know that

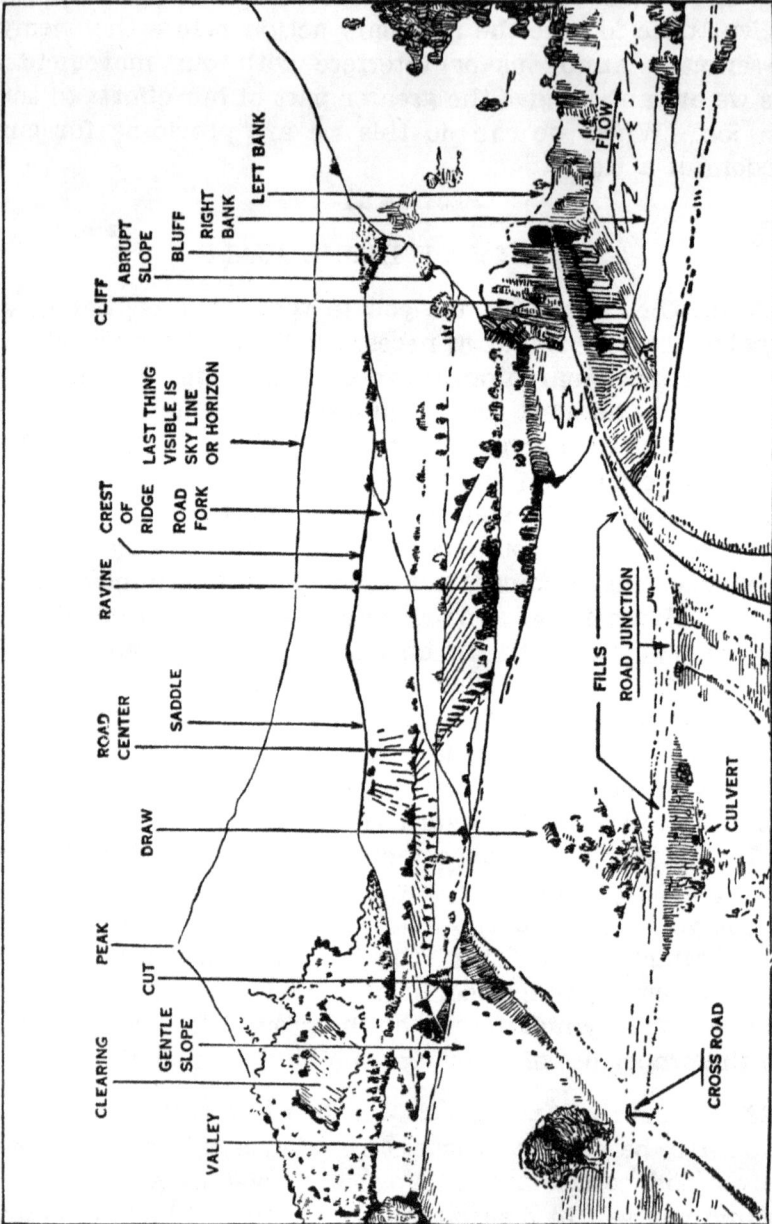

FIGURE 65.—Military features of terrain.

the terrain feature is occupied. "Cover," on the other hand, means that you are both concealed and protected against enemy fire.

b. Concealment may be provided by bush or tall grass; cover may be a trench, fox hole, a building, an air-raid shelter, an armored vehicle, or the side of a hill away from the enemy.

c. You are provided with an olive-drab uniform because that color blends in with the colors of nature and is difficult to see even at a short distance. If there is not sufficient natural concealment at hand, you can still further increase the concealment which your uniform affords you by using leaves, grass, nets, sacking, or other material which may be at hand. No piece of your equipment should glisten in the sun. When the ground is covered with snow concealment may be provided by wearing a cape or jacket of white sheeting.

d. In observing, take the position which will most reduce your exposure to enemy view. Whenever possible this should be the prone position. Keep off the skyline and avoid taking cover behind single trees and bushes which stand out against the skyline or are in sharp contrast to the surrounding terrain. When observing from woods or a building, keep back in the shadows (figs. 66 and 67). You should look and fire around the right side of trees or other concealment.

e. When in the open, lie motionless with your body stretched out flat against the ground. To observe, lift your head slowly and steadily. Hostile eyes may see abrupt and quick movements.

f. If you must move to a new position for better observation, select your route carefully before you start. If your route carries you over open ground, spring up, run at top speed with body bent low to your next cover, and remain motionless (fig. 68).

g. If a wall or hedge is available, move behind it, keeping well out of sight. If you have a slight rise of ground between you and the enemy, crawl with all parts of your body close to the ground.

h. Before starting toward a new position, pick out those places around you where the enemy may be located and then move as though you were being watched from these places.

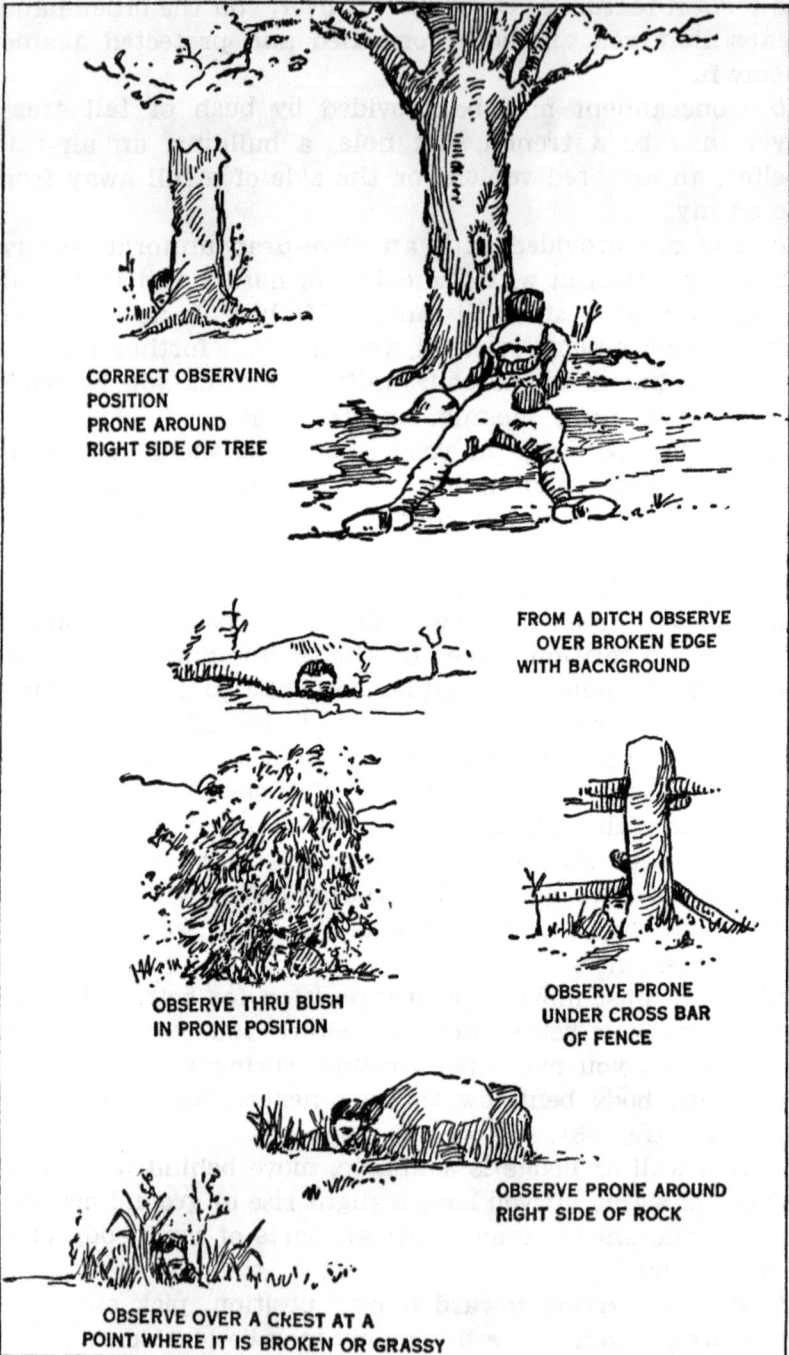

CORRECT OBSERVING POSITION PRONE AROUND RIGHT SIDE OF TREE

FROM A DITCH OBSERVE OVER BROKEN EDGE WITH BACKGROUND

OBSERVE THRU BUSH IN PRONE POSITION

OBSERVE PRONE UNDER CROSS BAR OF FENCE

OBSERVE PRONE AROUND RIGHT SIDE OF ROCK

OBSERVE OVER A CREST AT A POINT WHERE IT IS BROKEN OR GRASSY

FIGURE 66.—Correct use of cover.

Observe the new position closely to see that an enemy is not concealed there. In searching an area look first at the ground nearest you. Look carefully at every place that may afford an enemy concealment. Search a narrow strip close to you from right to left parallel to your front. Then search a sec-

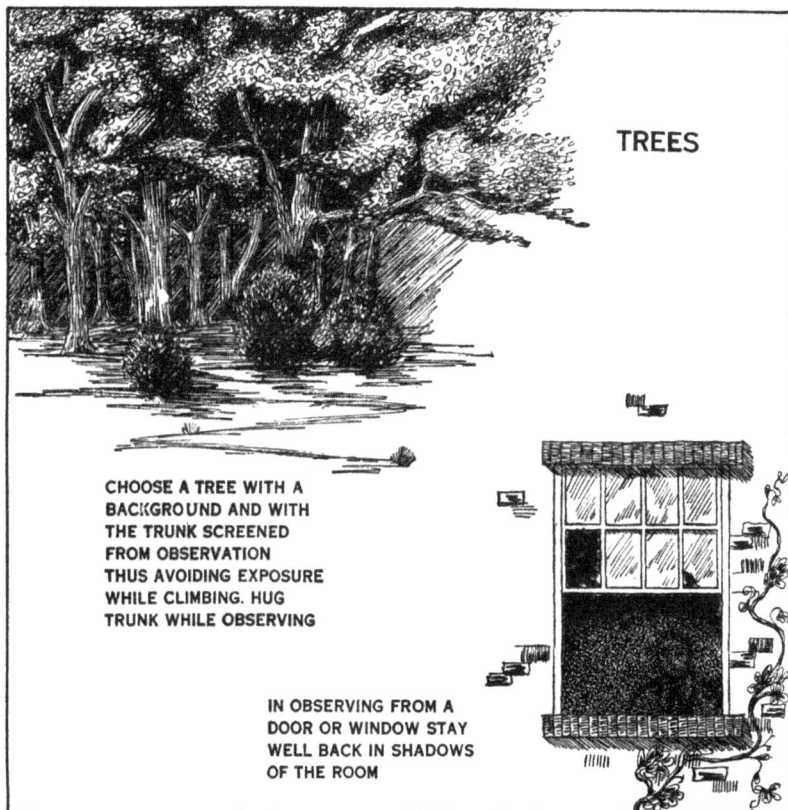

FIGURE 67.—Observing positions, showing correct occupation.

ond strip a little farther away but overlapping the first. Keep this up until the entire area is carefully covered (fig. 69).

i. Know where you are at all times and do not become lost or confused as to the direction of your own troops. Remember all that you see, and report exactly what you have seen when you rejoin your organization.

j. If your duties require you to move close to the enemy lines at night make sure that no piece of your equipment will glisten in the light of a flare, or make a jingle or other telltale noise when you move.   Cover the luminous dial of your watch.

k. In movement at night it is just as important as in the

FROM A PLACE OF CONCEALMENT
THE SCOUT OBSERVES POSITION
FOR SIGNS OF HOSTILE OCCUPATION

THEN HE APPROACHES IT BY
A COVERED ROUTE

FIGURE 68.—Method of approaching an observing position.

daytime to keep off the skyline and make use of shadows. If you are able to creep, crawl, and cross wire silently you will make good progress at night, as you will be unseen. You must learn to distinguish different types of noises such as men digging with shovels, cutting wire, and walking. Also the sounds made by helmets and equipment when struck by wire and brush. Stop often and listen.

l. If you hear the sound of a flare, drop to the ground and remain motionless before the flare bursts. If you look at a

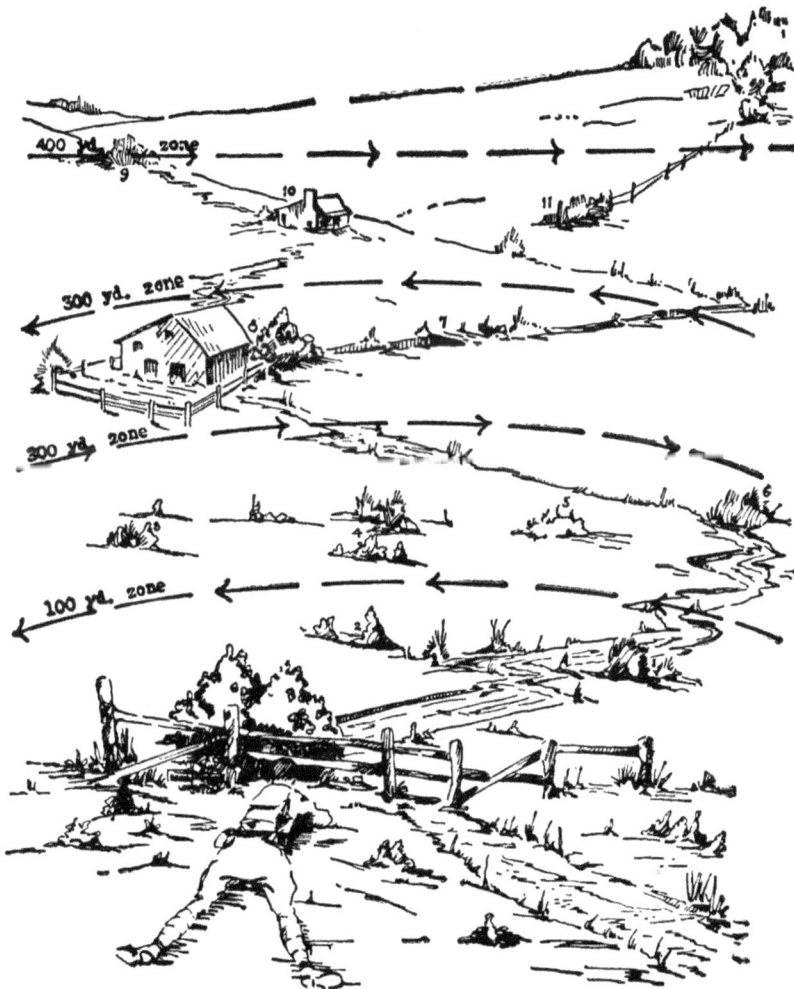

FIGURE 69.—Method of searching ground.

bursting flare you will be blinded momentarily. If possible, inspect by day the area you will move over at night. Select your route out and back, and carefully note all features of the terrain that will assist in guiding you at night. Take advantage of any sound, such as firing or wind, to cover the noise of your movement and move boldly. Consider all people or sounds beyond your own lines as hostile.

m. During combat if you should be wounded and able to walk, report to your commander, turn over your ammunition, and leave the battlefield alone. *Unless you have been detailed for that purpose, do not carry wounded men to the rear without a written order from an officer.* That duty will be performed by medical or specially detailed personnel.

n. If you become separated from your own unit, report to the commander of the nearest organization and fight with it until the action is over. Then ask for a written statement that you were present with the organization and present it to your unit commander when you rejoin.

o. If you should be made a prisoner remember that by the international rules of warfare you are required to give *only* your name, grade, and serial number. Answer no other questions and do not allow yourself to be frightened by threats into giving any information. Any facts about our troops or equipment may be of great interest to the enemy and result in defeat to the Army and death to your comrades. Do not give false answers to questions, as they are dangerous; merely refuse to answer.

p. Do not take into combat letters, diaries, or other written papers. If maps or documents have been given to you, destoy them if it appears that you cannot escape capture.

q. Remember that acts of violence against peaceful civilians and the damaging or looting of property are forbidden. They are punishable by trial before military court. Prisoners and enemy wounded are not to be mistreated nor is their property to be taken from them. If civilians adopt hostile acts against you, force may be used to resist them.

■ 224. SENTINELS.—*a.* A sentinel may be posted by a unit to insure its safety or readiness for action, or he may be a part of a security detachment sent out to protect a larger body. If you should be posted as a sentinel, you must be on the job every minute you are on post. You should have the following information, obtained from the person who posted you:

(1) Direction and probable route of approach of the enemy.

(2) Sector you are required to watch.

(3) Names of terrain features of military importance within sight (villages, roads, streams).

(4) Location of the nearest security detachments on the flanks and the means of communicating with them; number and location of your own outguard or security detachment, its support, and the routes to them.

(5) Whether patrols or other friendly troops are operating to your front. If so, any signs or signals of recognition or other means by which you can identify them, especially at night.

(6) Other special signals.

(7) Instructions concerning challenging.

(8) What you will do in case of attack.

b. If practicable, you will be provided with field glasses and a means of signaling. You should place yourself where you can see your assigned sector at all times and not be seen by the enemy. If possible, in the daytime you should also be able to see the sentinels on your flanks. A position in a tree may be just what you want. If you see signs of the enemy, notify your commander at once. In the daytime you should let pass only officers, noncommissioned officers, and detachments that you recognize. Stop all you do not recognize and call your commander, who will make the necessary examination of their passes. At night when persons approach your post halt them and call your commander. When halting anyone keep him covered. If a person fails to stop at your third command to halt, or attempts to escape or attack you, shoot him. If the enemy attacks or there is other great danger, give the alarm by firing rapidly. You do not need to challenge if you are certain you have recognized the enemy. If deserters or a small hostile party displaying a white flag approach, make them lay down their arms; call your commander. Pass on to the sentinel who relieves you all information and instructions relating to your post. (Fig. 70.)

■ 225. MESSENGERS.—At any time during active operations you may be called upon to deliver a message. It is your duty to deliver it in the shortest time possible. If you should delay, it may mean the defeat or capture of your unit. Before starting out repeat back the message, if it is an oral one, to the person who gave it to you in order to fix it firmly in your mind. Ask questions about any points that are not clear and be sure that you thoroughly understand what is expected of you. Next, locate yourself on the ground and map, if you have one, and

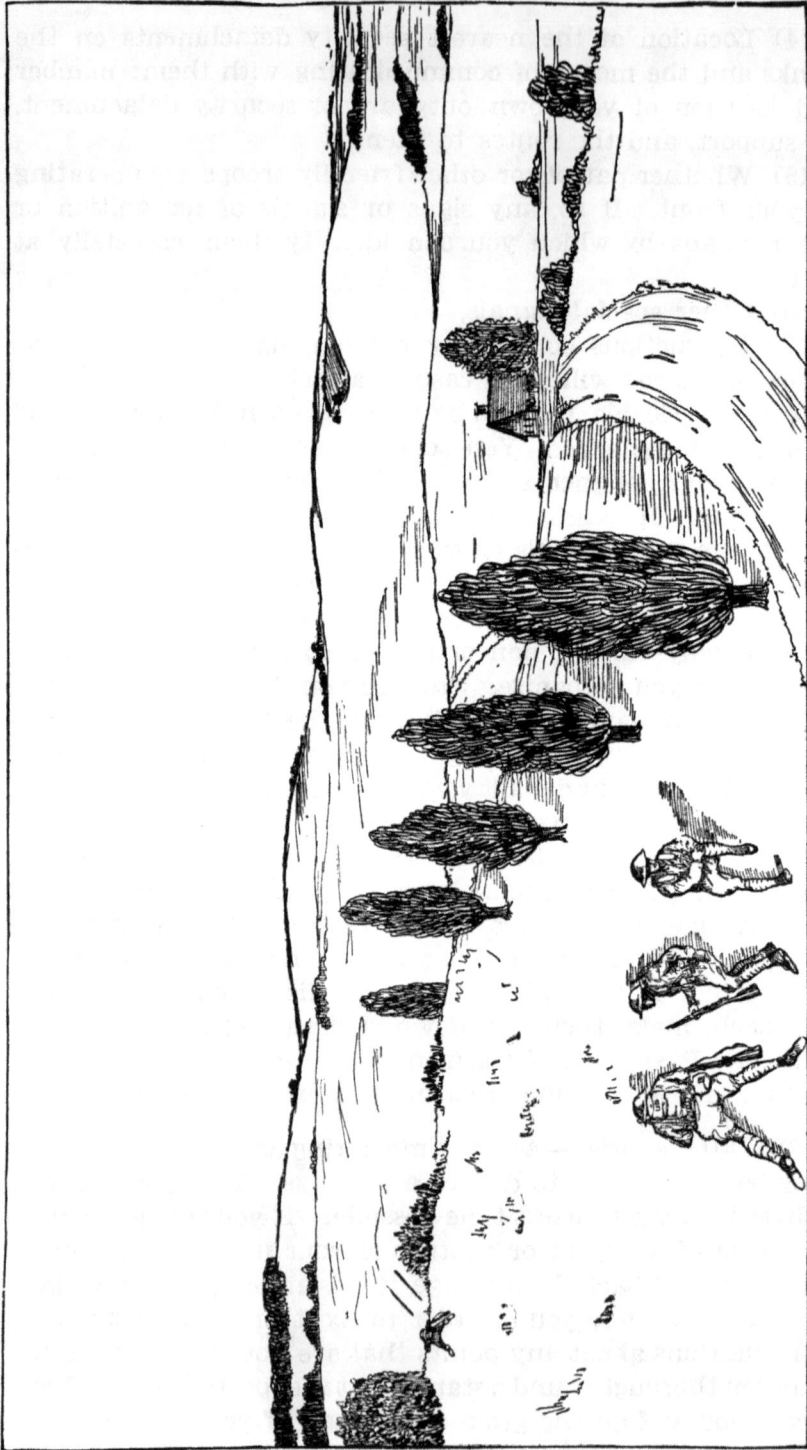

FIGURE 70.—Sentinel on duty.

select land marks to help you find your way. In order to accomplish your mission it will generally be necessary for you to take full advantage of the concealment afforded by the ground, as has been explained in paragraph 223. Be especially careful not to make careless movements which would enable the enemy to locate the station sending the message or the one receiving it. By using different routes in entering and leaving message centers and command posts you will avoid marking out paths which can easily be seen from the air. If necessary, ask any troops you pass the whereabouts of the person or headquarters for whom your message is intended. If you should be delayed or lost, show or explain your message to an officer and ask his advice. Any information of importance you may have obtained along your route should be reported to the person to whom you are delivering the message. Be sure than you explain to him what you have seen and heard yourself and what has been told you by someone else. After delivering your message and before returning, ask if there are any messages or orders to be taken back. Upon your return to the place from which you started report that you have accomplished your mission.

■ 226. CONNECTING FILE.—Connection between the different parts of a marching column or between the detachments of a unit is maintained by connecting files. In a marching column a connecting file usually consists of two men. One keeps in touch with the element in front, the other with the rear. They halt only when the element in front halts or upon signals from the rear. They repeat signals from front to rear. The distance between connecting files is usually about 100 yards by day. At night, or when there is poor visibility, the distance is decreased to the limit of visibility. If you are a connecting file the principal thing to remember is to regulate your movement so that you can always see the other connecting file as well as the groups ahead or in rear of you. You should see that the element following takes the correct road. This will require especial care in turning off a road in forests, towns, or villages, and in darkness or fog.

■ 227. ANTIAIRCRAFT SECURITY AND PROTECTION.—*a.* As long as the enemy has any combat aircraft which will fly, our troops may expect to be attacked from the air. To provide security against such attacks each ground unit establishes antiaircraft lookouts to watch for enemy airplanes and warn the troops. These lookouts are provided on the march, in shelter, and in combat. They may remain at one post, march abreast of the marching unit, or move from one post to another by motor vehicles. If you are detailed on this duty you should observe in every direction, and especially that from which attacks are to be expected. The direction of the sun, or of hills, woods, or other cover which might screen low-flying attacks until they are close to your unit is particularly dangerous. Antiaircraft lookouts usually work in pairs and relieve each other at intervals of not more than 15 minutes. They are equipped with field glasses and sun glasses and instructed as to the alarm signal to be used. They are trained to recognize hostile as well as friendly airplanes. The alarm is given as soon as low-flying airplanes are seen which are not positively identified as friendly. Observers stationed at our antiaircraft weapons and at command and observation posts will be on the watch for signals from the antiaircraft lookouts.

b. In case of daylight air attack, *never attempt to escape by running.* The airplane probably has not seen you before but is sure to see you when you run. Your best protection is to lie flat on the ground. At ditch, shellhole, depression, or shadows along the road will give you good protection. When attacked from low altitudes, unless you have received definite orders not to fire, every soldier should fire on the enemy airplanes with rifle, automatic rifle, and machine guns. This will cause the enemy airplanes to keep above the range of small arms fire.

c. Dense woods provide complete concealment from aircraft and it is doubtful that you will be seen even in sparse woods provided you do not move around. If you are to be in the open for some time you can conceal yourself by pulling branches or bushes over you, which will blend with the landscape, and by *lying still.*

d. At night enemy airplanes may drop flares to light up the ground. When a flare is first dropped, it glows for about a second and then burns brightly. When you see that a flare has been dropped, stop where you are and remain motionless until it has burned out.

■ **228. ANTITANK SECURITY AND PROTECTION.**—*a.* To give warning of the approach of enemy tanks or armored vehicles, antitank lookouts are provided. Sometimes the same lookouts will watch for enemy aircraft as well as tanks and armored vehicles. Prearranged sound and visual signals are used to warn our troops. The approach of tanks may be suspected by the noise of their motors and tracks or by unusual columns of dust. When your unit is at a distance from where the enemy is known to be, the probable approach of tanks or armored vehicles will be over roads. When you are close to the enemy, however, the entire area to your front, flanks, and rear must be watched.

b. For the same reason that you should not run from an airplane attack do not run from an attack by enemy tanks or armored vehicles. You can't run fast enough to get away from them and they are sure to see you and have a much better shot at you than if you remained still. If you are with your unit, upon seeing or hearing the antitank warning signal, await orders from your commander.

c. If you are alone, your best protection from vehicles of this kind is to take advantage of natural obstacles that they cannot cross. These are deep streams, canals, or other bodies of water, marshes or boggy ground, deep ditches or ravines, thick, heavy woods, stump land, and ground littered with good-sized boulders.

d. You will also be safe from these vehicles in a trench or "fox hole" if you get down below the surface of the ground and allow the tank to pass over you. If you get a chance to shoot at the tank, aim at the vision slots or other openings but withhold your fire until the vehicle is at close range. If the belly of the tank is exposed you have a good chance of shooting through it with your .30 caliber armor piercing ammunition. Hand grenades have been used to good effect against armored vehicles, as well as bottles of gasoline which will break on the vehicle and set it afire. Above all, remember that armored vehicles can be stopped and destroyed, so don't be panicky when they approach your position.

■ 229. PROTECTION AGAINST GAS.—*a.* Gas is another weapon which the enemy may use on the battlefield to gain surprise. Your security against being surprised is to learn to know when gas attacks are being made and how to use your gas mask. If you can do this, act promptly and keep cool, you have nothing to fear from a gas attack.

b. The enemy may use gas in one of the following ways:

(1) From candles and cylinders. You can tell these by the hissing sound of the escaping gas and during daylight by the cloud of gas itself.

(2) From gas projectors and artillery and mortar shells. Projector attacks make a big explosion, a brilliant flash, and a large cloud of smoke and dust. Artillery and mortar shells filled with gas sound almost like duds when they explode. Usually a thin haze or mist surrounds the burst for a few moments.

(3) From airplanes and tanks. The airplane bomb filled with gas also sounds like a dud when it explodes. If the gas is sprayed from the airplane or tank it can usually be seen.

(4) From bulk containers and chemical land mines, placed in position and exploded by electricity or by contact fuze.

c. You should remember the following rules as your security against gas:

(1) Carry nothing in your gas mask carrier but your mask.

(2) Prevent damage to your gas mask by handling it carefully.

(3) Keep your gas mask. You may need it at any time, and it may save your life.

(4) Give a gas alarm only when gas is present.

(5) Hold your breath after the gas alarm is given until you are sure that your mask is well adjusted to your face and that you have cleared the facepiece of gas by blowing vigorously into it while holding the outlet valve.

(6) Keep your gas mask on until permission to remove it is given by an officer or a gas noncommissioned officer.

(7) Do not enter a dugout during or immediately after a gas attack.

(8) During or immediately after a gas attack keep your mask on, even if in a gasproof dugout.

(9) Remain quiet and avoid unnecessary moving around during a gas attack.

(10) Keep cool, and remember your protective equipment will save you if properly used.

(11) Remember that the enemy uses many different kinds of gases, sometimes one kind at a time, and sometimes mixed with other chemical agents, smoke, or high explosive.

(12) Remember that clothing which has been in contact with mustard gas should be removed as soon as possible.

(13) Use gloves to remove another man's clothing or to handle equipment that has come in contact with mustard gas.

(14) Remember that mustard gas remains in an area for days.

(15) Avoid all areas in which there has been mustard gas. If your duties require you to go into such an area, remain as short a time as possible even though you are wearing protective clothing and a gas mask.

(16) Remember that the best conditions for a gas attack are during a calm, in foggy or cloudy weather, a drizzling rain, and at night. Be on the alert.

(17) Avoid drinking water or eating food that has been subjected to a gas attack.

(18) Remember that all gas cases require first, rest; second, warmth; third, fresh air.

(19) If gassed, do not talk, walk, or move about.

(20) Do not bandage the eyes of a gassed case. It is harmful and may result in blindness.

SECTION III

SECURITY OF SMALL UNITS

■ 230. For your commander to use his troops successfully he must first know where the enemy is and what he is doing. Without this information your commander is like a man trying to feel his way in the dark. He cannot know how to plan his attack to defeat the enemy, for he does not know where he will meet him. Nor does he know at what moment, or from what direction, the enemy may attack him and take him by surprise.

■ 231. You may be detailed as a member of a detachment sent out to provide security for a larger body of troops. These detachments have different names which indicate whether the main body is resting, marching, or fighting and what the security detachment is doing. No matter what they are called, always remember that the principal mission of every security detachment is to prevent the main body from being surprised. They do this by finding out where the enemy is and what he is doing by giving warning of the enemy's approach, and by delaying him so that the main force can get ready to fight.

They are the eyes and ears of the commander. They get back to him the information he needs to know so quickly that he will have plenty of time to make or change his plans. Another important thing to remember is, no matter how small the unit may be it *always* provides for its own security even though this security may consist of only one or two men.

■ 232. Scouts.—*a*. The smallest security detachment is the scout. The scout is a soldier whose duty it is to see what the enemy is doing without being seen, and to hear the enemy without being heard. The scout must be intelligent, have a strong body, great endurance, keen eyesight, delicate hearing, and an excellent memory.

b. As a scout your commander may use you in all types of combat operations. When your organization is in camp or bivouac, scouts are sent out from the outpost to gain information of the enemy, to prevent his scouts from gaining information of your organization, or both. When your organization is on the march, scouts perform important duties with the advance, flank, and rear guards by discovering hostile troops and promptly sending this information back so that your own commander will not be surprised. In movements by night or in dense woods, scouts serve as guides.

c. As your unit moves forward to the attack, scouts precede it and keep the proper direction for it to follow; they investigate danger areas before the unit crosses them, and select locations where it will be protected from enemy fire. During the progress of the attack they also protect your unit from surprise fire or counterattack by the enemy; they select and occupy firing positions and point out enemy targets.

d. When their organization is on the defense, scouts serve as lookouts, observers, listeners, and snipers. They may serve as members of patrols to enter the enemy lines, both by day and night, to get information of the enemy. They drive off enemy scouts and patrols who are trying to do the same thing.

e. A trained scout will be able to see and hear things that the average soldier does not. You must be able to pick up indistinct and motionless objects as well as moving ones. Long periods of painstaking search are often required before the position of a hostile soldier is located. As a scout you will conceal yourself as has been described in the preceding section, but as you will be "on your own" you will have greater freedom of movement.

f. Scouts usually work in pairs, with each scout having the utmost confidence in the ability of his fellow scout. Train with your partner and make a buddy of him so that each of you know what the other will do under any circumstances. Scouts always work in pairs when scouting in front of their organization in the advance. They move ahead of their organization as ordered by the commander. Here their duty will be to cause hostile riflemen and machine gunners to open fire and disclose their position, and to overcome resistance from small hostile outposts and patrols (fig. 71).

g. As you scout in front of your advancing unit, pick out probable positions that may conceal enemy machine guns or rifle groups. When you signal that these positions are clear your unit will advance by bounds and you should move forward for further reconnaissance.

h. Your distance in front of your organization varies with the ground and position of the enemy. In approaching houses, woods, and villages, one scout of each pair covers while one reconnoiters (fig. 72).

i. When the enemy opens fire, stop, seek cover, and determine where the fire is coming from. Scouts open fire with tracer ammunition to show to their leader the position of the enemy.

j. Scouts must be alert for intervals or gaps in the enemy line. When you discover them, push in, take up a position from which flanking fire may be brought to bear on the hostile position, then either you or your fellow scout notify your leader at once.

k. You can see that if you are appointed a scout a great deal will depend upon how well you perform your duties. You must always remember why the commander sent you out and what he wants you to do. That is your "mission." Sometimes this will require a great deal of courage on your part and you may have to try out several of different plans until one of them works. You will be "on your own" and often will find yourself in a situation which neither you nor your commander could have thought of in advance. But if you remember your "mission" at this time, and just what information your commander is anxiously waiting to receive from you, you will succeed.

RUNNERS CONNECTING UP THE SCOUTS WITH
THE PLATOON LEADER

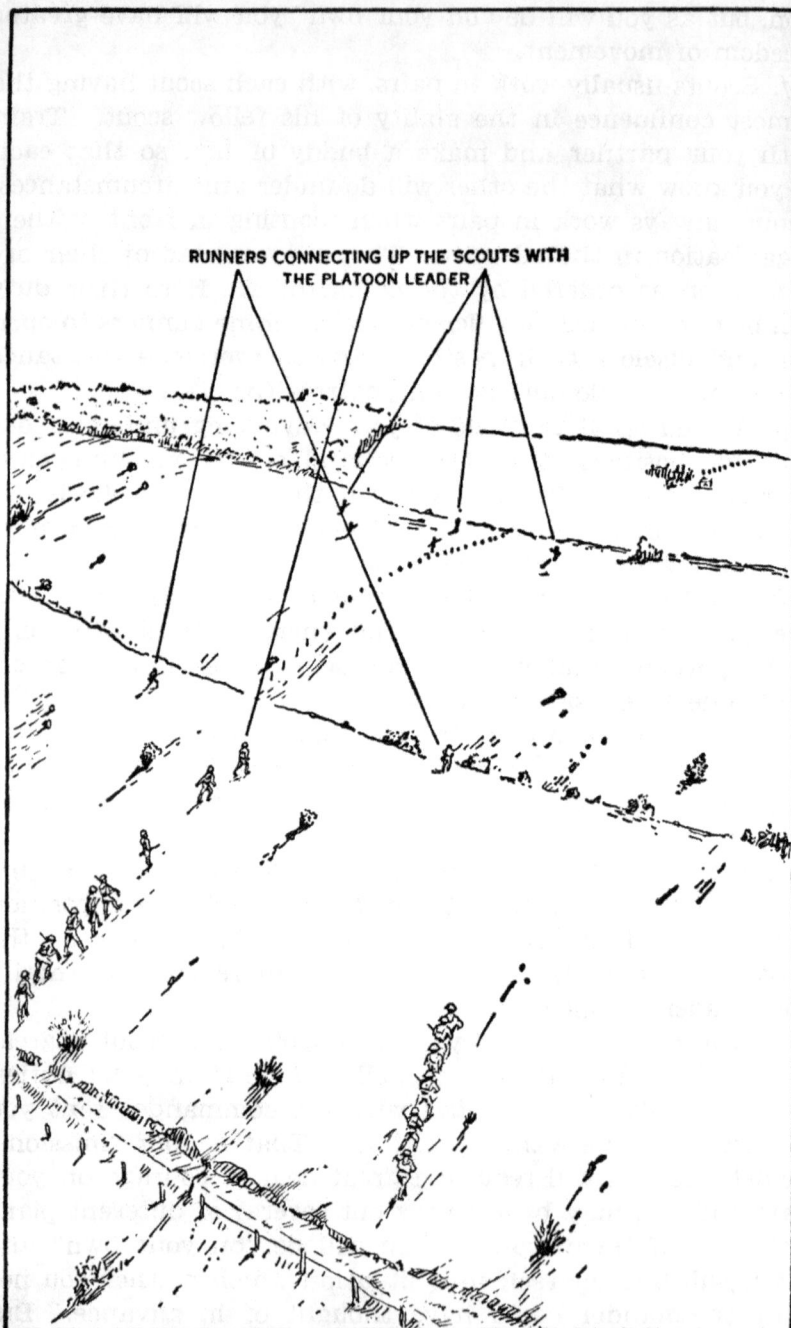

FIGURE 71.—Position of scouts in advance.

WITH PLATOON IN WOODS SCOUTS REACH OPEN AND SEE HOUSE AHEAD. THEY SIGNAL HALT, MEANING THAT THE PLATOON SHOULD NOT ADVANCE BEYOND THIS POINT. RECONNAISSANCE SHOWS HOUSE TO BE CLEAR. SCOUTS SIGNAL FORWARD AND PROCEED

CROSSING OPEN SPACE SCOUT SEES POSITION FROM WHICH MACHINE GUN MAY SWEEP THIS AREA. HE SIGNALS DOUBLE TIME AND POINTS TO THE MG POSITION, MEANING THIS AREA IN DANGER. FROM THAT POINT PLATOON SHOULD HURRY ACROSS

SCOUT RECONNOITERS FOR A SHORT DISTANCE INTO WOODS, FINDING EDGE OF WOODS TO BE UNOCCUPIED. A SCOUT RETURNS TO EDGE OF WOODS AND SIGNALS "FORWARD", THEN BOTH ENTER WOODS AND WAIT FOR PLATOON TO CLOSE UP

FIGURE 72.—Conduct of scouts during advance.

■ 233. PATROLS.—*a. General.*—The squad or a part of a squad oftens acts as a patrol. Patrols are assigned either reconnaissance or security as their primary mission.

(1) *Reconnaissance patrols* are used primarily to get information, maintain contact with the enemy, or observe points or areas. They do not fight unless they must in order to accomplish their task. They move so as best to do their job; they are not bound by either position or distance to the unit from which they were sent out.

(2) *Security patrols* provide security for a larger force. Their mission often will require them to fight. They must regulate their movements on the force or unit they are protecting.

(3) Patrols executing missions which will probably call for combat are given the means and the strength to enable them to engage in combat.

b. Reconnaissance patrols.—(1) Reconnaissance patrols are usually small, consisting of a leader and two or three men. They avoid unnecessary combat and accomplish their missions by stealth.

(2) The patrol leader is given the enemy situation and our own situation insofar as he needs to know them. He is given a definite job to do; he is told the general routes to be followed, the friendly troops through which he will pass, the time of return, and the place where messages are to be sent or the patrol is to report.

(3) Before starting out, the patrol leader studies the map and the terrain and selects a suitable route. He appoints alternate leaders, gives the other members of the patrol careful instructions about the task the patrol has to perform, assigns individual tasks, points out the route on the map and on the ground, arranges special signals, and designates an assembly point if the patrol is forced to separate. He makes sure that all members of the patrol know their jobs and checks to see that the arms and equipment are so carried that they will not glisten or rattle. The members of the patrol do not carry written matter which might be of value to the enemy if they are captured.

(4) All must clearly understand that in event of a fight wounded comrades are not abandoned but brought in with the patrol, whenever possible.

(5) All patrols provide for a point, flank protection, and a get-away man, who must always be able to return to his commander no matter what may happen to the remainder of the patrol. When a patrol is at a halt for any reason it must provide itself with all around protection (fig. 73).

(6) When moving in open country near the enemy, the patrol should pick its next stopping place before each advance. Moves should be made by one man at a time and at top speed. Before crossing a skyline one man should go to a point where the skyline is broken and observe, the rest of the patrol covering his advance. When he signals "forward" the way is clear and the remainder of the patrol comes up (fig. 74).

(7) Patrols should avoid enclosures and villages if possible. If it is necessary to pass through villages or to patrol them, great care must be taken, as each house or cellar may conceal an enemy. Watch windows, doors, and tops of houses closely. Advance slowly and cautiously (fig. 75).

(8) If a patrol is attacked and must fight, the man who first notes the danger calls out "Front," "Right," "Left," or "Rear." All members face toward the man attacked. The men on the flanks advance a short distance straight ahead and then close on the enemy from the flanks. The patrol leader and the men with him rush the enemy. During the combat, the members of the patrol repeat their recognition signals. If necessary, the leader designates a man near him to stay out of the fight.

(9) The patrol leader decides whether information gained will be sent back at once by messenger or reported on the return of the patrol. He alone is authorized to talk to, or arrest civilians or to seize telegrams and mail matter. Patrols do not allow civilians to pass through or precede them.

(10) An example of a message which you, as a patrol leader, might send back is shown in figure 76. After writing the message you would point out to the messenger who will carry it the location of the stone fence, woods, and machine guns and tell him your intentions. The sketch can be made quickly and requires no special ability. It contains all the information that is needed but no unnecessary information. If the commanding officer of Company A

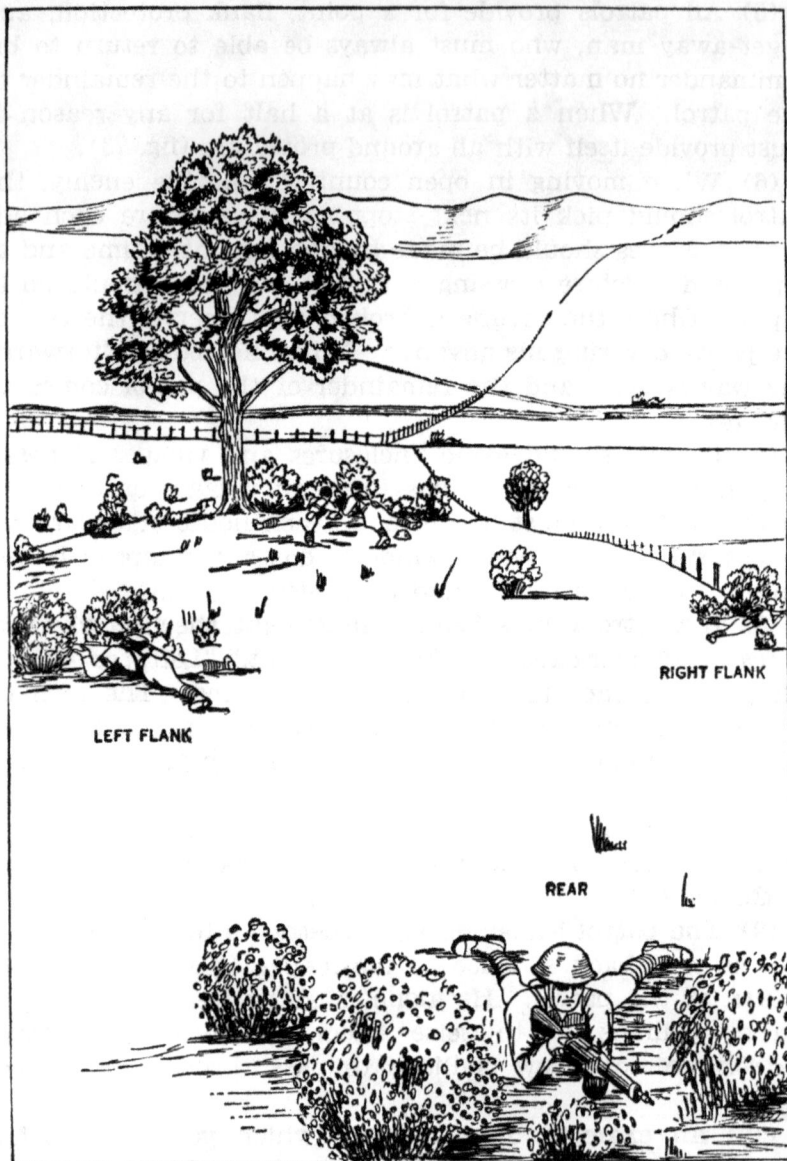

FIGURE 73.—Distribution of patrol halted in observation.

wants to know what you are going to do, he will ask the messenger. The advantage of this lies in the fact that, should the messenger and the message be captured by an enemy patrol, there is nothing in the message to tell them where **Corporal Jones** is *now*. To write "squad will remain at B" invites capture.

FIGURE 74.—Method of approaching house; of crossing stream.

FIGURE 75.—Formation of patrol passing through village.

(11) A soldier who is a good individual scout will ordinarily be a good member of a patrol. However, it must be remembered that as a member of a patrol you must obey the signals or commands of the designated leader instantly and without fail. You are not then scouting "on your own."

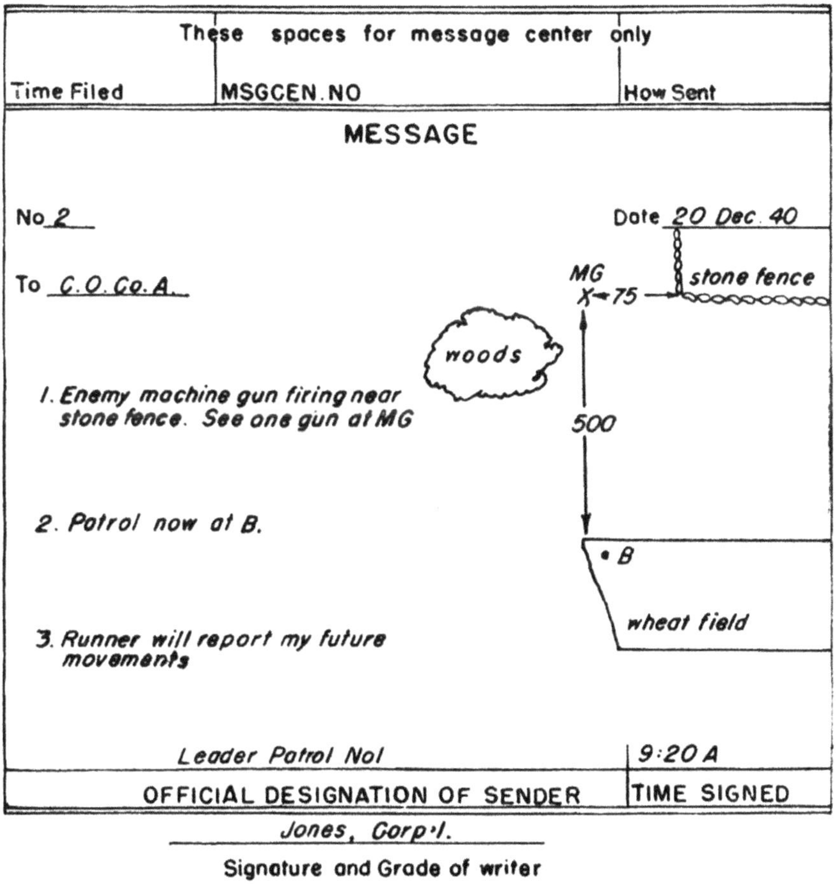
These spaces for message center only

Time Filed | MSGCEN. NO | How Sent

MESSAGE

No 2 Date 20 Dec. 40

To C. O. Co. A.

1. Enemy machine gun firing near stone fence. See one gun at MG

2. Patrol now at B.

3. Runner will report my future movements

Leader Patrol No1 | 9:20 A

OFFICIAL DESIGNATION OF SENDER | TIME SIGNED

Jones, Corp'l.

Signature and Grade of writer

FIGURE 76.—Example of message.

(12) Since many night patrols are for the purpose of capturing prisoners and executing tasks which may require combat, the patrol should rehearse plans for night combat and laying ambushes until it reaches a high state of efficiency. Only through repeated rehearsals and training will each member of the patrol learn to do his part unhesitatingly and correctly, and thus gain confidence in the ability

of the patrol as a unit (fig. 77). Failure to do this will sooner or later result in heavy losses in the patrols.

c. *Security patrols.*—(1) A squad or a part of a squad may act as a point (of the advance guard or rear guard) or as a flank patrol of a force on the march or in combat.

(2) *Point of advance guard.*—The point of an advance guard is a security patrol. It moves along the route of march and prevents an enemy on or near the route of march from opening surprise fire on the troops in rear. Behind the point comes the advance party. The distance between them will vary with the kind of terrain and whether it is day or night, but usually the point will not precede the advance party by more than 300 yards. As a member of the point you will find that it is so arranged as best to let the leader control it, to make it a poor target for enemy fire, and to permit all members to fire quickly to the front or either flank. It frequently marches on both sides of the road. It fires on all hostile forces within effective range. When unable to drive off the enemy, it holds its position and covers the action of the advance party. The presence of a distant enemy beyond effective rifle range is reported by signal. The point observes toward the front and flanks but does not reconnoiter on the flanks of the route of march. When the column halts, the point sends forward one or more observers.

(3) *Point of rear guard.*—As a member of a rear point you are assisting in protecting the rear of your marching column. The formation of the rear point is similar to that of the point of an advance guard. However, as a member of a rear point you stop to fire *only* when the enemy threatens to interfere with the march. No other troops will move to your assistance, but when the enemy presses closely, other troops will take up firing positions in rear to cover you. When you are forced back, withdraw to a flank so that the troops behind you can fire into the enemy.

(4) *Flank patrol.*—(a) A flank patrol is a security patrol. Flank patrols operate in one of two ways; either they go to a designated place, remain there for a specified time, and there rejoin the column, or they march along a designated route. They report, by signal or messenger, enemy forces they observe.

PAIRS OF SCOUTS ATTACK
PREVIOUSLY DESIGNATED
MEMBERS OF THE ENEMY
PATROL BY RUNNING IN
UPON THEM FROM BEHIND.

A PAIR OF MEN WITH
BROWNING AUTOMATIC RIFLES
ARE PLACED ON EACH FLANK
NEAR END OF AMBUSH SO THAT
THEY CAN COVER ITS FLANKS.

FIGURE 77.—Night ambush.

(b) A flank patrol of a column on the **march moves** so that it can protect the column against hostile small-arms fire at midranges (300 to 600 yards).

(c) In combat the flank of the unit to which you belong may become exposed. In such a situation flank security patrols are sent out to protect the exposed flank. Not only do these patrols report observed hostile forces and their movements but they also report the movements of friendly forces which they can see.

■ 234. SECURITY AT HALT.—a. Detachments of troops detailed to protect a body of troops at rest or not on the march are called outposts. The general purposes of an outpost are to get information, to observe places where the enemy might sneak up on the main body, and to fight off enemy troops coming toward your position. In particular the outpost must protect the main body so the troops can rest, or work undisturbed, and in case of attack hold the enemy off long enough so that the main body can get ready to fight. **If you are a sentinel on outpost duty you must be on the job every minute you are on post, but you must avoid unnecessarily alarming the command.**

b. For an organization the size of a company, troop, or battery the outpost need be only a few sentinels and patrols. In a larger organization a larger and more elaborate outpost will be needed. On account of the presence of motorized and armored forces in all modern armies, outposts must give all around protection to their commands. The part of the outpost nearest the enemy is an observation group called an cutguard. Behind the outguard are more troops in detachments called supports (figs. 78 and 79).

c. If you are a member of an outguard, no fires will be built or smoking permitted unless you are told you can do so. You should avoid loud talking or making other noise. The position of each outguard may be entrenched and will be concealed. You keep your weapons at hand all the time, and do not remove your equipment. Your duties as a sentinel are described in the preceding section.

d. You may be called upon to perform outpost patrol duty. Outpost patrols operate either within our lines or beyond our lines. Some patrols operate beyond our lines to reconnoiter in the direction of the enemy. Other patrols operate within

our lines in order to keep in touch with the parts of the
outpost and check up on the performance of duty on the line
of outguards.   Outpost patrols have at least two men and

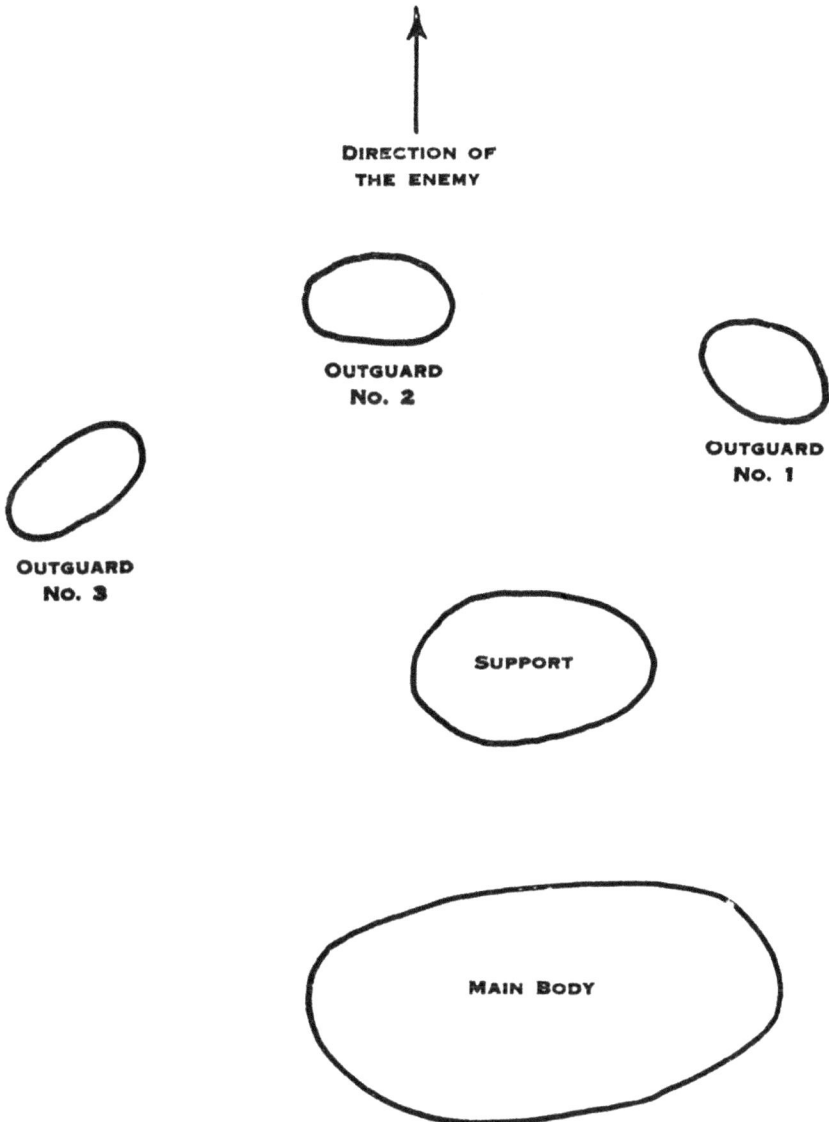

DIRECTION OF
THE ENEMY

OUTGUARD
No. 2

OUTGUARD
No. 1

OUTGUARD
No. 3

SUPPORT

MAIN BODY

FIGURE 78.—Outpost of small force.

a good leader who, on important tasks, may be an officer.
The patrols get information of the ground and of where the
enemy is and what he is doing.   Any ground near the line

one line in order to keep in touch with the patrols, the
outpost and close in on the performance of duty by means
of examples. Outpost duty is, for the most part, one

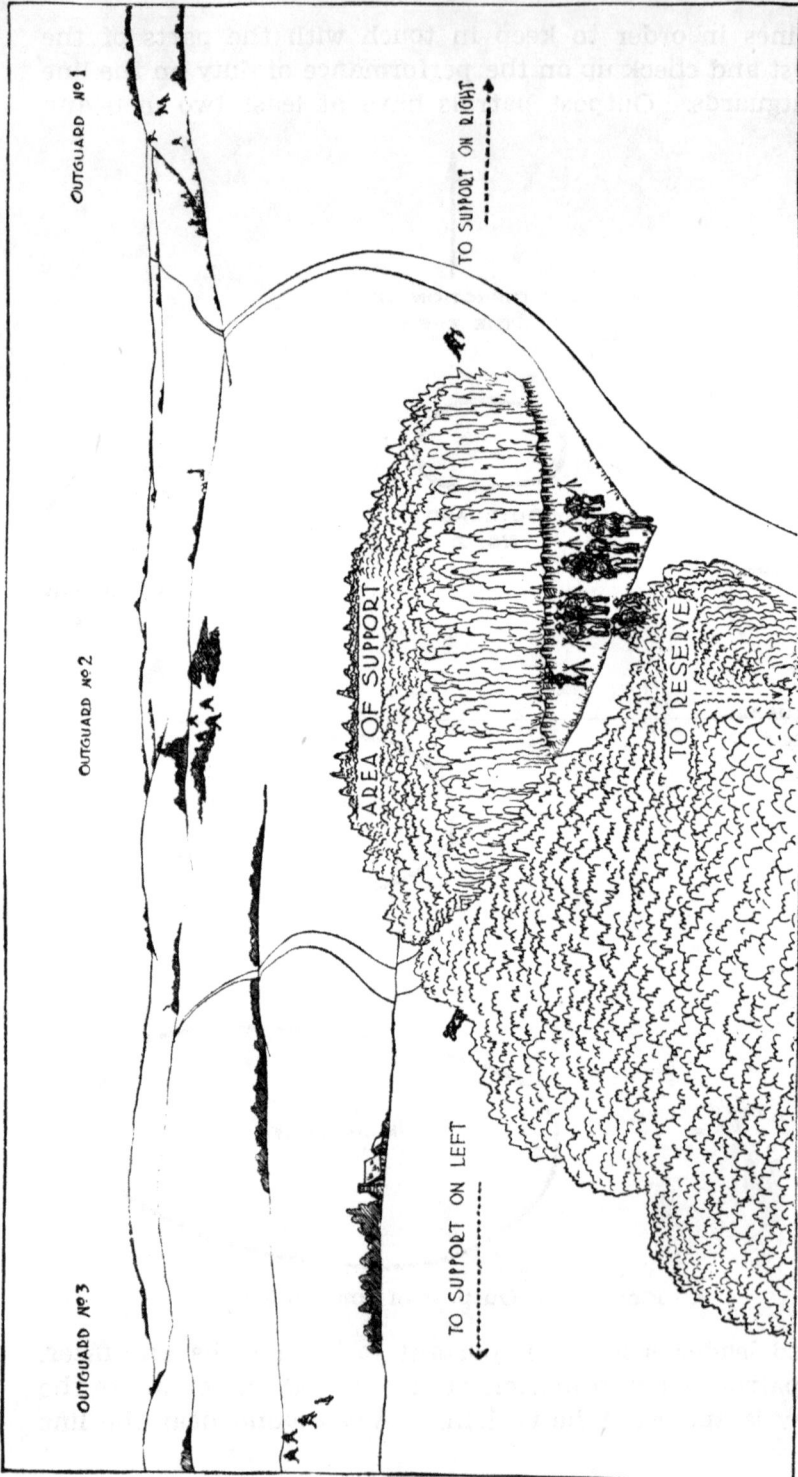

OUTGUARD Nº 1

OUTGUARD Nº 2

OUTGUARD Nº 3

TO SUPPORT ON RIGHT

AREA OF SUPPORT

TO RESERVE

TO SUPPORT ON LEFT

FIGURE 79.—Several outguards on duty.

of outguards that might give concealment for hostile troops is searched frequently by patrols if the enemy could get to it without being seen. When you are on patrol duty you fire only in self-defense or to give the alarm. Patrols and reliefs should not move in the open in vicinity of the outguards and so give away the location of the sentinels and outguards.

e. If you have to establish a cavalry outguard, remember that your horses must be kept as near at hand as practicable. This will require careful planning so that they can be fed and watered and still be protected from enemy observation and fire.

■ 235. SECURITY ON THE MARCH.—*a.* An *advance guard* is a detachment of a body of troops that goes ahead of and protects the main body on the march. The chief job of an advance guard is to protect the main body against surprise attack and drive back small detachments of the enemy. Particularly its duties are—

(1) To guard against surprise and get information by patrolling.

(2) To push back small detachments of the enemy and prevent them from observing, firing on, or delaying the main body.

(3) To remove obstacles and make repairs to the road to help the steady advance of the column.

(4) To delay the enemy's advance in force long enough to let the main body get ready to fight.

(5) When the enemy is found on the defensive to take a good position, locate his lines, and protect the main body during its preparation for action.

b. An advance guard provides for its own security and gets information by putting out smaller detachments to the front and flank. The most advanced part of the advance guard is called the *point* (figs. 80 and 81). The point is usually a squad, or part of a squad. It is really a patrol with a fixed mission.

c. Your part in an advance guard may be as a part of the point or one of the other patrols sent out to make sure that the enemy does not ambush the main body.

d. If the point of an advance guard is fired upon, it should deploy and try to continue to advance fighting. This is done

195

in order that small enemy detachments will not succeed in delaying the advance of the main body. Flank patrols assist in this, and if the enemy does not fall back they try to locate his flanks. If necessary, each part of the advance guard goes into action to clear the way for the main body.

e. A rear guard is a detachment whose job is to protect the main body from an attack from the rear. In a retreat it fires on and delays in every possible way enemy pursuing troops, so that the main body can gain distance from the

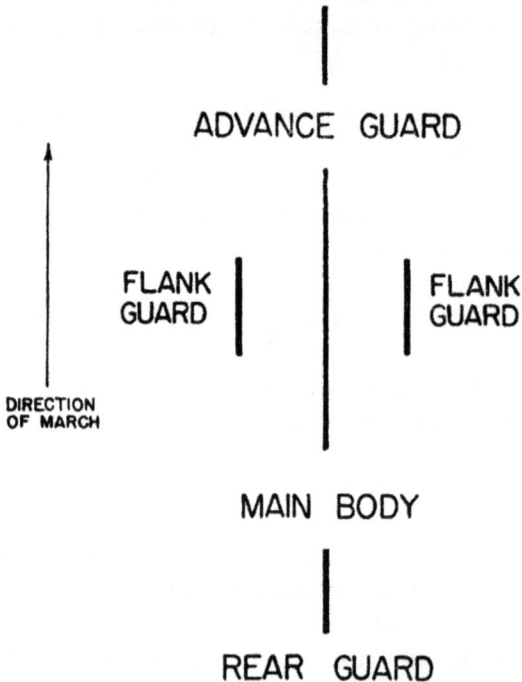

ADVANCE GUARD

FLANK
GUARD

FLANK
GUARD

DIRECTION
OF MARCH

MAIN BODY

REAR GUARD

FIGURE 80.—Relation of security detachments on march to main body.

enemy. The formation of a rear guard is like that of an advance guard, reversed. That is, the various parts follow the main body instead of going ahead of it. Also the rear party follows the support, and the rear point follows the rear party. The rear guard makes the most of opportunities to block the road and takes up good positions from which it can fire on the enemy and make him deploy. The fight is not kept up so long that the rear guard will not be able to fall back to other positions (fig. 82).

f. A *flank guard* is a detachment whose job is to cover the flank of a column exposed to enemy attack. It may be placed in position to cover the march of the main body or it may march generally opposite the main body to protect it. The object of the flank guard is to prevent attack of the main body or, if this cannot be done, then to delay the enemy long enough so that the main body can get ready to fight. The flank guard must keep contact with the main body. A flank guard must provide its own protection and if necessary have

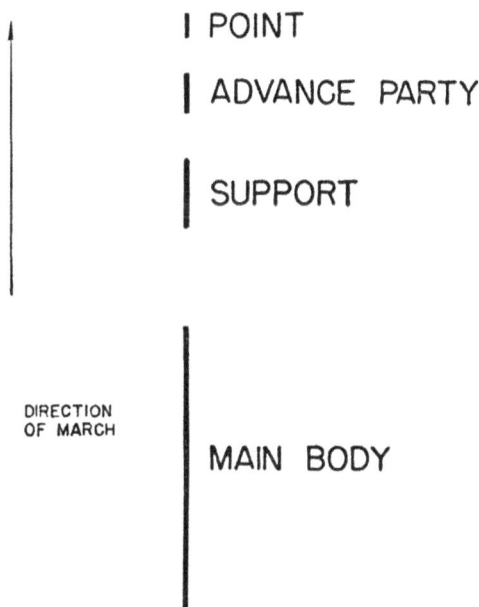

I POINT

| ADVANCE PARTY

| SUPPORT

DIRECTION
OF MARCH

MAIN BODY

FIGURE 81.—Advance guard of small force.

its own advance guard or rear guard and flank patrols (fig. 80).

g. (1) When a march is made near the enemy, special measures are taken during halts for protection against surprise or attack. When the halt is only for a short time (less than a half hour), the advance party and support rest along the route of march. The point and flank patrols move to positions where they can keep a good lookout. If necessary more patrols will be sent out from the advance party and support. Antiaircraft and antitank lookouts are detailed to watch out for the approach of enemy airplanes and tanks or armored vehicles.

(2) If the halt is longer than a half hour, a march outpost will probably be formed. Outguards are sent out to the front and flanks, and unless friendly troops are close in the rear they will be put out to protect the rear also. The outguards to the front and flanks are furnished by units of the advance guard. Outguards to the rear, when necessary, will be taken from the rear guard. When the march is to be resumed, the various outguards are signaled to close in, and when all are back in their march formations the march is resumed. March

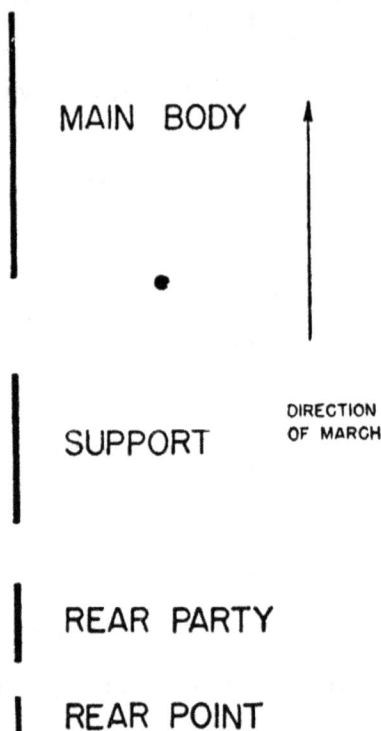

MAIN BODY

SUPPORT   DIRECTION OF MARCH

REAR PARTY

REAR POINT

FIGURE 82.—Rear guard of small force.

outposts watch particularly roads and routes of approach leading to the main body for the approach of enemy mechanized and motorized detachments. March outposts work like other outposts in protecting the main force.

h. All arms of the service follow the same general plan for providing security for themselves. In the cavalry, armored, or motorized units, however, the distances between the security detachments and the main body are greater than with foot troops because of the greater speed which cavalry, armored, and motorized units have. Security elements of these rapidly moving forces sometimes advance by bounds, much as a scout will do in advancing toward the enemy. That is, the point of the advance guard will move rapidly forward to some ridge or other favorable terrain feature from which it can observe toward the enemy and, if all looks well, it signals for the next larger unit to come forward. The leader of the point then selects another favorable terrain feature and repeats his advance, taking advantage of cover. While the point is doing this the next larger detachment in rear is prepared to defend the point by firing on any hostile element which might seek to stop the advance of the point. Sometimes, however, when the advance of the main body is very rapid, or during darkness or fog, movements by bounds will not be made but a steady rate maintained.

■ 236. SECURITY WHILE DEFENDING.—*a.* When your organization is defending, security against a surprise attack is provided by sentinels, patrols, outguards, outposts, a warning system, and natural and artificial obstacles. The natural obstacles which provide some protection by making it difficult for the enemy to attack are rivers, canals, lakes, marshes or boggy ground, ravines, steep mountains, and other difficult parts of the terrain. They can all be crossed, however, and must be watched and defended.

b. The artificial obstacles which provide protection are trenches and dugouts, barbed wire entanglements, road blocks, road craters, traps, and mines. Just as with the natural obstacles, the enemy can remove or cross artificial obstacles if he is not interfered with. The thing to remember is that after a natural or artificial obstacle has been selected or put in place it should be covered with the fire of your weapons, especially machine guns. The obstacles will slow up the enemy. When he attempts to remove or cross them your fire will stop him.

c. (1) There are specially organized units in the Army to provide protection against aircraft and armored vehicles. If you are assigned to one of these units, you will be given special instruction in the use of the weapons. If you are not a member of such a unit, however, you should make every effort to provide your own security with the weapons and other means available to you. As was explained before, your best protection against low-flying aircraft is concealment, remaining quietly in place, and firing on the airplane with all weapons unless you have received orders not to fire.

(2) Even where natural obstacles exist, additional security should be provided against armored vehicles by an all around protection of artificial obstacles. Tank traps and mines can be set out, although this will usually be done by engineers or larger troop units. Road blocks are especially effective in stopping armored vehicles or slowing them up and making them go across country. These may be easily constructed by deepening and enlarging shell holes on the road, by felling trees or telephone poles, or by putting old automobiles or trucks crosswise on the road where the armored vehicles cannot get off the road because of steep banks or ditches. The value of these obstacles is increased by covering them with fire which will interfere with the enemy's attempts to remove the obstacles.

(3) You must be on the alert to prevent enemy sympathizers or parachute troops which have been landed behind our lines from removing these obstacles. If you are detailed to guard an obstacle never allow any persons to tamper with it or remove it unless you are sure of their authority to do so. If there is any doubt in your mind hold them under guard until one of your officers or noncommissioned officers arrives. If they attempt to attack you or to escape, shoot them.

■ 237. SECURITY WHILE ATTACKING.—*a*. As your unit approaches the actual or probable location of the enemy, security is provided by covering its advance with scouts. These scouts go in advance of the larger units and "comb" the ground thoroughly. Their action will make the enemy disclose his position by opening fire before the larger elements of your organization have come within his range. As your unit comes closer to the enemy's position additional security will be provided by breaking up into smaller units known as squad or platoon columns, or by deploying as skirmishers. This increases the readiness for action of your unit by putting it into formation from which it can move in any direction and cannot be surprised by any action of the enemy. Additional security is provided by the fire of machine guns and other weapons which keep down the enemy's fire until your organization can reach his position and drive him out of it.

b. If your organization halts during the attack, one or more combat outposts are immediately sent out to the front where they can screen and protect your organization until it is ready to continue the attack. A combat outpost usually operates from several alternate positions. If the enemy advances the combat outpost opens fire at long range. Upon close approach of the attacking troops the combat outpost withdraws. Routes of withdrawal are used which will not interfere with your own organization in rear firing at the enemy.

c. If the battle is interrupted by darkness, combat outposts will be promptly established. At night they will be closer to your organization than in the daytime. The combat outpost will establish listening posts to warn the front line organizations of the approach of hostile raiding or attacking parties. It will maintain a vigorous reconnaissance during the night in order to discover any change in the hostile dispositions, intentions, or situation.

d. During battle it may happen that a flank of your organization may be exposed. That means that there are no friendly troops close to that flank. When this happens a flank patrol must be sent out to that flank. Its duties are to prevent the enemy from working his way around and attacking your exposed flank or rear, or to give due warning of such an intention. Such a patrol regulates its own movements on that of the unit it is protecting. It may remain in one position or, if your organization is advancing, it will move rapidly from one position to another. When the patrol occupies a position each member selects two locations, one from which he can fire to the front or flank and another from which he can fire to the flank or rear. The patrol must be in constant communication with the unit it is protecting. One man is selected who must always be able to escape and get back to your organization in case the patrol is captured. Information of enemy activities or of friendly troops which may appear on that flank are reported back to your commander as he directs.

CHAPTER 14

MILITARY SANITATION AND FIRST AID

SECTION I

MILITARY SANITATION

■ **238.** Before you entered the Army, you were given a thorough physical examination to see that you had no disease. Now that you have been accepted in the military service it is your duty to our country and yourself to keep well and ready for any service. If you will remember and follow the few simple rules given below, you will find yourself repaid many times. Following these rules, in connection with the daily exercise of your military training, will keep you in excellent physical condition, and you will return to civil life with a better and stronger body than when you entered the Army.

■ **239.** If at any time you do not feel perfectly well, or believe that you have any disease, go at once to your first sergeant, or the noncommissioned officer in charge of quarters, who will send you to a medical officer for examination. Never try to treat yourself, as you may not only seriously harm yourself, but may also become a source of danger to your comrades. The danger of giving a disease to another man is usually greatest when the illness is just starting, and often before you feel really sick. If you have a cold, a headache, diarrhea, sore eyes, a rash on your body, or feel feverish, you must be examined by a medical officer as soon as possible. Many contagious diseases begin with these symptoms, so you must not wait until you have exposed your comrades before seeing a medical officer. You will also usually have a less severe illness yourself if you report for a treatment as early as possible.

■ **240.** Stay away from any person having a disease unless it is your duty to take care of him.

■ 241. An unclean body may be the cause of disease. Take
a bath at frequent, regular intervals and at least twice a
week. Pay particular attention to your armpits, the parts
between the legs, the feet, and under the foreskin. Always
wash your hands thoroughly before eating and after using
the toilet, as you may have gotten some disease germs on your
hands which will get on the food you eat and into your system. You are especially likely to get such germs on your
hands when going to the toilet. If bathing facilities are not
available, scrub your body frequently with a wet cloth, paying
particular attention to your armpits, crotch, and feet.

■ 242. Have your underwear, shirts, and socks washed frequently and change them at least twice a week. If water is
not available, crumple up your clothing, shake it well, and
hang it in the sunlight for at least 2 hours. Be on the lookout
for body lice and crab lice. If you have a continued itching
on your body or head, report to a medical officer at once.

■ 243. When your clothing or shoes get wet, change them
as soon as possible. Sitting around in wet clothes or with
wet feet is almost certain to give you a cold or other serious
illness.

■ 244. Keep your mouth clean by thoroughly brushing your
teeth at least twice a day; one brushing should always be
before going to bed. Brush your teeth on the inside and outside, away from the gums and toward the cutting surfaces of
the teeth. If particles of food remain between the teeth, they
should be promptly removed, care being taken not to injure
the gums. If your teeth are bad, or ache, report to the
dental officer.

■ 245. Get into the habit of having your bowels move regularly once each day at as nearly the same time as possible.
Always go to the toilet to urinate, or when your bowels move.
Using the ground for this purpose is a source of great danger
to everyone. Flies or other insects may alight where you
have relieved yourself, pick up germs, and later deposit them
on food. These germs may also be carried by rain, or
drainage, into wells or a stream which serves as a water
supply for some city or your own camp or post.

■ 246. Drink plenty of water at intervals during the day but do not drink a large amount at one time, especially when you are overheated after exertion. Drink from your own glass or cup, or from a bubbling fountain. Never use a cup which is used by others, as someone may have left live germs on it from his mouth or hands, and you may catch a disease when drinking from it. For the same reason do not exchange pipes, cigars, musical instruments played by the mouth, handkerchiefs, towels, or shaving outfits.

■ 247. Be sure to use your mosquito bar when mosquitoes are present. See that it is well tucked in and that it has no holes in it.

■ 248. Flies and cockroaches frequently carry disease germs and leave them on food and other articles over which they walk. Get rid of flies in every way. Whenever you see a fly in barracks, kill it. Be sure that screens in windows and doors are kept tightly closed. Food containers and garbage cans must be kept tightly closed. Scraps of food, fruit skins, and manure should never be left on the ground about the post or camp.

■ 249. Keep your barracks and squad room clean. If you find bedbugs in your bed, or in the barracks, report that fact to your company commander.

■ 250. Keep your hair cut short and your fingernails clean. This is especially important if you are detailed as a cook, baker, or in other positions in which you handle food.

■ 251. *a.* Avoid venereal diseases. These diseases are almost always caught by sexual intercourse with an infected woman. If you have had sexual intercourse, report at once for "prophylaxis." The prophylactic treatment must be carried out thoroughly and the directions followed exactly. The sooner you report for this treatment, and *at least* within 2 hours after exposure, the more certain you are of avoiding disease.

b. If you should feel that you have caught a venereal disease, report to the medical officer at once and do exactly as he tells you. Any venereal disease can be cured much more quickly if proper treatment is begun early. Above all, do not try to treat yourself or go to an advertising quack doctor. Doing either of those things may result in serious damages to your body and health which will remain with you the rest of your life.

■ 252. While all of the rules given above are of the same importance in the field as they are in your post or cantonment, the following are of especial importance in your field service:

a. Be more careful of the water you drink. Never drink any water from a stream, spring, well, or faucet until it has been passed as pure by a medical officer and a sign posted that the water is safe to drink. When orders have been issued that all drinking water must be boiled, be sure that the water you drink has *actually been boiled for 20 minutes* and not merely heated a little. Often water will be provided for drinking which has been purified in a sterilizing bag known as a Lyster bag. These bags are usually placed in your company street or near the company kitchen. When this is done drink only the water from the bag. Do not mind the peculiar taste; it will not hurt you in the least and comes from a powder issued by the Quartermaster Corps to purify the water. Water purified in this way may make your urine sting a little but this means nothing harmful. Let the water run from the faucet of the bag into your own cup. Do not dip a cup into the bag and do not drink by putting your lips to the faucet.

b. Be especially careful not to relieve yourself except in the latrine, or the night urine can, provided in your company street.

c. Be sure that your mess kit and knife, fork, and spoon are thoroughly washed in hot, soapy water and rinsed in boiling water after they are used. Unless this is done in boiling water your mess gear may pick up disease germs from the men who used the water before you and you may contract disease.

d. Use the mosquito bar whenever there are mosquitoes, or when directed by your company commander.

e. Get a bath whenever possible. Watch for lice or other vermin on your body and clothing and, if found, report immediately to the medical officer.

f. Do not sit or lie directly on the damp ground. When you are hot or perspiring, or when your clothes are damp, do not remain where a draft can strike you. If you do, you will get chilled and as a result may contract a cold, rheumatism, or pneumonia.

g. Every day, if possible, hang your blankets and clothing out to air in the sun and shake or beat them with a stick Wash your shirts, underwear, and socks frequently. Whenever possible, roll up your tent so the air and sun can get in it. Keep it ventilated at night.

h. Ditch your tent as soon as you can after it is put up, even if your camp is only for one night. If you do not, a little rain may spoil a whole night's rest.

i. Always prepare your bed before dark. If you have no cot, level off the ground and scrape out a little hollow for your hips. Use some straw, dry grass, leaves, or small branches. Sleep on your raincoat. This keeps the dampness from coming up from the ground and chilling your body.

■ 253. The most important thing in your marching ability as a soldier is the care of your feet. You will find instructions on this matter in section II, chapter 11.

SECTION II

FIRST AID

■ 254. During your military service you may find yourself in a situation where you will have to give first aid to the injured until a member of the Medical Department arrives. The following points are important for you to remember:

a. Do not get excited; act quickly but quietly.

b. Be gentle; do not handle a wounded man roughly; keep bystanders away.

c. Do not try to do too much.

d. A Medical Department man should be called as soon as possible.

e. Make the injured man sit or lie down.

f. Never move an injured man until medical help comes, unless it is impossible to keep him warm where he is, or unless he must be removed from the battlefield to reach help. The less an injured man is moved right after being hurt, the better chance he will have to recover.

g. Warmth is most important to prevent chilling and shock, even on a warm day. Fill canteens with hot water and place them under his armpits and between his legs, always outside of his clothing, so as not to burn him. Wrap him in blankets, coats, newspapers, or anything else available to keep him warm. If he is conscious and not wounded in the stomach, throat, or mouth, he may be given a hot drink.

h. Do not pour liquids into his mouth if he is unconscious; they may choke him.

i. Do not try to bring an unconscious wounded man to consciousness. Just let him be quiet, stop his bleeding, and keep him warm.

j. Never touch a wound with anything unclean, such as dirty hands, or water and bandages that are not sterile. You may cause blood poisoning. Do not wash the wound.

k. Expose the wound by unbuttoning, unlacing, or cutting the clothes, shoes, leggings, or boots. Open all articles of clothing which interfere with the circulation of blood or breathing but do it gently.

■ 255. FIRST-AID PACKET.—Among the items of equipment issued to you is a first-aid packet. It consists of a little airtight container and is carried in a small web pouch attached to your belt. When you place this packet in the pouch always have the ring down, at the bottom of the pouch, so that when the packet is taken out of the pouch the ring will not be caught and the packet accidentally opened. Never open the packet until it is necessary for you to use it in the treatment of a wound.

■ 256. USE OF FIRST-AID PACKET.—The following information will assist you in using the first-aid packet:

a. The packet contains two sterile dressings, each wrapped in waxed paper. Each dressing consists of a gauze bandage (4 inches wide and 84 inches long), to which is sewed in the middle a "compress" or pad of gauze. The dressing is arranged so that the compress (folded) is on the inside and a roll of the bandage is on each of the two outer sides. When the rolls are pulled, the compress on the inside opens. This packet also contains two safety pins wrapped in waxed paper.

b. To apply the first-aid packet, carefully remove the wrapper and carefully remove the paper from one of the packages without unfolding the compress or bandage, between the thumb and fingers. When ready to dress the wound, open the compress by pulling on the two rolls, being careful not to touch the inside of the compress with the fingers or anything else. Still holding one roll of the bandage in each hand, apply the compress to the wound, then wrap the bandage around the limb or part, and tie the ends together or fasten with safety pins. The second compress and bandage may be applied over the first or it may be used for a sling if the arm is wounded, or to bind both legs together if one is injured.

c. For two wounds opposite each other, apply to one wound an unopened compress, to the other an opened compress, and hold both dressings in place with the bandage of the latter.

d. For two wounds not opposite each other tie a compress over each.

e. For a wound too large to be covered by the compress, find and break the stitch holding the compress together, unfold it, and apply as directed above.

f. If the contents of one packet are not large enough to cover a wound thoroughly, use several.

g. All wounds bleed more or less. Some bleed very freely because a large blood vessel has been wounded, and you must know how to stop this heavy bleeding, or hemorrhage, as it is called. Remember that while all wounds bleed a little, as a rule, this bleeding will stop in a few minutes if the patient is quiet, and that the firm pressure of the pads and bandage will keep it controlled. All severe flesh wounds should be dressed and splinted, if possible to do so, as is done for a fracture. This will insure immobility and help to prevent bleeding.

■ 257. HEMORRHAGE.—*a.* Bleeding from the arteries is the most dangerous because the blood flows fast and will soon cause a man to bleed to death unless the flow of blood is stopped. In arterial bleeding the blood squirts from the artery with each pulsation of the heart and is bright red in color.

b. Blood from a vein flows in a slow, steady stream, and the color is dark red or purple.

c. Capillary bleeding is an oozing of blood from a cut surface and is generally the least dangerous.

■ 258. To CONTROL BLEEDING.—*a.* To control bleeding from the arteries quickly, press upon the blood vessel between the wound and the heart.

b. To stop bleeding from the scalp apply pressure with the tips of the fingers in front of the ear just above where the lower jaw can be felt working in its socket. A branch of the artery crosses the temple on a line from the upper border of the ear to above the eyebrow. (See fig. 83A.)

c. To stop bleeding from the neck and head press the thumb and fingers deeply into the neck in front of the big, plainly seen muscle which reaches from behind the ear to the upper part of the breast bone. (See fig. 83B.)

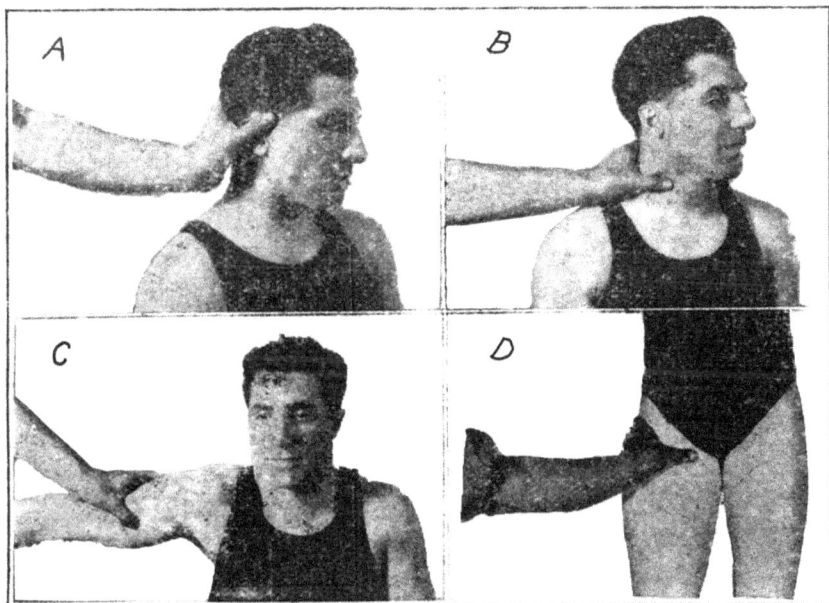

FIGURE 83.—Pressure points.

d. In bleeding from wounds of the shoulder or armpit press the thumb deeply into the hollow behind the middle of the collar bone.

e. To stop bleeding from the arm or hand press outward against the bone just behind the inner border of the large muscle (biceps) of the arm. (See fig. 83C.)

f. In bleeding from the thigh, leg, or foot, press strongly with the thumbs on the artery at the upper part of the inside of the thigh, where the artery passes over the bone. (See fig. 83D.)

■ 259. TOURNIQUET.—a. If the bleeding from an arm or leg continues in spite of pressure exerted by the thumb or fingers, the bleeding must be stopped by the use of a tourniquet. This consists of a pad, which is placed on the line of the artery, and a strap or band that goes over the pad and around the limb, so that when tightened it will press the pad down upon the artery and interrupt the flow of blood. For the arm and hand the tourniquet pad is applied over a point on the inside of the arm about a hand's breadth below the arm pit. (See fig. 84.) For the thigh and leg the tourniquet is applied 4 or 5 inches below the groin, and on the inside of the thigh where the main artery passes over the bone. (See fig. 85.)

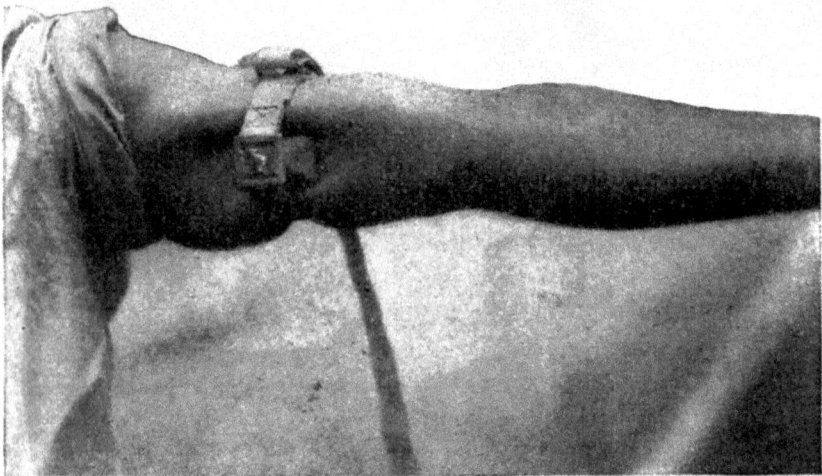

FIGURE 84.—Use of tourniquet application.

b. The pad may consist of a roll or bandage or a small stone or other hard object wrapped in something to make it less rough; and a bandage, belt, handkerchief, or necktie may be used for the strap. After tying the strap loosely around the limb, the required degree of pressure can be made by passing a stick or bayonet under the band, but directly opposite the pad, and twisting it so that the pad is pressed down firmly upon the blood vessel.

c. Turn the stick slowly and stop at once when the blood ceases to flow, fixing the stick in place with another bandage. Harm may be done if too much force is used or if pressure is kept up too long. It is a good rule to loosen the pressure at the end of each 20 to 30 minutes and allow the stick to remain loose, but in place, if no bleeding appears. The tourniquet can be tightened if bleeding begins again.

d. Do not make the tourniquet any tighter than necessary to check the bleeding. At best it is painful.

e. A tourniquet should never be hidden by clothing or a bandage so that it cannot be seen.

f. Mark the patient's tag plainly, "Tourniquet," with the date and hour of application. If he is conscious, instruct him to tell every medical officer that he has a tourniquet.

g. If a tourniquet is left on tight for as much as six hours, the patient will probably lose his arm or leg.

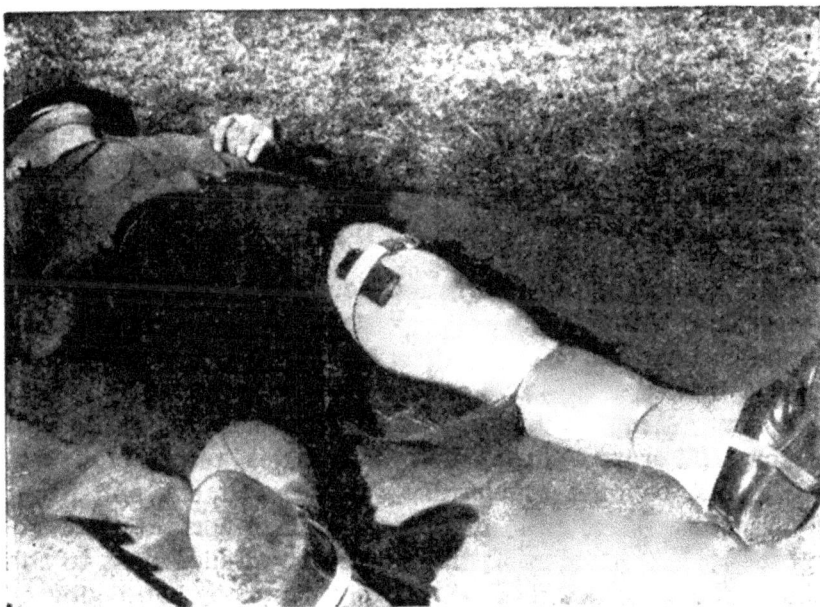

FIGURE 85.—Application of tourniquet to thigh.

■ 260. FRACTURES.—The following are some of the more common injuries for which you may be required to give first aid and the method you should use to treat them until some member of the Medical Department arrives:

a. A fracture is a break in a bone. Fractures occur most frequently in the arms or legs. When the long bones of the arm or leg are broken the wounded man loses power of control over the limb and it gives way and may be crooked instead of straight.

b. A *simple fracture* is one in which there is no wound extending from the broken bone through the skin. A *compound fracture* is one in which the broken bone has pushed through the skin and therefore is exposed to the dangers of infection from the outside. A *complicated fracture* is one where there is damage to adjoining large blood vessels, nerves, or muscles from movement of the sharp and jagged edges of the broken bone.

c. In no injury is the outcome more influenced by the character of first-aid treatment than in fractures. Improper handling or immediate movement may produce or increase shock and deprive the patient of a chance for recovery. All fractures, or suspected fracture cases, should be handled gently. It is equally as important to know what *not* to do as to know *what* to do.

d. Immediate movement or transportation of the patient is usually very dangerous to him. The first-aid treatment should be given where he lies and medical assistance should be brought to the patient instead of carrying the patient to the doctor.

■ 261. TREATMENT OF FRACTURES.—*a.* Except when the bone has broken through the skin, if the condition of the injured person is such that he can walk or be carried to medical assistance, a broken leg or arm can be fixed in position by splints or other available material. Many common materials will do for temporary splints, such as shingles, pieces of board, rifle boots, bayonet scabbards, a rain spout cut and fitted to the limb, or bunches of twigs. It is important that the splints be well padded on the side to be applied next to the arm or leg and that they be securely bound by bandaging or by tying above and below the point of fracture but not over it.

b. In fractures with wounds or hemorrhage the flow of blood should be stopped and the wound bandaged before splints are applied. If possible, it is best to wait for expert medical care to apply the splints in such cases.

c. Fractures of the arm should be supported by a sling after splinting. Arm slings can be made of bandages, or can be improvised from clothing by using safety pins to fasten the coat sleeve to the front of the coat in order to support the arm. The coat flap can be used for the same purpose by pinning it or by punching a hole through the lower edge of the flap and buttoning this to a coat button.

d. In splinting, the limb should first be straightened out gently and the broken bone alined by quickly but firmly pull-

ing upon the end of it, if necessary, and then fixed or re-
tained in position by splints.

e. For a broken upper arm apply two splints, one in front,
the other behind, if the bone is broken near the elbow; or to
the inner and outer sides if the fracture is in the middle or
near the shoulder. Support the arm by a sling.

f. For a broken forearm place the forearm across the breast,
thumb up, and apply to the inner surface a splint extending
to the tips of the fingers, and another to the outer surface,
extending to the wrist.

g. For a fracture of the collarbone bend the forearm to
a right angle in front of the body and support it by a sling.

h. For a broken thigh apply a long splint, reaching from the
armpit to beyond the foot on the outside and another from the
groin to the foot on the inside. A rifle can be used as an outside splint, and a rifle boot for the inner. A blanket rolled into
two rolls, to form a trough, will help to keep a broken leg firm.

i. For a broken lower leg or ankle apply two splints, one on
the outside, the other on the inside of the limb, extending from
the knee to beyond the foot. A bayonet and scabbard are
serviceable when nothing better can be had. Support can be
given by a roll of clothing and two sticks.

j. If no better means are at hand for splinting, tie a broken
leg to the other leg or bind a broken arm to the body.

■ 262. POISONED WOUNDS.—*a.* Snake venom acts quickly. The
main object is to prevent the poison from passing into the
blood circulation. If the wound is on a limb, apply a tourniquet just above the wound to increase bleeding. A necktie,
handkerchief, or bandage can be used as a tourniquet. It
should be tight enough to prevent the blood flowing back
through the veins but not tight enough to prevent the blood
flow in the arteries. Do not leave it on longer than 1 hour.
Whether or not the bite is on a part of the body where you can
use a tourniquet, make a cut ½ by ½ inch, over each fang
mark and, if possible, a cut connecting the two fang punctures.
The cut must be deep enough, ¼ to ½ inch, to secure free
bleeding; then get the poison out of the wound by suction.
This may be done by sucking with your mouth, or by heating
a bottle and applying its mouth tightly over the wound. The
cooling of the bottle produces the suction. Snake venom is
harmless in the mouth unless there are cracks or wounds in

the mouth or lips. Keep the patient quiet and secure medical aid as quickly as you can. *Do not give the patient liquor.* The best aid you can give him is to produce free bleeding followed by suction.

b. Bites of spiders, scorpions, and other insects should be treated in the same manner as snake bites. The proper removal of the stinger is important. This should be done by grasping the stinger with a pair of small forceps and removing all of it. A paste made of baking soda, or a cold, moist dressing, using a diluted solution of salt, soda, or ammonia is helpful.

c. The first-aid treatment for animal bites is the same as that for ordinary wounds. You should get medical advice as soon as possible, however, even though the wound appears unimportant, since animal bites may become quickly infected unless dressed properly.

■ 263. FAINTING.—If the patient can be made comfortable, it is usually best to allow him to lie where he falls; lower his head and shoulders by elevating his hips; loosen the tight clothing. Sprinkling his face with cold water, and inhalations of ammonia or smelling salts are helpful.

■ 264. BURNS.—*a.* Burns may be caused by dry or moist heat, electricity, and chemicals. They are classified in degrees according to the depth to which the tissues are injured. Shock and infection are to be feared in dry burns.

(1) First degree—The skin is reddened but there is no blister.

(2) Second degree—The skin is blistered.

(3) Third degree—The skin is destroyed or charred, as from contact with flames.

b. The following general rules apply to the first-aid treatment of all burns:

(1) Do not pull the clothing from the burned part; snip or cut it off.

(2) Do not break or prick blisters if present.

(3) Treat shock early in all severe burns.

(4) When possible, protect the burn quickly with a sterile dressing, applying medication as indicated in *c* to *f* below.

c. First-degree burns.—The treatment is directed toward the relief of pain since the skin is unbroken and there is no danger from infection. Any substance that will relieve the pain is satisfactory. An oily substance such as petrolatum (vaseline), olive oil, or castor oil is usable. Cold water or soda in water is soothing when immediately applied. It must be remembered that if the burn is at all serious, such as found in second- or third-degree burns, oily substances are not to be applied.

d. *Second-degree burns.*—Here the injury must be regarded as an open wound; only material that is known to be clean can be used. Remove the loose clothing, but do not try to remove material that sticks to the skin. The application of sterile gauze soaked in a solution of Epsom salts (2 tablespoonfuls to a pint of boiled water) is very good. The dressings should be kept moist and warm until further aid is obtained. The best treatment is application of gauze saturated with 2 percent picric acid solution applied securely but not tightly. A 5 percent tannic acid solution similarly applied is of equal value. *Never apply iodine or similar substance to a burn and never apply absorbent cotton to a burned surface.* Shock is always present to some degree in every case.

e. *Third-degree burns.*—These are always serious and require medical attention promptly. The first-aid treatment consists chiefly of keeping the patient warm and treating shock. If medical attention can be obtained promptly, it is best merely to lay a sterile dressing lightly on the wound. If over 30 minutes will elapse before help can be obtained, one of the dressings used for second-degree burns should be applied.

f. *Chemical burns.*—Burns caused by acids or alkalies should be washed with large quantities of water, preferably lukewarm, until the chemical is thoroughly removed. All clothing should be cut away with scissors. Apply a salve dressing after the chemical is completely removed, and secure a medical officer's services. Eye burns require careful attention. The best first-aid treatment is to flush the eye thoroughly with clean olive oil, mineral oil, or castor oil. If these are not available, use water; a drinking fountain that throws a stream is excellent for this purpose. After washing, the eye should be covered with a moist dressing and further medical aid secured.

■ 265. SUNSTROKE.—a. Sunstroke is a very dangerous condition, usually caused by direct exposure to the rays of the sun,

215

especially when the air is moist. The symptoms are head-ache, dizziness, oppression, and sometimes vomiting; the skin is hot and dry, and the face flushed; the pulse is rapid and full; the temperature is high, often ranging between 107° and 110°. Unconsciousness usually occurs, and the body becomes relaxed; however, convulsions may occur.

b. *Treatment.*—Remove the person to a shady, cool place, if possible, and loosen or remove the clothing. Lay the patient on his back with shoulders elevated. Apply cold to the head by means of wet cloths, ice bags, or ice. The brain cannot withstand the effects of high temperatures. Cool the body by giving cold baths for 20 minutes at a time combined with brisk massage of the limbs and trunk. Cold wet cloths or ice bags may be used. Wrapping the body in a sheet and pouring on cold water every few minutes is very effective. Do not overdo any of these procedures. Stop every few minutes to observe the effects on the patient. If the skin again gets hot repeat the treatment. Do not give him stimulants to drink while unconsciousness lasts.

■ 266. HEAT EXHAUSTION.—This is caused by exposure to high temperature as found in boiler rooms, foundries, bakeries, and similar places. The first signs of heat exhaustion are dizziness, nausea, and uncertain gait. The face is pale, the body is covered with a heavy perspiration, and the skin is cold and clammy. Breathing is shallow, the pulse is weak, and the temperature may be normal or somewhat elevated. Fainting may occur, or prostration may become severe. Remove the patient to circulating cool air; place him on his back and let him drink freely of cool salt water (1 teaspoonful of table salt in a pint of water). Call a medical officer if the patient does not recover promptly.

■ 267. FREEZING.—a. The symptoms of freezing are cold in the part, then pain, and finally, loss of sensation. The affected part becomes white or bluish white. Slowly thaw the frozen part by using extra clothing, applying it to another part of the body, or wrapping it in cloths soaked in cool water. Do not expose frozen tissues to a hot stove or radiator. Do not rub the frozen part either with the bare hands or with snow; the tissues will be bruised and torn, and gangrene may result. Medical attention is usually necessary after freezing.

b. When a man becomes unconscious from cold, if possible carry him into a cool room, cover him well with blankets, and move his arms and legs gently but steadily. When consciousness returns, give him warm drinks and let him lie quietly.

■ **268. PAIN IN THE ABDOMEN.**—Pain in the abdomen or what is known as a common "stomach ache," may be due to a number of causes, many of which may be serious. Any case where there is nausea and vomiting, accompanying or following pain and tenderness over all or any part of the abdomen, and with pain and tenderness in the lower right parts of the abdomen may mean appendicitis. Appendicitis may also occur without nausea. If you or one of your comrades should have these symptoms, see a medical officer at once. In the meantime no food, no water, and especially no laxatives, should be taken until directed by a medical officer.

■ **269. ATHLETE'S FOOT.**—Ringworm of the feet or "athlete's foot" is a very common skin disease. In some cases it may become so severe as to be disabling. It consists chiefly of an inflammation of the skin between the toes and on the soles of the feet, but it may also appear on the hands. Usually there is considerable itching. It is usually spread by contact of the bare feet with the floors, mats, and benches of showers and swimming pools; but you may also acquire it by using or wearing the towels, slippers, shoes, or other articles of some one who has it. The care of the feet, as described in section II, chapter 11, is important in the prevention and control of this disease. Keep your feet dry, and after a bath dry carefully the spaces between your toes before putting on your socks and shoes. If your feet perspire a great deal, apply the issue foot powder twice a day. Your corporal or the noncommissioned officer in charge of your unit will issue this powder to you when you ask for it. If you think you have athlete's foot you should see a medical officer as soon as possible so that you may be cured and will not spread the disease among other members of your organization.

■ **270. GASES USED IN WARFARE.**—The following simple general rules will help you in giving first-aid treatment to men suffering from gases used in warfare.

a. In handling a gassed man always wear your mask and,

if you have them, gloves. If you do not have gloves, rub your hands with dry lime, or wash them with soap and water as soon as possible after handling the man.

b. Move the man from the gassed area as soon as possible. If possible move him from low ground or woods to a hillside or knoll. Do not carry him into a dugout or cellar. Gas is heavier than air and will descend and cling to the lower levels. *Do not allow a gassed man to talk or walk.*

c. Remove the man's equipment and clothing, unless undue exposure to the cold will result, but leave his mask on until you are certain there is no gas in the air.

d. Remember that mustard gas from the clothing, equipment, or body of a man gassed with mustard will cling to you or your clothing. Avoid blankets, litters, or areas on the ground occupied by such cases.

e. Prevent men gassed with mustard from rubbing their eyes, mouths, or bodies. Do *not* bandage their eyes.

■ 271. PEACETIME GASES.—The chief poisonous gases encountered in civil life are illuminating gas, carbon monoxide (motor exhausts), charcoal, and mine gases. The first thing to do in all of these gases is to get the patient into fresh air. The fresh air of a warm room is preferable to extremely cold air. If breathing is weak or irregular or has stopped, artificial respiration by the Schaefer method should be started and continued until normal respiration has been established. A medical officer should always be called, since the patient may die even after breathing is apparently normal.

■ 272. ARTIFICIAL RESPIRATION.—Asphyxia, suffocation, or cessation of breathing occurs most frequently in drowning, electrical shock, and gas poisoning. The safest and most effective method of applying artificial respiration is the prone pressure or Schaefer method. Oxygen respirators, which are available at many bathing beaches and military stations, are very efficient in trained hands, but for unskilled personnel, are less satisfactory than the Schaefer method.

■ 273. DROWNING.—*a.* Being under water for over 5 minutes is usually fatal, but an effort to revive the apparently drowned should always be made. It is very important that artificial respiration be started at the earliest possible moment after the patient has been removed from the water.

b. (1) Lay the patient face down, force his mouth open, pull the tongue forward, and remove false teeth, juice, vomitus, or debris from his mouth and throat.

(2) Raise him by the hips in order to drain the water from his lungs.

(3) Lay him on his belly, preferably at a spot where his head will be lower than his feet. One of his arms should be extended over his head, the other bent at the elbow so that his face can be turned on the side and rest on the hands.

(4) Kneel astride the patient's thighs, with your knees placed at such a distance from his hips as will allow you to exert the pressure on his lower ribs as described below. Place the palms of your hands on the small of his back with your fingers on his lower ribs, your little fingers just touching his lowest rib, with your thumbs and fingers in natural position and the tips of your fingers out of sight just around the sides of his chest wall. The heels of the hands should be placed as far from the backbone as possible without slipping off.

(5) With your arms held straight, swing forward slowly so that the weight of your body is gradually brought to bear upon the patient. Do not bend your elbows. This operation should take about 2 seconds. (See fig. 86.)

(6) Now immediately swing backward so as to remove all pressure completely and suddenly. Leave the hands in place if possible. (See fig. 87.)

(7) After about 2 seconds repeat the operation. The cycle of compression and release should take about 4 or 5 seconds and should be repeated at the rate of 12 to 15 times per minute.

(8) Continue the operation without interruption until natural breathing is restored, or until the subject is unquestionably dead. Remember, many patients have died because artificial respiration has been stopped too soon. Always continue the operation for 2 hours or longer.

(9) Aside from the resuscitation, the most valuable aid that can be rendered is keeping the patient warm. After artificial respiration has been started, have an assistant loosen the clothing and wrap the patient in any clothing that is available. Use hot bricks, pads, heaters, or similar means, but be sure the person is not burned by your treatment.

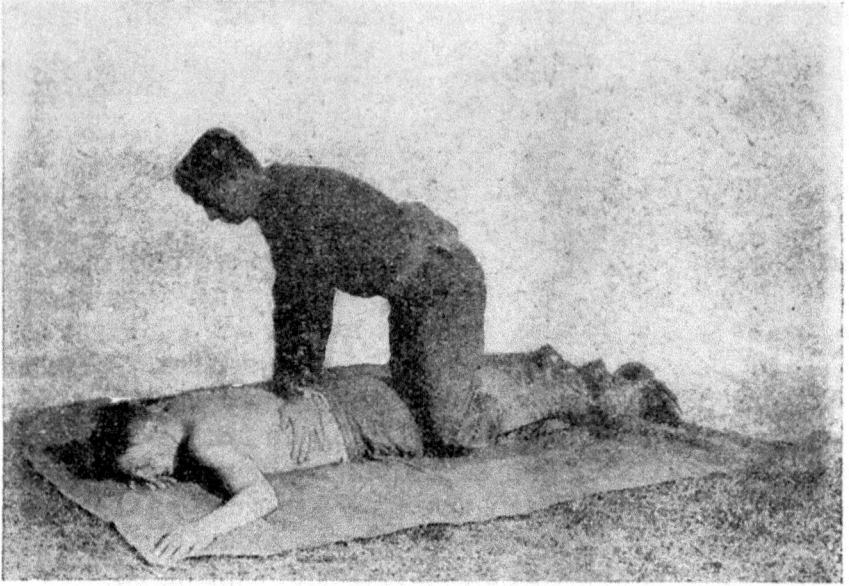

FIGURE 86.—Artificial respiration, first position.

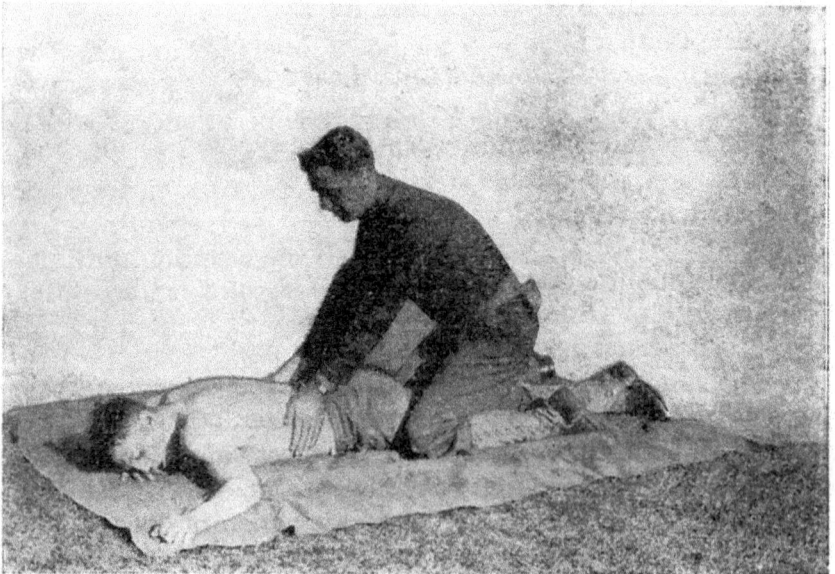

FIGURE 87.—Artificial respiration, second position.

(10) When the patient revives he should be kept lying down and not allowed to stand or sit up; this will prevent undue strain on the heart. Stimulants such as hot tea or coffee, or aromatic spirits of ammonia, can be given as soon as the patient is perfectly conscious.

(11) At times a patient, after temporary recovery of respiration, stops breathing again; artificial respiration should be resumed *at once*.

(12) Due to the length of time this operation may be kept up, one, two, or more operators may be necessary. A change of operators can be made without loss of rhythm of respiration. If this point is remembered no confusion will result when the change occurs and the respiratory count will be kept even. The great danger is stopping artificial respiration too soon. In many cases, breathing has been established after 3 or 4 hours of artificial respiration, and there are instances where normal breathing has been reestablished after 8 hours. The ordinary and general tests for death should not be accepted; a medical officer should make several careful examinations at various intervals before the procedure is allowed to be stopped.

■ 274. ELECTRICAL SHOCK.—The rescue of the victim from a live wire is always dangerous. If the switch is near, turn the current off, but lose no time in looking for the switch. Use a dry stick, dry clothing, dry rope, or some other dry nonconductor in removing the victim from the wire. Start artificial respiration immediately by the Schaefer method as previously described. Do not regard early stiffening as a sign of death; always keep up the artificial respiration for several hours.

■ 275. LITTERS.—If it becomes necessary to move an injured man for even a short distance, it is best to use a service litter which is furnished by the Medical Department. If a litter is not available, one of the following means may be used to construct one:

a. Camp cots, window shutters, doors, benches, and ladders, properly padded.

b. Sacks, bags, or bedticks, by ripping the bottoms or snipping off the corners, passing two poles through them, and tying crosspieces to the poles to keep them apart.

c. A shelter half, a blanket, piece of matting, or carpet may be fastened to poles by tacks or twine.

d. Hay, straw, or leafy twigs, over a framework of poles and cross sticks.

e. Rope, wire, or rawhide may be woven between poles and this network covered with a blanket.

f. The usual way is to use blankets or shelter tents, and poles about 7 feet long. The blanket is spread on the ground.

FIGURE 88.—Litter improvised with blankets.

One pole is laid across the center of the blanket which is then folded over it. The second pole is placed across the center of the new fold and the blanket is folded over the second pole as over the first and the free end of the blanket fixed. (See fig. 88.)

g. A litter may also be prepared by turning two or three blouses inside out and buttoning them up, sleeves in, then passing poles through the sleeves; the backs of the blouses form the bed.

■ 276. OTHER MEANS OF TRANSPORTING THE INJURED.—When the condition of the injured man is such that it is not necessary to carry him on a litter he may be moved for a short distance in one of the following ways:

a. *Rifle-coat seat.*—A good seat may be made by running the barrel of a rifle through each sleeve of an overcoat, turned inside out and buttoned up, sleeves inside, so that the coat lies back up, collar to the rear. One bearer rolls the tail tightly around the barrels and takes his grasp over them; the other bearer holds the rifles by the butts, trigger guards up. (See fig. 89.)

FIGURE 89.—Rifle-coat seat.

b. *Rifle-blanket seat.*—Fold blanket once from side to side. Lay a rifle transversely upon it across its center so that the butt and muzzle project beyond the edges; fold one end of the blanket upon the other end and lay a second rifle upon the new center in the same manner as before. The free end of the blanket is folded upon the end containing the first rifle so as to project a couple of inches beyond the first rifle. The litter is raised from the ground with trigger guards up.

c. One bearer.—A single bearer may support a slightly injured man or carry a patient in his arms (fig. 90) or on his back (fig. 91) or across his shoulders (fig. 92). If the patient is helpless, the last named is best. This is done as follows:

FIGURE 90.—Patient carried in arms.

(1) Turn the patient on his face, and step astride his body, facing toward the patient's head with hands under his armpits, and lift him to his knees; then, clasping your hands over his abdomen, lift him to his feet; next seize the right wrist of the patient with your left hand and draw the arm over your head and down upon your left shoulder; now shift yourself in front, stoop, pass your right arm between the legs and grasp the patient's right wrist; with your left hand grasp

the patient's left hand and steady it against your side when you rise.

(2) In lowering the patient the motions are reversed. Should the patient be wounded in such a manner as to require these motions to be conducted from the right side instead of left, as described above, the change is simply one of hands;

FIGURE 91.—Patient carried on back.

the motions proceed as directed substituting right for left and vice versa.

d. Two bearers.—The bearers take position at patient, one man between the patient's legs and one at his head, both facing toward his feet. The rear bearer, having raised the patient to a sitting posture, clasps him from behind around the body under the arms, the front bearer passes his hands from the outside under the flexed knees; both rise together.

This method requires no effort on the part of the patient but is not applicable to severe injuries of the extremities.

e. Horseback.—(1) The help required to mount a disabled man will depend upon the site and nature of his injury. In many cases he is able to help himself materially. The horse, blindfolded if necessary, is held by an attendant.

FIGURE 92.—Patient carried across shoulders.

(2) Once mounted, the patient should be made as safe and comfortable as possible. A comrade may be mounted behind him to guide the horse; otherwise a lean-back may be provided, made of a blanket roll, a pillow, or a bag filled with leaves or grass. If the patient is very weak, the lean-back may be made of a sapling bent into an arch over the cantle of the saddle, its ends securely fastened.

CHAPTER 15

THE RATION

■ 277. THE RATION.—A ration is the allowance of food for the feeding of one person for one day. Each soldier is authorized to receive one ration each day that he is on the active list of the Army.

■ 278. KINDS OF RATION.—There are several different kinds of rations used in the Army of the United States, but the ones in which you will be interested are the following:

a. The *garrison ration* is that which the Government prescribes in time of peace for all persons entitled to a ration except under special circumstances when other rations are prescribed. The different items such as meat, fresh vegetables and fruit, beverages, bread, and other articles of food which make up the ration are called "ration components." The number of components and the amount of each required to give a soldier a well-balanced and nourishing daily diet have been carefully determined by food experts. The money value of the ration is figured each month from the wholesale costs of food to the Government, and your organization mess account is credited with the total amount required to feed all the men in your unit. The meals served by your organization mess sergeant in time of peace, and while your organization is in a post, camp, or cantonment, will usually be prepared from the components of the garrison ration. After the mess sergeant has made up his menus he will buy the various articles of food required from the money which the Government has credited to your organization mess account. Some of these items he may buy from the quartermaster commissary. Others he may buy from local markets or farmers, in order to take advantage of certain foods in season or because the commissary may not have them in stock. Any savings which he makes are called "ration savings" and become part of your unit mess fund, to be expended by your organization commander on extras for the mess on holidays or other special occasions.

b. The *field ration* is that prescribed for use in time of war or other emergency. In time of peace it may be used some-

227

times for training purposes. Its components are prescribed by the War Department or the commanding general of the field forces. No ration savings are permitted and the components are issued "in kind." This means that instead of your mess sergeant buying the various components of the ration from the quartermaster or in local markets, the quartermaster will issue to him certain items of food sufficient to feed all the members of your organization. There are four kinds of field rations—

(1) *Field ration A* corresponds as nearly as practicable to the peacetime garrison ration and contains "perishable" items such as fresh meat and vegetables. It is issued as often as the circumstances will permit.

(2) *Field ration B* corresponds as nearly as practicable to field ration *A*, except that nonperishable or canned products replace the perishable items.

(3) *Field ration C* consists of previously cooked or prepared food, packed in sealed cans, and which may be eaten either hot or cold. Each ration consists of three cans of meat and vegetables and three cans of crackers, sugar, and soluble coffee.

(4) *Field ration D* consists of three 4-ounce bars of concentrated chocolate.

(5) Sometimes the field ration may be a combination of types *C* and *D*. In this case it will usually consist of two cans of meat and vegetables, two cans of the crackers, sugar, and soluble coffee, and two of the 4-ounce bars of concentrated chocolate.

■ 279. Our Government spends more money for the food of its soldiers than any other nation in the world. A great deal of time is spent on the training of mess sergeants and cooks and you will soon discover that your food is better prepared, there is more of it, and it has a greater variety than that of most families in civil life. It is especially selected to build up your body and give you the energy and endurance which will carry you to success on the battlefield. If at first it seems strange to you and you miss the meals with which you are familiar, do not be tempted to eat in neighboring civilian restaurants. You will profit both in your pocket and stomach if you eat all of your meals in your organization mess.

■ 280. When you go into the field your mess sergeant and cooks will accompany you. There is special cooking equipment in your organization which will follow you. On this your food can be prepared in the same way as it is cooked on the stoves of your barracks or cantonment. During combat all organization kitchens are usually grouped in sheltered locations in rear where the meals can be prepared without interference by the enemy. Immediately after dark, trucks bring the cooked meals forward so that they can be distributed by carrying parties.

■ 281. DURING CAMPAIGN.—During a campaign the commanding general of your division or a higher commander may direct that each soldier carry a field ration as part of his field equipment. He may decide to do this because he feels that the condition of the roads or transportation may delay the arrival of the cooked meals and in such a case he wants to be sure that no soldier goes hungry. A ration which is carried by a soldier is called an individual reserve. It will probably be field ration C or D, or a combination of both.

■ 282. a. It may sometimes happen during campaigns that you and one or more of your comrades may be separated from your unit. If there is another organization near you, you will always be able to get a meal from it by reporting to its first sergeant or mess sergeant; giving your name and organization and explaining how you happen to be separated from your own unit.

b. If there is no other organization near, it may then be necessary for you and your comrades to cook your own meals, using your mess kits for this purpose and the food you have with you. Since you will probably have field ration C with you, this will be very easy. Simply heat one or more of the cans in hot water, and open them. If you, or any of your comrades, have had boy scout training you will probably be able to prepare a very good meal from the ration.

■ 283. FIRE FOR COOKING.—a. Remember that the best fire for cooking is a small clear one, or, better yet, a few brisk coals. With your bayonet, dig a trench in the ground, laid with the wind, about a foot long, 4 inches wide, and 6 inches deep. Gather a number of sticks about 1 inch in diameter. Dead limbs taken from a tree are dryer than those picked up from the ground. Split some of these and shave them into kindling. Start the fire in the trench gradually, piling on the heavier wood as the fire grows. When the trench is full of burning wood, allow it a few minutes to burn down to coals. Then rest the meat can and cup over the trench and start the cooking. You may support them, if necessary, with green sticks.

b. If the ground is rocky or stony, and you cannot scrape a trench in the soil, you may make your fire between two small, flat stones, or with two parallel logs. These should be placed so that the draft will pass between them. The meat can can be placed on the stones, across the fire, and the cup for boiling coffee at the end, away from the draft, where it will get the most heat. Always see that the fire is completely out before you leave.

CHAPTER 16

PAY AND ALLOWANCES

■ 284. RATE OF PAY.—When you first enter the military service, your rate of pay will be $21.00 per month. This pay is in addition to the food, clothing, medical, and dental attention which the government provides you without charge. After a period of 4 months, however, and provided you have not demonstrated inefficiency or other unfitness, your pay will be raised to $30.00 per month. From that point on your pay need only be limited by your ambition, your attention to duty, and the manner in which you qualify yourself for promotion. Remember that promotion is on a strictly competitive basis. Your organization commander will promote the man who he believes is best qualified for the next vacancy, and on whom he has found he can depend. The various grades, with their rates of monthly pay as authorized by Congress in the act of September 16, 1940, are given below:

First grade—Master sergeant_____ $126.00
Second grade—First sergeant and technical sergeant_ 84.00
Third grade—Staff sergeant_____ 72.00
Fourth grade—Sergeant_____ 60.00
Fifth grade—Corporal_____ 54.00
Sixth grade—Private, 1st class_____ 36.00
Seventh grade—Private with over 4 months' service_ 30.00
Private with less than 4 months' service during first
   enlistment period or whose inefficiency or other
   unfitness has been determined under regulations__ 21.00

■ 285. SPECIALIST.—If you are a private or a private, 1st class, you may have certain qualifications which will enable you to be rated as a specialist and receive the following pay in addition to the pay of your grade. Specialist ratings are given in a limited number to men trained to do certain kinds of work such as electricians, mechanics, radio operators, riveters, woodworkers, clerks, or cooks:

Per month

Specialist 1st class_____ $30. 00

Specialist 2d class_____ 25. 00

Specialist 3d class_____ 20. 00

Specialist 4th class_____ 15. 00

Specialist 5th class_____ 6. 00

Specialist 6th class_____ 3. 00

■ 286. AIR CORPS.—If you are in the Air Corps, during such
time as you are authorized to take part regularly and frequently in aerial flights, you will receive additional pay of
50 percent of the pay of your grade. If you are a private,
private, 1st class, corporal, or sergeant and are rated as an air
mechanic, 1st class, you will receive the pay of the second
grade; or if you are rated as an air mechanic 2d class, you
will receive the pay of the third grade during the time you hold
your rating.

■ 287. DECORATIONS.—For certain decorations, or awards for
distinguished service, you will receive an additional amount
of money each month.

■ 288. FURLOUGH ALLOWANCE.—If you are granted a furlough, you are entitled to an allowance for rations during the
period of the furlough. This allowance will be paid to you
when you report back to your station on or before the date
of expiration of the furlough. It will not be paid if you over-
stay your furlough unless you are excused for overstaying by
your commanding officer. It will not be paid if you fail to
report back to your own station.

■ 289. DEPOSITS.—While you are in active military service
you may deposit with the Government, as savings, any amount
not less than $5.00.   Your deposits will be repaid to you when
you are discharged and, if they have been deposited for 6
months or longer, will draw interest. Your deposits are not
subject to collection for debts unless you authorize, in writing,
collection of amounts due the United States or for your
discharge by purchase.

■ 290. ALLOTMENTS.—You may make an allotment of your pay
for the support of your family or dependent relatives, or for
payment of premiums for commercial life insurance if such
insurance is on your own life. The amount allotted will be

deducted from your pay each month and paid directly to the insurance company or person you have designated in your allotment.

■ 291. GOVERNMENT INSURANCE.—You may take out a policy for National life insurance on your own life. The premiums may be paid by you directly to the Veterans Administration in monthly payments, or you may authorize their deduction from your pay each month.

■ 292. If you desire any further information regarding allotments, deposits, or Government insurance, see your first sergeant. He will be glad to help you.

■ 293. DEDUCTIONS.—Deductions will be made from your pay if you are found responsible for loss or damage to Government property and if you are absent without leave or absent sick, not in line of duty. You do not lose pay for sickness or injury in line of duty or for absence in confinement; however, the time lost by absence in confinement, by absence without leave, or by absence due to sickness not in line of duty has to be made up at the end of your enlistment period. Two-thirds of your monthly pay may be taken to satisfy any amount which you may owe the United States or which you may owe to the company fund, post exchange, or United States Motion Picture Service.

■ 294. TRAVEL PAY.—Upon honorable discharge from the service you will be entitled to travel pay at the rate of 5 cents per mile for the distance from the place you are discharged to the place you were accepted for enlistment, enrollment, or muster into the Army, not including sea travel.

■ 295. BURIAL EXPENSES.—The Government provides the burial expenses for a soldier who dies while in active service.

CHAPTER 17

LAST WILL AND TESTAMENT

■ **296.** Certain advantages may accrue to the estate of any person who has made a will. Hence, you should consider carefully whether or not to make a will. You should decide *now.* Do not put it off until tomorrow.

a. A will is invalid if it does not meet certain legal requirements established by the laws of the State where it is to be filed for probate. These requirements vary in each State. It is almost impossible to forecast the particular set of requirements which will have to be met by a given will unless the facts in each case are known. This is so because where land is involved the will must ordinarily satisfy the requirements of the State where the land is situated, whereas in the case of personal property (property other than land, such as money, stocks, bonds, a business, a car), the will must satisfy the requirements of the State in which the testator "legally resides" or has his "permanent home" (sometimes called "domicile") at the time of his death. Your military station is ordinarily not your "legal residence" or "permanent home." You can perceive that many difficult legal questions may arise in connection with making a will.

b. If your property is substantial in value, or if you own land, or if you wish to provide for two or more people as beneficiaries, your case may be complicated. Consequently, under ordinary circumstances you are advised to consult competent legal counsel in the preparation of a will. Assistance in the selection of counsel may be obtained by communicating with the nearest advisory board for registrants or by letter to the American Bar Association, Washington, D. C. Officers of the Judge Advocate General's Department will also lend assistance.

c. However, instances may arise in which you wish to make a will, when circumstances make it difficult or impossible to obtain legal assistance such as on the eve of battle.

d. For your assistance in such an emergency and in such case only, the following form may be used. It is legal in form

234

in nearly all States and the District of Columbia. The will must be dated, signed by you *in the presence of all the witnesses assembled together and by each of them at the same time it is signed by you.* This must be done with the greatest of care. It should also be filed or kept in a safe place or perhaps mailed to your home or to a trusted friend.

e. Above all, because the form on page 237 is intended for use only to meet the needs of an emergency, it should be made as a temporary will only and should be replaced by a more carefully drawn will with assistance of legal counsel as soon as time and circumstances permit. *The form in this manual can be completed, signed (by yourself and the three witnesses), detached by clipping along the black line and filed or mailed.*

FORM OF WILL[1]

I, _____, of _____,
           (Name of soldier)   (City or town)
_____, now in the actual military service of the
   (State)
United States and stationed at _____, hereby
revoking any and all prior wills or any part thereof, do de-
vise and bequeath all of my estate to _____
                               (Name of beneficiary)

my _____, for $\frac{her}{his}$ own use and benefit for-
  (Relationship. if any)

ever, and I hereby appoint $\frac{her}{him}$ my $\frac{executrix}{tor}$ without bond,
with full power to sell, mortgage, lease, or in any way dispose
of the whole or any part of my estate.

(See note *c* below)

_____
(Signature of soldier in presence of three
witnesses all together)

Signed, published, and declared by _____,
                               (Name of soldier)
testator above named, as and for his last will and testament
in the presence of each of us, who at his request and in his
presence, in the presence of each other, at the same time,
have hereunto subscribed our names as witnesses this _____

day of _____, 194__, at _____, _____.
                     (City or town)   (State)

    1. _____, _____
         (Name of witness)   (Address of witness)

    2. _____, _____
         (Name of witness)   (Address of witness)

    3. _____, _____
         (Name of witness)   (Address of witness)

[1] See *notes* on back of this sheet for instructions for completion
of form.

NOTES

a. Your will must be signed by three witnesses as provided by the form.

b. In some States a male under 21 years of age is not competent to make a will. If you are under 21, make it for the time of the emergency, but consult competent counsel at the first opportunity thereafter.

c. Wife and children.—In every State a wife and children have certain legal rights in the estate of the testator. A wife generally cannot be willed less than the share to which she is entitled by law where no will is made. In most States a child takes the full share provided for by law, unless the will expressly provides otherwise.

Note that the above form of will is designed for only one beneficiary. Usually this will be a near relative or trusted friend. If you have one or more children and wish each of them to receive his share as provided by law, this will be the result in most States if you add nothing to the above form.

But if you wish one or more children to receive nothing, you must add at the end of the above form where starred (*):
"My child [ren] is to have no part of my estate."

"My child [ren] $\frac{is}{are}$ to have no part of my estate."

Or as may be desired in most cases, if you wish to provide primarily for your beneficiary and to entrust the care of your children to him or her, you may insert at the end of the above form where starred (*): "Provision for my children is purposely omitted as I have the utmost faith in my beneficiary."

d. In the event of marriage, divorce, or birth of a child after the will has been made or in the event of the death of any beneficiary named in the will, the soldier should consult competent counsel even though his will was prepared carefully and with the assistance of counsel.

e. Soldiers residing in or having their home in Louisiana may use the above form of will under emergency circumstances, *Provided*, they write it *entirely in their own handwriting.*

f. Except for soldiers residing in or having their home in Louisiana, the will may be either typewritten or written in longhand by the soldier or some other person for him, or may be made on the form provided in FM 21–100.

g. Remember that this form should be used *only* when assistance of competent counsel is not possible and never if it is available. In any event, use it only to meet a situation of extreme emergency and even then consult competent counsel as soon as possible after the emergency has passed. It is for temporary needs only.

APPENDIX

GLOSSARY OF COMMON MILITARY EXPRESSIONS

AWOL.—Absent without authority.

Aide, or Aide-de-camp.—A personal assistant to a general officer.

Base.—The element on which a movement is regulated.

Blind.—A money fine of a court-martial sentence.

Bob-tail—A dishonorable discharge.

Bucking for orderly.—Extra efforts for personal appearance when competing for post of orderly to the commanding officer.

Bust.—To reduce a noncommissioned officer to the grade of private.

Chow.—Food.

Cits.—Civilian clothing.

CO or KO.—Commanding officer.

Distance.—Space between elements in the direction front to rear.

Dogtags.—Identification disks.

Doughboy (dough).—An infantryman.

Dud.—An unexploded shell.

Field, in the.—Campaigning against an enemy under actual or assumed conditions.

File.—A column of men one behind the other.

Fox hole.—Pit dug by a soldier to protect his body.

GI.—Government issue; galvanized iron.

Guard house lawyer.—A person who knows little but talks much about regulations, military law, and soldiers' "rights."

Hash mark.—A service stripe.

Hike.—To march.

Hitch.—An enlistment period.

IC.—Inspected and condemned.

Interval.—Space between elements in the direction parallel to the front.

Jawbone.—Credit. To buy without money. To shoot a weapon over a qualification course when it doesn't count for record.

Kick.—A dishonorable discharge.

KP.—Kitchen police.

Lance jack.—A temporary or acting corporal with the same duties and authority of a regularly appointed corporal, but without the pay of the grade.

Mess gear.—A soldier's individual mess kit, knife, fork, spoon, and cup.

MP.—Military police.

Mule skinner.—A teamster.

Noncom.—A noncommissioned officer.

OD.—Olive drab or officer of the day.

On the carpet.—Called before the commanding officer for disciplinary reasons.

Over the hill.—To desert.

Pace.—A step 30 inches long.

Piece.—The rifle or weapon.

Pup tent.—Shelter tent.

Reup or takeon.—To reenlist.

Shave tail.—A second lieutenant.

Skipper.—The company commander.

Sniper.—An expert rifle shot detailed to pick off enemy leaders or individuals who expose themselves.

The old man.—The company commander; commanding officer.

Top sergeant or top kick.—The first sergeant.

INDEX

241

BASIC FIELD MANUAL

SOLDIER'S HANDBOOK

CHANGES |
No. 1 |

WAR DEPARTMENT,
WASHINGTON, May 4, 1942.

FM 21–100, July 23, 1941, is changed as follows:

■ 31. In your home   *   *   *   career as a soldier.

*   *   *   *   *   *   *

e. The salute is always given whenever you recognize an offi-cer.   It is likewise given whether or not you are wearing a head covering.

*   *   *   *   *   *   *

[A. G. 062.11 (3–18–42).]   (C 1, May 4, 1942.)

■ 32. The following situations will assist you in remembering when you do not or need not salute:

*   *   *   *   *   *   *

j. Rescinded.

[A. G. 062.11 (3–18–42).]   (C 1, May 4, 1942.)

■ 37. HAT CORD.—At a distance   *   *   *   color of the piping.

*   *   *   *   *   *   *

n. Armored Force—Green piped with white.

[A. G. 062.11 (3–18–42).]   (C 1, May 4, 1942.)

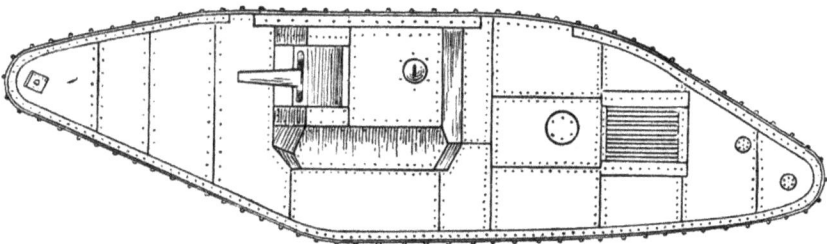

Figure 1½.—Armored Force insignia.

[A. G. 062.11 (3–18–42).]   (C 1, May 4, 1942.)

■ 44. All officers wear a band of brown braid 3 inches from the end of each sleeve of the service coat.   All warrant officers and enlisted men who served honorably as officers in the **first** World War wear a similar band of forest green braid.

[A. G. 062.11 (3–18–42).]   (C 1, May 4, 1942.)

■ 45. Noncommissioned officers wear * * * and the fatigue
uniform. The chevrons for the different grades are shown in
figures 5 and 5½.

INSIGNIA, SLEEVE, CHEVRON

**TECHNICIAN
(3º GRADE)**   **TECHNICIAN
(4ᵀᴴ GRADE)**   **TECHNICIAN
(5ᵀᴴ GRADE)**

Figure 5½.—Insignia for technicians, third, fourth, and fifth grades.

[A. G. 062.11 (3–18–42).]   (C 1, May 4, 1942.)

■ 64. The United States rifle * * * with a safety lock.
(See fig. 7.)

*   *   *   *   *   *   *

d. Care of the rifle.

*   *   *   *   *   *   *

(3) *Cleaning gas cylinder, M1 rifle.*—Carbon will accumulate
* * * and failure to feed.

(a) *Spline type.*—To remove accumulated deposits of carbon
from the gas cylinder, remove the lock screw and remove carbon,
using the screw driver blade of the combination tool. The gas
cylinder lock may be removed and the lock screw reinserted in
the gas cylinder and threaded in enough to break loose the carbon. The inside of the gas cylinder should be thoroughly wiped
clean and oiled at the conclusion of firing.

(b) *Screw-on type.*—Scrape the carbon from the exposed
surface of the front of the gas cylinder and gas cylinder plug
and piston head after extensive firing. Clean the gas cylinder

plug and the grooves in the gas cylinder to insure correct seating of the plug. The frequency of this cleaning depends on the amount of firing. A sharp-bladed instrument similar to a mess kit knife should be used to remove the carbon from the gas cylinder plug and piston head.

(*c*) **Both types.**—If firing is contemplated the next day tip the muzzle down, place a few drops of oil into the gas cylinder between the piston and the walls of the cylinder, and operate the rod by hand a few times. Wipe clean the exterior of the gas cylinder, the operating rod, and the front sight and oil lightly. If no firing is contemplated in the next week or two remove the operating rod and the gas cylinder lock screw (or gas cylinder plug), leaving the cylinder open at both ends. Clean the cylinder with a rod and patches in exactly the same manner as the bore is cleaned. Hold the rifle so that no water will get into the gas port. *Do not remove the gas cylinder for cleaning.* Clean the piston head and rod with cleaner or with water and dry thoroughly. Oil the rod and the cylinder before reassembling. Carbon may be removed at this time. If abrasive cloth is used care should be taken that the corners of the plug (or lock screw) or piston head are not rounded.

*　　*　　*　　*　　*　　*　　*

[A. G. 062.11 (3–18–42).]　(C 1, May 4, 1942.)

■ 81. Soon after your equipment is issued to you, * * * you will receive instructions as to how it will be carried.

Field equipment, enlisted men (other than clothing worn on person)

Article	Dismounted	Mounted on horse (except artillery drivers)	Driver, horse (artillery only)	Driver, vehicle	Men mounted in vehicle*
*			*		*
Blankets, wool	In pack carrier. Carried on back or in cargo vehicle.	In cantle or blanket roll.	In cantle or blanket roll.	In pack carrier or in blanket roll. Carried on back or in/on vehicle.	In pack carrier or in blanket roll. Carried on back or in/on vehicle.
Bucket, watering, canvas.		Attached to off (right) saddlebag, under canteen, with thong or coat strap.			
Canteen, cup and cover.	On belt, left rear.	Slung from off (right) cantle ring and attached to off saddlebag.	Slung from near (left) cantle ring, off horse and attached to saddlebag.	On belt, left rear or in/on vehicle.	On belt, left rear or in/on vehicle.
Cap, field	Worn, or in haversack.			Worn, or in haversack.	Worn, or in haversack.
Carrier, wire cutters	On belt, left front.	On belt, left front.			On belt, left front.
Case, canvas, dispatch.	On right side, slung by strap passing over left shoulder.	On right side, slung by strap passing over left shoulder, or modified so as to attach to left front of field belt.			On right side, slung by strap passing over left shoulder, or in/on vehicle.

Item					
Compass, lensatic or prismatic.	On belt, right front	On belt, right front	On belt, right front		On belt, right front.
Compass, watch	In pocket	In pocket	In pocket	In pocket.	In pocket.
Flashlight	In bag, canvas, field, or in haversack.	In near (left) saddlebag.	In near (left) saddlebag.	In haversack, in saddlebag, or in vehicle.	In bag, canvas, field, or in haversack.
Glasses, field	On right side, slung by strap passing over left shoulder.	On right side, slung by strap passing over left shoulder.	On right side, slung by strap passing over left shoulder.	On right side, slung by strap passing over left shoulder.	On right side, slung by strap passing over left shoulder.
Gloves, any type	Worn, or in haversack.	Worn, or in near (left) saddlebag.	Worn, or in near (left) saddlebag.	Worn, or in haversack.	Worn, or in haversack.
Goggles		Worn, or in near (left) saddlebag.	Worn, or in near (left) saddlebag.	Worn, or in shirt pocket.	Worn, or in shirt pocket.
Handkerchiefs	In blanket roll	Near (left) saddlebag.	Near (left) saddlebag, off horse.	In blanket roll, or in saddlebag.	In blanket roll.
Hat, service		Attached to near (left) saddlebag.	Attached to off (right) saddlebag, off horse.		
Haversack	On back, attached to belt.	*	*	On back, attached to belt.	On back, attached to belt.
Horseshoes, 2 extra, with nails.	*	In off (right) saddlebag.	In off (right) saddlebag, off horse.	*	*
Housewife	In haversack	In near (left) saddlebag.	In near (left) saddlebag, off horse.	In haversack	In haversack.
Intrenching tool (machete or bolo).	Attached to rear of haversack				Attached to rear of haversack.

*See note on page 55.

Field equipment, enlisted men (other than clothing worn on person)—Continued

Article	Dismounted	Mounted on horse (except drivers) artillery	Driver, horse (artillery only)	Driver, vehicle	Men mounted in vehicle*
Jacket, field	In haversack	Attached to pommel, over feed bag.	Strapped across seat of saddle, off horse.	In haversack, in bag, canvas, field, or in/on vehicle.	In haversack, in bag, canvas, field, or in/on vehicle.
Kit, grooming, complete, and saddle soap and sponge.	*	In off (right) saddlebag.	In off (right) saddlebag, off horse.	*	*
Laces, shoe, extra	In haversack	In near (left) saddlebag.	In near (left) saddlebag, off horse.	In bag, canvas, field, in haversack, or in left saddlebag.	In haversack or in bag, canvas, field.
Lariat		In near saddlebag.			
Mask, gas, horse		Strapped to halter under throatlatch.	Strapped to halter under throatlatch.		
Mask, gas, service	Slung under left arm by strap passing over right shoulder.	Slung under left arm by strap passing over right shoulder.	Slung under left arm by strap passing over right shoulder.	Slung under left arm by strap passing over right shoulder.	Slung under left arm by strap passing over right shoulder.
Ointment, protective	In haversack, or in bag, canvas, field.	In near (left) saddlebag.	In near (left) saddlebag, off horse.	In haversack, in bag, canvas, field, or in saddlebag.	In haversack, or in bag, canvas, field.

Overcoat	Attached to haversack. *	Strapped to pommel over feed bag. *	Strapped across seat of saddle, off horse. *	Attached to haversack, to bag, canvas, field, or in/on vehicle. *	Attached to haversack, to bag, canvas, field, or in/on vehicle. *
Scabbard, rifle		Attached to near (left) side of saddle, under skirt. *	*	Attached to vehicle. *	
Set, antidim	In carrier, gas mask.	In carrier, gas mask.	In carrier, gas mask.	In carrier, gas mask.	In carrier, gas mask.
Set, toilet	In haversack *	In near (left) saddlebag. *	In near (left) saddlebag, off horse. *	In blanket roll or in saddlebag. *	In blanket roll. *

*See note on page 55.

[A. G. 062.11 (3-24-42).] (C 1, May 4, 1942.)

■ 223. Conduct of Individuals.

* * * * * * *

o. Do not take into combat letters, diaries, or other written papers. If maps or documents have been given to you, destroy them if it appears that you cannot escape capture.

p. If you should be made a prisoner remember that by the international rules of warfare you are required to give *only* your name, grade, and Army serial number. Answer no other questions and do not allow yourself to be frightened by threats into giving any information. Any facts about our troops or equipment may be of great interest to the enemy and result in defeat to the Army and death to your comrades. Do not give false answers to questions as they are dangerous; merely refuse to answer. Read the "Rules to be remembered if captured" in appendix II until you are thoroughly familiar with them. DO IT NOW.

* * * * * * *

[A. G. 062.11 (3-18-42).]   (C 1, May 4, 1942.)

APPENDIX I

GLOSSARY OF COMMON MILITARY EXPRESSIONS

*   *   *   *   *   *   *

APPENDIX II (ADDED)

RULES TO BE REMEMBERED IF CAPTURED

■ 1. IMPORTANCE.—One of the enemy's objectives in war will be to capture prisoners. From these prisoners he hopes to obtain valuable information of our plans. The best way to prevent the enemy from securing this information is not to get captured. If you should be captured, however, remember that the lives and freedom of the other members of your organization, as well as your own treatment while in the enemy's hands, will depend on your following these simple rules. **DON'T FORGET THEM.**

■ 2. THINGS TO DO.—*a.* Before going into action make it a regular rule to go through your clothing and equipment and destroy or leave behind all envelopes, letters, diaries, or other papers which may identify your organization.

b. If your official duties require you to carry maps or documents in action, destroy them if it appears that you are in danger of capture.

c. When questioned, give *only* your *name, grade* and *Army serial number.* This is *all* you are required to give by the international rules of warfare. The enemy requires his troops to give only the same information when captured by us.

d. Maintain absolute silence when asked any other questions. The enemy has experts who will obtain valuable information from you if you enter into conversation with them on what may appear to be unimportant subjects. Keep your wits about you and refuse to answer. SILENCE alone is safe.

e. Try to remember directions and permanent landmarks while being taken to the prisoner of war camp or other destination. Keep your eyes and ears open to obtain information which will help you in an early escape and enable you to report what you have learned when you return to our lines.

f. Make thorough plans for escape but discuss those plans *only* out-of-doors and with fellow prisoners *whom you have known before your capture.* The enemy is extremely clever in installing microphones or other listening devices in unexpected places. He will also plant his agents among the prisoners. They will wear our uniform or those of our allies, and may appear to be wounded. Trust NO ONE.

g. Keep physically fit.

■ 3. THINGS NOT To Do.—*a.* Don't carry or permit anyone under you to carry into action any papers *of any kind* which may identify your organization.

b. Don't give any information except your *name, grade,* and *Army serial number.*

c. Don't try to be clever and give false or misleading answers when questioned by the enemy. If you do his experts will trap you. REMAIN SILENT.

d. Don't allow yourself to be frightened by threats into giving any information. The enemy will not harm you. He will be afraid of retaliation on his own people in our hands.

e. Don't discuss any of our Army, Navy, or air force matters with *anyone,* including your best friends among your fellow prisoners. *The walls have ears.*

f. Don't refer in any circumstances to your unit or its position. A careless word may cost old comrades their lives.

g. Don't write to anyone *a single word relating to any incident whatsoever* preceding your capture. The enemy censor who will read your letter is clever and he may deduce valuable information of our plans from statements that appear perfectly harmless.

h. Don't believe the enemy if he tells you that he will drop messages over the lines addressed to your unit or organization telling them you are safe.

i. Never address letters to officers or men of our Army which will indicate in any way their unit or the position of their unit. Give only the *name* and *grade* of the person to whom you are writing, and address it care of the United States Army *through the Prisoner of War Information Bureau.* Such a bureau is established by us for transmitting information to the enemy regarding his prisoners in our hands, and by the enemy for furnishing information to us regarding our prisoners. The enemy will announce how many letters and post cards each prisoner of war will be allowed to send each month and he is required to forward promptly your correspondence through his information bureau. If you write to any of your relatives *who are not in the armed services* telling them you are safe, you may use their home address, and your correspondence will reach them through the information bureau.

j. Don't believe anything you are told by the enemy or from spies he may have planted among you as fellow prisoners. Be patient and above all BE SILENT.

k. Don't be downhearted if captured. Opportunities for escape will present themselves.

l. Don't give parole. This would prevent you in honor from attempting to escape. The enemy cannot compel you to accept your liberty on parole.

[A. G. 062.11 (3–18–42).]   (C 1, May 4, 1942.)

BY ORDER OF THE SECRETARY OF WAR:

G. C. MARSHALL,
Chief of Staff.

OFFICIAL:

J. A. ULIO,
Major General,
The Adjutant General.

www.ingramcontent.com/pod-product-compliance
Lightning Source LLC
Chambersburg PA
CBHW051945090426

42741CB00008B/1284